Illustrations by V. Cosentino

Published in 1977 by
Sampson Low
Berkshire House, Queen Street,
Maidenhead, Berkshire SL6 1NF.

SBN 562 00058 5

© 1975 Europa Verlag
© 1975 Arnoldo Mondadori, Milan

Printed in Italy

SAMPSON LOW GUIDES

World AIRCRAFT

1918-1935

ENZO ANGELUCCI and PAOLO MATRICARDI

Sampson Low

Contents

Introduction

The two decades between the two World Wars represent a fascinating period in the history of aviation. Commercial aviation was born during this time, and this is the underlying theme of the second volume in this series of guides to the aeroplanes of the world: the discovery of the aeroplane as a means of civil transport, the growth of commercial aviation, and the enormous contribution it has made to the development of the modern world.

This volume is identical in layout to *Origins – World War 1*, which details over two hundred and eighty aircraft types. *World Aircraft 1918–1935* continues the story by discussing a further one hundred and eighty aircraft types which are described and illustrated. This information is supplemented by technical tables, a perspective view of the period, and an outline history of each type.

Often the colour illustration and line drawings refer to different models of the same basic aircraft. The aim of this is to give the broadest possible coverage in a limited space.

Although commercial aircraft claim pride of place in this volume, together with five of the most important dirigible airships, military planes are also included. These planes are all especially significant, both historically and technically, in the development of aviation in the individual nations that produced them, and in the evolution of world aviation in general. Racing planes are also included. Competition racing and trans-oceanic flights played an important part in the history of aviation, both civil and military, during the years between the two World Wars.

Ligne Paris-Londres

Plusieurs Compagnies assurent le service sur ce parcours. Le tableau ci-dessous indique les horaires des Compagnies groupées. Le courrier étant choisi, il suffit de se reporter à la Compagnie qui l'assure pour avoir les tarifs et conditions.

Nota. — Les heures indiquées sont les heures de l'Europe Occidentale

	C D - QUOTIDIENS SAUF LE DIMANCHE - V W							
	A B E F G H - QUOTIDIENS - S T U X Y Z							
	Messageries et POSTE	Passagers et Messageries				Passagers Messageries et POSTE	Passagers et Messageries	
	A	B	C	D	E	F	G	H
Paris-Le Bourget	6.00	11.30	11.30	11.30	12.30	13.15	16.00	15.45
Londres-Croydon	8.30	13.45	14.30	14.30	14.45	16.15	18.15	18.15
Compagnies	Messageries aériennes	Instone	HandleyPage	Grands Express	Daimler	Messageries aériennes	Instone	Daimler

	Messageries et POSTE	Passagers et Messageries				Passagers Messageries et POSTE	Passagers et Marchandises	
	S	T	U	V	W	X	Y	Z
Londres-Croydon	6.00	9.30	11.30	11.30	12.00	12.30	12.45	16.00
Paris-Le Bourget	8.30	12.00	13.45	14.30	15.00	15.30	15.15	18.15
Compagnies	Messageries aériennes	Daimler	Instone	Grands Express	HandleyPage	Messageries aériennes	Daimler	Instone

AERODROMES

Le Bourget, Croydon, voir Annexe C.

Correspondances ferroviaires.

A PARIS. — I. Au départ des avions :   arrivant à

Express E. de Lisbonne, Madrid, Bayonne, Bordeaux	Gare d'Orsay	6 h. 10
Express F de Rome, Gênes, Nice	Gare de Lyon	6 h. 30
Express Orient-Constantinople, Athènes, Bucarest, Milan, Lausanne	Gare de Lyon	7 h. 40
Rapide J de Rome, Gênes, Nice	Gare de Lyon	8 h. 45
Express 72 de Toulouse	Gare d'Orsay	9 h. 37
Rapide L de Rome, Gênes, Nice	Gare de Lyon	10 h. 15
Rapide C de Lisbonne, Madrid, Bayonne, Bordeaux	Gare d'Orsay	12 h. 10

From *L'Indicator Aérien*, June 1922. Train connections with the Paris–London and London–Paris flights are also given.

War and Peace

The first unofficial flight took place on August 10, 1910, taking off from Blackpool, England. The first official postal flight took place on February 18, 1911, when the Frenchman Henri Pequet carried letters and packages some five miles in a Humber biplane. This was the first time letters carried an airmail cancellation. In the same year a regular postal flight ran for three weeks in Great Britain. The flights, carried out by the Grahame-White Aviation Company, were established to commemorate the coronation of George V. In three weeks a total of 25,000 letters and 90,000 post cards were carried between London and Windsor. Before the year was out, other airmail flights were made in the United States and Italy.

Postal transport was the first organized civil use of the aeroplane. In the pioneer years of aviation, passenger transport was purely experimental, and its chief aim was to publicize aviation. It was only in 1914, in the United States, that a first attempt was made to create a regular passenger service. The St. Petersburg–Tampa Airboat Line was founded in Florida, and a Benoist seaplane made two flights a day between the two cities. The company went out of business after four months.

Nevertheless, the St. Petersburg–Tampa Airboat Line was not the first passenger transport company in the history of aviation. Five years earlier, on October 16, 1909, Count von Zeppelin (the inventor of the rigid airship) founded the first commercial air transport company in Germany, the Deutsche Luftschiffahrt Aktien Gesellschaft (DELAG). But the company used dirigibles, not aeroplanes. Between March 1912 and November 1913, they made 881 flights, flew 60,000 miles (over 100,000 kilometres), carrying 19,100 passengers.

The First World War interrupted the development of civil aviation. For almost five years the aeroplane was considered a war machine. Reconnaissance planes, fighters, and bombers were the order of the day. The war years, however, provided the impulse for further development of aircraft generally. The experience that designers and manufacturers gained during the war led the heavier-than-air craft into its first years of maturity.

The years of peace reaped the harvest of the technical advances made during the war. The aeroplane played a fundamental role in the reconstruction of post-war Europe. The first hesitant attempts to organize regular civil transport in Europe were carried out with aircraft left over from the War. This was especially true in France, Great Britain, and Germany, the three countries that had made the most important contribution to the development of aviation. But soon planes were to appear that had been conceived as means of transport, and from that point in history the development of civil and military aviation followed separate paths. The era of commercial aviation had begun.

Benoist XIV

This small single-engine seaplane in-augurated the first regular passenger service in the world. Its maiden flight, on January 1, 1914, between St. Petersburg and Tampa, Florida, was $21\frac{1}{2}$ miles (34.5 km). The plane, carrying one passenger beside the pilot was designed and built by Thomas Benoist, a St. Louis businessman who had made a fortune in automobiles before going into the aircraft business. Benoist signed a contract with the St. Petersburg authorities on December 13, 1913, to support and finance a regular air service to Tampa. Although a certain A. C. Pheil paid $400 for the privilege of being the first passenger, the ticket price was $5 per person, with varying charges for cargo. Despite its enthusiastic beginnings, the St. Petersburg–Tampa Airboat Line was a commercial failure and went out of business in a few months.

Aircraft: **Benoist XIV**
Manufacturer: **Thomas Benoist**
Type: **Civil transport**
Year: **1914**
Engine: **Roberts, 6-cylinder in-line, liquid-cooled, 75 hp**
Wingspan: **45 ft (13.72 m)**
Length: **26 ft (7.92 m)**
Height: —
Weight: **1,190 lb (540 kg) (empty)**
Maximum speed: **64 mph (103 km/h)**
Maximum cruising altitude: —
Range: —
Crew: **1**
Passengers: **1**

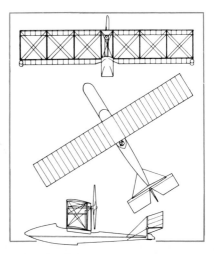

Lévy-Lepen Type R

The first airline in Equatorial Africa
was inaugurated with this three-seat
seaplane, which was built in 1917 for
the French navy during World War I.
The first stretch, between Léopold-
ville (mod. Kinshasa, Zaire) and
N'Gombé, was inaugurated July 1,
1920, under the auspices of the
SNETA, the official Belgian airline. A
second stretch, from N'Gombé to
Lisala, was inaugurated March 3,
1921. The whole Congo line, the Ligne
Aérienne Roi Albert (LARA), was
inaugurated July 1, 1921, the terminus
being Stanleyville. It was not one of
the easiest lines to run. The chief
difficulties were heat and humidity.
The fabric covering of the plane had to
be checked after each flight. Lévy-
Lepen seaplanes were also being used
by other companies, including the
Transport Aériens Guyanais, which
had five planes in service in French
Guiana in 1922.

Aircraft: **Lévy-Lepen Type R**
Manufacturer: **Hydravions Georges Lévy**
Type: **Civil transport**
Year: **1917**
Engine: **Renault, 12-cylinder V, liquid-
cooled, 300 hp**
Wingspan: **60 ft 8 in (18.49 m)**
Length: **40 ft 8 in (12.39 m)**
Height: **12 ft 7 in (3.85 m)**
Weight: **5,400 lb (2,450 kg)**
Maximum speed: **90 mph (145 km/h)**
Maximum cruising altitude: —
Range: —
Crew: **1**
Passengers: **2**

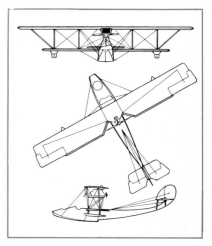

Breguet 14 T

The Breguet 14, which remained in production until 1926, was a sturdy aircraft fully adapted to the early needs of transport. When in 1919 a group of aircraft manufacturers, including Breguet, Caudron, Blériot, Farman, and Morane, founded the Compagnie des Messageries Aériennes (CMA) to open commercial routes to Great Britain and Belgium, twenty-four Breguet 14s were put in service on the Paris–Lille, Paris–Marseilles, Paris–Brussels, and Paris–London lines. The plane was modified for passenger transport and the new model was called 14 T. The plane's success was assured by the extensive use made of it by the Lignes Aériennes Latécoére, the company founded by the Toulouse businessman Pierre Latécoére for service in South America. No fewer than 106 Breguet 14 Ts were in service until 1923, and some were specially modified for postal service.

Aircraft: **Breguet 14 T**
Manufacturer: **Société Anonyme des Ateliers d'Aviation Louis Breguet**
Type: **Civil transport**
Year: **1919**
Engine: **Renault 12 FCX, 12-cylinder V, liquid-cooled, 300 hp**
Wingspan: **47 ft (14.32 m)**
Length: **29 ft 6 in (8.99 m)**
Height: **10 ft 10 in (3.30 m)**
Weight: **4,374 lb (1,984 kg)**
Cruising speed: **78 mph at 6,500 ft (125 km/h at 2,000 m)**
Maximum cruising altitude: **14,700 ft (4,500 m)**
Range: **290 mile (460 km)**
Crew: **1**
Passengers: **2**

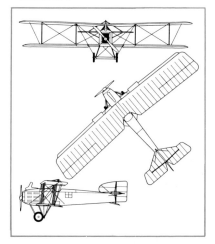

de Havilland D.H. 4A

In Great Britain, as in France, the first commercial planes were overhauled veterans of World War I. The D.H. 4, a light bomber in the war, was one of the first aircraft to be 'demobbed'. After two earlier modifications, the third and most important variation, the D.H. 4A, was introduced. These planes were altered in much the same way as the Breguet 14. The fuselage was enlarged to accommodate two passengers. The D.H. 4A first saw regular service with Aircraft Transport and Travel Ltd. and with Handley-Page Air Transport Ltd. A route to Amsterdam was opened in August 1919, as well as a line from Hounslow to Le Bourget, France. The plane proved itself on routes to France and Holland. On December 4, 1920, the plane set a record, carrying two passengers from London to Paris in one hour and forty-eight minutes. Lt. Vaughan Fowler, the pilot, acknowledged that the winds had been favourable.

Aircraft: **de Havilland D.H.4A**
Manufacturer: **Aircraft Manufacturing Co., Ltd. (Airco)**
Type: **Civil transport**
Year: **1919**
Engine: **Rolls-Royce Eagle VIII, 12-cylinder V, liquid-cooled, 350 hp**
Wingspan: **42 ft 5 in (12.93 m)**
Length: **30 ft 6 in (9.29 m)**
Height: **11 ft (3.35 m)**
Weight: **2.600 lb (1,180 kg)**
Maximum speed: **121 mph (195 km/h)**
Maximum cruising altitude: —
Range: —
Crew: **1**
Passengers: **2**

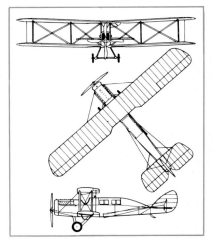

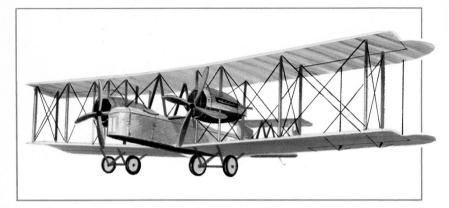

Vickers F.B.27 Vimy IV
Vickers F.B.27 Vimy
   Commercial

The Vimy was designed as a heavy bomber late in World War I, and only three planes were in service before the armistice. But it was very popular in military and civil aviation well into the 1920s.

Although the military model was in great demand, the commercial model was significant in the post-war development of aviation. One of the most historic events of this time was the first non-stop crossing of the Atlantic Ocean. On June 14–15, 1919, John Alcock and Arthur Whitten

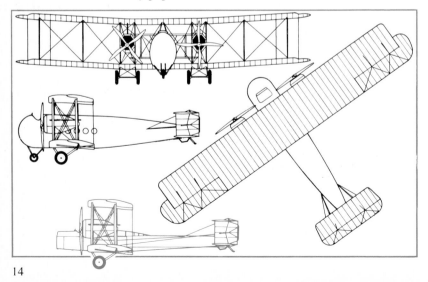

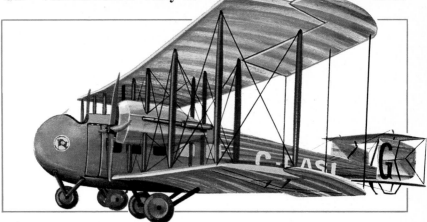

Brown flew 1,960 miles (3,154 km) from Lester's field, St. John's Newfoundland, to Derrygimla bog near Clifden, Ireland in 16 hours 27 minutes. Their aircraft was a normal Vickers Vimy bomber from which the military equipment had been removed to make room for supplementary fuel tanks. This increased the fuel capacity of the aircraft by 865 gallons (3,932 L).

The achievement of Alcock and Brown won them the Daily Mail prize of £10,000 and both men were created K.B.E. It also marked the Vimy's introduction into civil aviation. The fuselage was closed and enlarged, and could accommodate up to ten passengers. The F.B.27 'commercial' prototype made its maiden flight on April 13, 1919, and final modifications were completed in 1920. This new model made its inaugural passenger flight on May 9, 1920, on the Croydon–Brussels route. It was in almost continuous service thereafter on the Paris, Brussels, and Cologne routes. By July 1921 the plane had clocked 360 hours

Aircraft: **Vickers F.B.27 Vimy IV**
Manufacturer: **Vickers Ltd.**
Type: **Civil transport**
Year: **1919**
Engine: **Two Rolls-Royce Eagle VIII, 12-cylinder V, liquid-cooled, 360 hp each**
Wingspan: **67 ft 2 in (20.47 m)**
Length: **43 ft 6 in (13.26 m)**
Height: **15 ft 3 in (4.65 m)**
Weight: **12,500 lb (5,670 kg)**
Maximum speed: **100 mph (160 km/h)**
Max. cruising altitude: **10,500 ft (3,200 m)**
Range: **1,880 mile (3,020 km)**
Crew: **2**

Aircraft: **Vickers F.B.27 Vimy Commercial**
Manufacturer: **Vickers Ltd.**
Type: **Civil transport**
Year: **1920**
Engine: **Two Rolls-Royce Eagle VIII, 12-cylinder V, liquid-cooled, 360 hp each**
Wingspan: **67 ft 2 in (20.47 m)**
Length: **42 ft 8 in (13.00 m)**
Height: **15 ft 8 in (4.72 m)**
Weight: **12,500 lb (5,670 kg)**
Cruising speed: **84 mph (135 km/h)**
Max. cruising altitude: **10,500 ft (3,200 m)**
Range: **450 mile (720 km)**
Crew: **2**
Passengers: **10**

in the air, and had carried 10,600 passengers. By April 1, 1924, when it was given to Imperial Airways Ltd., it had flown 107,931 miles (173,691 km). The total production of this model was 43 aircraft.

France

France, the cradle of aviation, was only the second country in Europe to establish a regular civil airline. The first was inaugurated in Germany on February 5, 1919, by the Deutsche Luft-Reederei, between Berlin and Weimar. But the next month, on March 22, Lucien Bossoutrot, at the controls of a Farman F.60 Goliath, inaugurated the Paris–Brussels route. The Farman company itself founded its own airline a couple of months later (the first in France and the second in Europe), the Lignes Aériennes Farman. It was the first step in the rapid development of civil aviation in France, and that nation again reached a position of pre-eminence in aviation, as it had in the pioneering days before World War I.

The official activities of the first French airline, however, were preceded by a number of isolated attempts. On December 24, 1918, an ambitious little company, which was later to become famous as the Lignes Aériennes Latécoère, made an exploratory flight from Toulouse to Barcelona. The scope of the flight was to test the possibility of establishing air communications with Africa and South America. On February 25,

1919, the company's Breguet 14 reached Alicante, and on March 20 it flew to Rabat, Morocco. On February 8, 1919, a Farman Goliath flew from Paris to London. The flight aroused considerable comment, and there was much debate whether it could be considered the first commercial international European flight. The plane took off from Toussus le Noble and landed at Kenley, carrying military passengers. The British objected that it was not a regular flight, and the French 'first' had to await the inauguration of the Paris–Brussels line.

After opening the route to Belgium, the Lignes Aériennes Farman made experimental flights to northern Europe and to Africa and established a Paris–London flight. Other companies were to follow Farman's lead. A second company was founded early in 1919 by a group that included some of the most famous French aviation industrialists, the Compagnie des Messageries Aériennes (CMA). The company began its activities on May 1, inaugurating a regular postal flight between Paris and Lille, a service that was soon extended to Brussels as well. On August 26, a flight to London was initiated, and on September 19 the first passenger flight to London was made. The company used a variety of aircraft: Blériot Spads, Farman Goliaths, and Breguet 14s. The third company to establish regular flights was the Compagnie des Transports Aéronautiques du Sud-Ouest, which opened a route to Spain in July 1919. The flight flew from Bordeaux to Biarritz, San Sebastian, and Bilbao. Several other companies were founded in the same year, including the Compagnie Générale Transáerienne, the Compagnie Aérienne Française, the Compagnie des Grands Express and the Aéro Transports Ernoul, and the Aéro Transport.

Commercial aviation was consolidated and expanded in the 1920s. The French government fully recognized the importance of this sector of the transport industry and gave large backing to the airlines. Indeed an under-secretariat of state for aviation and air transport was established in 1920. The bureau was subdivided into departments concerned with technical services, factories, air navigation, and a meteorological network. The airlines took full advantage of the government's interest. While new routes were studied, some 2,400 commercial flights were made in that year. It was in this climate that another airline was founded in April 1920, the Compagnie Franco–Romaine de Navigation Aérienne (CFRNA). On September 20, it opened its Paris–Strasbourg line, on October 7 the Paris–Prague line, on April 12, 1921, the Paris–Wroclaw–Warsaw line, and on May 1, 1922, the Paris–Vienna–Budapest line. And the farthest countries of Europe were

reached on October 15, 1922, with the opening of the line from Paris to Istanbul, by way of Strasbourg, Innsbruck, Vienna, Budapest, Belgrade, and Bucharest. The Lignes Aériennes Latécoère (which adopted the name of Compagnie Générale d'Enterprises Aéronautiques, CGEA, on April 21, 1921) continued its southern expansion toward Africa, while in the north, three companies flying the same routes consolidated their efforts in a single new company. First the Grands Express Aériens incorporated the Compagnie Générale Transáerienne. Then the CGEA was consolidated with the Compagnie des Messageries Aériennes to form a new company, the Air Union. The new company began its official activities on January 1, 1923, and concentrated its efforts on the Paris–London route with connections to Lyons, Marseilles, and Geneva.

Expansion and consolidation continued during the second half of the decade. The Air Union added southern routes to Corsica and North Africa, and amplified its services to Great Britain. On July 30, 1927, it inaugurated the Lioré et Olivier luxury flights in direct competition with the British airlines. The Farman company, which had been renamed the Société Générale de Transport Aérien (SGTA) increased and improved its service in northern Europe. And on May 26, 1926, a direct eight-hour Paris–Berlin flight was inaugurated. The next year Farman made an operating agreement with Deutsche Lufthansa and opened new routes to the Scandinavian countries. The Compagnie Franco–Roumaine de Navigation Aérienne (which on

January 1, 1925, officially became the Compagnie International de Navigation Aérienne, CIDNA) improved and developed its service to Warsaw and Istanbul. Exploratory flights were made to Moscow, but a regular line was not initiated, although routes were extended to Ankara, Baghdad, and Teheran. All these efforts reflected the level of success that commercial aviation was enjoying. A few figures will illustrate the point. In 1920 French lines carried barely 942 passengers, while five years later the number of passengers carried had risen to 20,000. By the beginning of the 1930s French lines flew to four continents (Europe, Africa, South America, and Asia). In 1932 alone, French airlines flew over 9,300,000 kilometres (5,780,000 miles) with 420,000 tons of cargo and 310,000 tons of mail.

The year 1933 was a decisive year in the development of French air transport policy. In an effort to improve France's position with respect to foreign competitors and in order to control civil aviation more efficiently, the government fostered the consolidation of the major airlines into a single company. Thus was born Air France, one of the most prestigious airlines in the world. The company was founded on August 30, 1933, by Air Orient, the Air Union, CIDNA, and SGTA (Farman), which had already joined together to form the Société Centrale pour l'Exploitation de Lignes Aériennes (SCELA), and had absorbed Aéro postale.

At the outset Air France found itself with about 23,000 miles (38,000 km) of route to cover and a fleet of 259 aircraft of various types, many of them outmoded monoplanes. One of the new company's first tasks was to try to standardize operations and improve carrier capacity. The formation of the new company thus gave enormous impetus to the French aircraft industry. French manufacturers were encouraged to build better and more competitive planes, and they responded with designs that often set the pace for aeronautic developments throughout the world. Such an aircraft design was the Dewoitine D.338, far ahead of other planes of the time. Air France also pioneered several intercontinental routes. In 1934 the first commercial routes between France and South America were inaugurated, thanks to the Couzinet Arc-en-Ciel flight. Two years later a regular passenger service to Dakar was begun. And in 1937 a special air line initiated experimental Atlantic flights connecting Europe and North America. The oriental route reached China in 1938. Again, a few figures will suffice to illustrate the expansion of French aviation in this period. In 1930 the four chief French airlines (Air Union, Farman, CIDNA, and Aéropostale) logged 55,000 passengers, more than half the total of the preceding five years. In 1939, on the eve of the Second World War, Air France had transported just under one hundred thousand passengers on all its routes. It was only the outbreak of World War II that put a halt to these dramatic advances.

Farman F.60 Goliath

On April 1, 1919, a Farman F.60, with four passengers on board, reached an altitude of 20,600 feet (6,300 m) in one hour and five minutes. It was the first of a series of world records. Two days later, fourteen passengers were carried to an altitude of 20,300 feet (6,200 m) in the same time. On May 5, twenty-five passengers reached an altitude of 16,700 feet (5,100 m) in one hour and fifteen minutes. In August the Farman flew some 1,270 miles (2,050 km) from Paris to Casablanca in eighteen hours and twenty-three minutes, carrying an eight-man crew. The debut of the Goliath F.60 in civil aviation could not have been more brilliant. In more than ten years of service, the Goliath became one of the most important transport planes of its time. It was used by the leading European airlines and saw service in Czechoslovakia, Romania, and South America.

Designed in 1918 as a bomber (a photograph survives showing an unfinished bomber with a mounted machine gun), the Farman F.60 was soon modified for civil aviation. It was a biplane with a wooden skeleton, fabric-covered, and a deep, widowed fuselage. The rear cabin had eight seats and was separated from the four-man forward compartment and the two-man cockpit. Originally the plane was equipped with two water-cooled radial engines, the Salmson Z-9. Subsequently other engines were used, including the 260 horsepower and 300 horsepower Salmsons, the 300 horsepower Renault, the 380 horsepower Gnome Rhône Jupiter radial, and the Lorraine-Dietrich and Maybach engines. The model name often varied because of the particular engine used.

The Farman F.60 was first adopted in regular service on March 20, 1920,

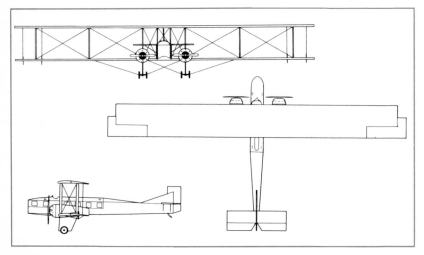

by the Compagnie des Grands Express Aériens on the Paris–London route. But it had already been named Goliath and had made several record-breaking flights, many of them under the auspices of the Farman works. The aircraft was soon in service on several European routes for other airlines as well. The Paris–London route, for example, was also served by the Compagnie des Messageries Aériennes, while the Paris–Brussels line was opened on July 1, 1920, by the Société Generale de Transport Aériens (also known as the Farman line, Lignes Farman). The latter company extended its flights to Amsterdam and Berlin in the following years.

The Farman Goliath saw service everywhere. It was used by the Air Union Company, the Compagnie Aérienne Française, Sabena, the CSA transport company in Czechoslovakia, and the Lares Company in Italy. A total of some sixty Farmans were in regular service until 1933. Considering that these were still the

Aircraft: **Farman F.60 Goliath**
Manufacturer: **Avions H. et M. Farman**
Type: **Civil transport**
Year: **1919**
Engine: **Two Salmson C.M., 9-cylinder radial, liquid-cooled, 260 hp each**
Wingspan: **87 ft (26.46 m)**
Length: **47 ft (14.33 m)**
Height: **—**
Weight: **10,516 lb (4,770 kg)**
Cruising speed: **75 mph at 6,500 ft (120 km/h at 2,000 m)**
Maximum cruising altitude: **13,000 ft (4,000 m)**
Range: **250 mile (400 km)**
Crew: **2**
Passengers: **12**

early years of civil aviation, the Farman was extremely popular. By 1930 one of the Farmans had clocked 2,962 hours and 25 minutes of flight time. Another one had clocked 3,843 hours by 1933.

Among the Farman's 'firsts' is the first collision of two planes in civil aviation. On April 7, 1922, a Farman Goliath of the Grands Express collided with another plane in the sky over Poix. This is hardly an enviable first, but it does indicate the great popularity of this aircraft after the First World War.

Blériot Spad 46

The Spad 46 was the second in a series of single-engine transport biplanes that Blériot-Aéronautique began producing in 1920. The first Spad 46 took to the air on June 16, 1921, and a total of fifty-one planes were eventually manufactured.

The first in the series was the 33, which made its debut in December 1920, and the last variation, produced in 1929, was the Spad 126. The 33 was a single-engine biplane powered by a Salmson Z–9 radial engine, liquid-cooled, and equipped with a four-passenger cabin. A fifth passenger could be carried alongside the pilot in the open cockpit. Forty aircraft were built in this popular model and saw service in some of the most important companies of the period, including the Compagnie des Messageries Aériennes, the Air Union, the Compagnie Franco–Rumaine de Navigation Aérienne, and Sabena.

What distinguished the Spad 46

Aircraft: **Blériot Spad 46**
Manufacturer: **Blériot-Aéronautique**
Type: **Civil transport**
Year: **1921**
Engine: **Lorraine-Dietrich 12 Da, 12-cylinder V, liquid cooled, 370 hp**
Wingspan: **41 ft 6 in (12.65 m)**
Length: **29 ft 8 in (9.05 m)**
Height: **—**
Weight: **5,070 lb (2,300 kg) (maximum loaded weight)**
Cruising speed: **103 mph (165 km/h)**
Ceiling: **16,500 ft (5,050 m)**
Range: **500 mile (800 km)**
Crew: **1**
Passengers: **4–5**

from its predecessor was a wingspan more than three feet wider and a new engine, a 370 hp Lorraine–Dietrich V-12. Although slightly heavier than its predecessor, the 46 was faster and had a higher ceiling. It saw service chiefly in the Compagnie Franco–Rumaine de Navigation Aérienne, which ordered a total of thirty-eight, on routes from France to the rest of Europe. There were five other variations of the basic model. The most noteworthy was the 56, which set a record in 1923 by reaching an altitude of 26,900 feet (8,200 m) carrying a cargo of 550 pounds (250 kg).

Caudron C.61

This large three-engine biplane was born in 1921, in a period when French aircraft manufacturers were all struggling to meet the growing demands of air transport. The commodious fuselage could accommodate eight passengers. The crew were less comfortably accommodated in the traditional open cockpit, just behind the central engine.

But relatively few C.61s were produced, twelve in all. Six of these aircraft entered the service of one of the leading airlines of the period, the Compagnie Franco–Roumaine de Navigation Sérienne (FRA), which first acquired the C.61 in 1923. The plane was used on the flight between Belgrade and Bucharest. There were night runs on this route.

In 1924 the C.61s were radically altered in order to increase their cargo capacity. The first and third engines were replaced by Salmson C.M.9 radial engines, liquid-cooled, of

Aircraft: **Caudron C.61**
Manufacturer: **Avions Caudron**
Type: **Civil transport**
Year: **1923**
Engine: **Three Hispano-Suiza 8Ab, 8-cylinder V, liquid-cooled, 180 hp each**
Wingspan: **79 ft 2 in (24.13 m)**
Length: **45 ft 11 in (14 m)**
Height: **—**
Weight: **7,670 lb (3,480 kg) (loaded)**
Maximum speed: **100 mph (160 km/h)**
Ceiling: **13,000 ft (4,000 m)**
Range: **400 mile (640 km)**
Crew: **2**
Passengers: **8**

260 hp each. This aircraft, known as the C.61 bis, had 160 hp more than its predecessor, and its cargo capacity was some 440–660 pounds (200–300 kg) greater. At the same time its range was significantly reduced, from 400 miles (640 km) to 230 miles (380 km); and its ceiling was reduced by 1,640 feet (500 m). The C.61 bis was in service for several years in the Compagnie Franco–Roumaine de Navigation Aérienne.

Blériot 135

One of the first four-engine planes designed expressly for civil transport, the Blériot 135 was one of a small number of aircraft used exclusively on the Paris–London run. The only company to use this plane was the Air Union. This was a company founded in 1923 by the merging of three smaller companies in order to improve the direct route between the English and French capitals.

The 135's predecessor, the Blériot 115, made its maiden voyage on May 9, 1923. It represented an innovation in aircraft design. Its four engines (all Hispano–Suiza 8Acs, 8-cylinder V, liquid-cooled, 180 hp each) were installed in pairs, two on the upper wing and two on the lower. Each was served by a fuel tank set just above it. The manufacturer made much of this arrangement, because it was safer. Moreover, the engines could be started in flight, and it was claimed that the aircraft could take off with only two engines in operation. The fact that 360 hp was sufficient to lift a full load of five-and-a-half tons was indirect witness to the plane's power. Aside from this, the Blériot 115 was fairly conventional. The ample fuselage had odd triangular-shaped windows, and the upper and lower wings were equal in span. The wings were fabric-covered, and the fuselage was covered in wood. The rectangular fuselage could accommodate eight passengers. The two crew-members sat side by side

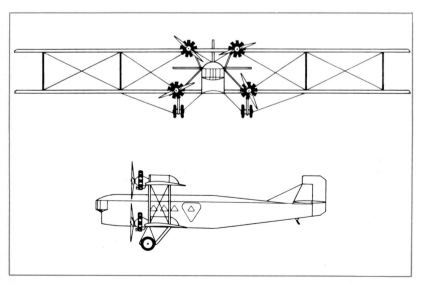

in an open cockpit. At the front of the fuselage was an observation post for the navigator. This cabin was completely closed with projecting windows.

Two 115s were assigned to the military and named the Jean Casale and the Roland Garros. These two aircraft set out on a remarkable enterprise in 1925. In nineteen days they flew from Paris, crossed the Sahara desert, and reached Gao, in the Niger. The Jean Casale crashed on take-off at the beginning of the return flight.

The only difference between the 115 and the 135 was in the engines. The Hispano–Suizas were replaced in the 135 by four Salmson 9Ab radials of 230 hp each. With this increase in power, the passenger capacity was raised from eight to ten. The first flight on the Paris–London route took place on August 8, 1924. The Air Union first used the 135 and in 1926 acquired two 155s, the last variation of the original model. The Blériot 155, which made its maiden flight on July 29, 1925, was

Aircraft: **Blériot 135**
Manufacturer: **Blériot Aéronautique**
Type: **Civil transport**
Year: **1924**
Engine: **Four Salmson 9Ab, 9-cylinder radial, air-cooled, 230 hp each**
Wingspan: **82 ft (24.99 m)**
Length: **47 ft 5 in (14.45 m)**
Height: **16 ft 2 in (4.93 m)**
Weight: **11,243 lb (5,099 kg) (maximum loaded weight)**
Cruising speed: **100 mph (160 km/h)**
Ceiling: **13,000 ft (4,000 m)**
Range: **370 mile (600 km)**
Crew: **2**
Passengers: **10**

slightly larger and heavier than its predecessors. The chief modifications were the substitution of 230 hp Renault engines and the enlargement of the cabin. By removing the observation post and moving the cockpit forward, room was made for seventeen passengers. The two aircraft, which were baptized Wilbur Wright and Clement Ader, saw brief service. They were destroyed in 1926, after barely five months service.

Potez 25 A.2

It was in July 1929 that a civil airline first crossed the Andes. The route was between Buenos Aires, Argentina, and Santiago, Chile, a route created exclusively for postal transport. The aeroplane was a Potez 25 A.2. (The Potez 25 was originally a two-seater military reconnaissance plane, while the B.2 variation was a bomber. However, a few of the original 25s were also used commercially.) The Potez that first crossed the Andes, piloted by Mermoz and Guillamet, was in the service of the French Aéropostale company, a development of the Latécoère line, which specialized in South American flights.

The Potez 25 was one of the most popular French military aircraft in the 1920s and 1930s. The aircraft was first shown in 1924, at the Salon de l'Aéronautique in Paris, and so impressed the military authorities that a massive production campaign was begun. A total of almost 4,000 planes

were manufactured in some 90 models. The prototype took to the air early in 1925, and one of the first of these aircraft set out in the summer of the same year on an endurance flight that contributed much to the plane's fame. It made the rounds of the capitals of Europe, covering a total distance of 4,632 miles (7,455 km) in thirty-nine hours.

The Potez 25 soon became famous throughout the world. In addition to the French air force, it saw service as a military aircraft in twenty-one other countries, including Algeria, China, Japan, Poland, Portugal, U.S.S.R., Romania, Yugoslavia, and Afghanistan. In South America, it saw service in Argentina, Brazil, and Uruguay. Several countries manufactured their own Potezs on licence, and a host of variations on the original were thus created. These variants were distinguished chiefly by engines that were substituted for the originals. The Potez 25 appeared with a wide variety of engines, in-line and radial, liquid- and air-cooled, and between 450 and

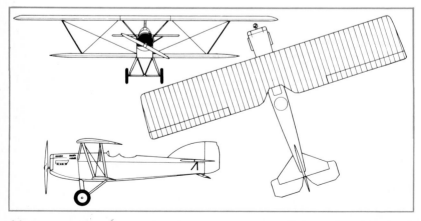

500 hp. Among these engines was the 500 hp Farman, the 500 hp Hispano–Suiza, the 550 hp Renault, and 480 hp Gnome-Rhône Jupiter radial and the 500 hp Salmson radial.

Two of the most important Potezs were the 25 M and the 25 O. The former was a monoplane; the lower wing was removed. The O model was designed for long range non-stop flying. It was equipped with a 420 hp Jupiter radial engine and several reserve fuel tanks, and the fuselage was metal-covered. This plane also had a detachable undercarriage, which was ejected immediately after takeoff; a kind of skating blade along the base of the fuselage was designed for landing the plane. It was this feature that made the plane impractical. The prototype crashed making a landing after a test flight.

Five Potez 25s were used in South America; three were delivered to the Aéropostale company in 1929, and two in 1930. When Air France took over Aéropostale in 1933, these planes

Aircraft: **Potez 25 A.2**
Manufacturer: **Société des Aeroplanes H. Potez**
Type: **Civil transport**
Year: **1925**
Engine: **Lorraine-Dietrich, 12-cylinder V, liquid-cooled, 450 hp**
Wingspan: **46 ft 7 in (14.19 m)**
Length: **30 ft 2 in (9.19 m)**
Height: **12 ft (3.65 m)**
Weight: **4,332 lb (1,965 kg)**
Cruising speed: **106 mph (170 km/h)**
Ceiling: **—**
Range: **310 mile (500 km)**
Crew: **2**
Cargo: **1,737 lb (788 kg) (including crew)**

were still in service and were only retired three years later. The quality and resilience of the Potez 25 were dramatically tested in an unusual accident that befell Henri Guillaumet on June 13, 1930, on a flight over the Andes. The pilot made a forced landing during a storm. Coming down onto a plateau at an altitude of 11,400 feet (3,500 m), the plane turned over and was half covered by the snow. It was dug out several months later and after repairs was put back into service.

Levasseur PL 8
Oiseau Blanc

The place is Le Bourget airport, the date is May 8, 1927, and the time is 5.21 a.m. After an unsuccessful attempt at take-off, due to excessive weight, a small biplane, all white, makes a long approach and finally lifts off the runway. Once aloft, it releases its undercarriage and heads slowly west. The last and most ambitious adventure of Charles Nungesser and François Coli is under way. The Oiseau Blanc (White Bird) as it was called, was carrying 886 gallons (4,025 l) of fuel, enough for just over thirty hours in the air, sufficient time to cross the Atlantic Ocean and reach the American continent. Perhaps Nungesser and Coli managed to see the coastline before the snowstorm hit them just over Newfoundland. That was the last that was ever heard from them. Twelve days later, Charles Lindbergh made his successful non-stop one-man flight across the Atlantic.

Charles Nungesser, the number three French ace in World War I (45 planes downed), was born in Paris on March 15, 1892. His war record made him a popular figure. He founded a flying school at Orly, but this was not very successful. Nevertheless, he flew constantly in his Morane-Saulnier monoplane, registered F-NUNG. The plane was decorated with the macabre insignia he had painted on during the war: a skull inside a black heart with crossed bones, a coffin, and two lighted candles. He went to the United States and appeared in mock combat at flying circuses. In America he flew a Hanriot HD–1, which he also decorated with his personal insignia.

It may have been his American experience that stimulated him to the adventure that was to cost him his life. When he returned to France, he persuaded Pierre Levasseur to build him an aeroplane that could fly across the Atlantic. They settled on the PL 8

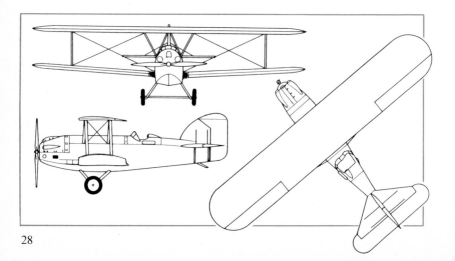

model, a three-seater reconnaissance plane that had originally been produced for the navy and was propelled by a 450 hp Lorraine–Dietrich engine. They modified this plane extensively. It was turned into a two-seater, and the forward part of the fuselage became a fuel tank. The landing gear was made detachable in order to lighten the aircraft and facilitate an eventual forced landing on water. And it was for this reason that the fuselage was separated into water-tight compartments.

After various trials and experiments, the Oiseau Blanc was ready for the flight. It took its name from the fact that it was painted white all over. The only elements not painted white were the French markings and Nungesser's personal insignia, on the wings and rudder. The second member of the crew was Captain François Coli, the navigator.

Immediately after takeoff, the Oiseau Blanc was escorted as far as Le Havre by another plane. Then it was

Aircraft: **Levasseur PL 8 Oiseau Blanc**
Manufacturer: **Société Pierre Levasseur**
Type: —
Year: **1927**
Engine: **Lorraine-Dietrich, 12-cylinder V, liquid-cooled, 450 hp**
Wingspan: **48 ft (14.63 m)**
Length: **32 ft (9.75 m)**
Height: **13 ft (3.96 m)**
Weight: **10,921 lb (4,954 kg)**
Maximum speed: **120 mph (193 km/h)**
Ceiling: —
Range: **3,700 mile (6,000 km)**
Crew: **2**

on its own. The anxious waiting throughout the world was suddenly interrupted by the following headline in a French newspaper: 'Nungesser and Coli have crossed the Atlantic. At 4.50 p.m. they reached New York harbor.' It was fake news. The truth about the fliers was brutally announced by a telegram from the American government. 'Nungesser not yet arrived. Weather terrible.' Nungesser and Coli never reached New York. All that remains of their attempt is the undercarriage of the Oiseau Blanc, which is now in the Musée de l'Air, Paris.

Farman F.180

Oiseau Bleu, the Bluebird. A delicate nickname – and one well-suited to the elegance of the Farman F.180. This plane was designed in 1927 for an Atlantic crossing and then assigned to civil transport. Although only three F.180s were built, they saw long and successful service with the Lignes Farman on the Paris–London route.

The design of the F.180 was extremely advanced for its time. This was especially true of its general aerodynamics and the purity of the line of the fuselage. Everything about this plane reflects precision of design and intelligent use of space, the result of the plane's original intention, long non-stop flying. The two wings of this biplane were of different size, and the elegant, windowed fuselage was almost oval in section. The wings were fabric-covered, and the fuselage was covered in wood. The large fuselage accommodated a passenger cabin that was 26 feet 3 inches (8 m) long, 7 feet 8 inches (2.35 m) wide, and 5 feet 11 inches (1.80 m) high. Twenty-four passengers could be accommodated in three rows of seats. The two-man was at the front of the plane and was completely enclosed, unlike most other civil aircraft of the time.

The arrangement of the engines was unusual and sensible. Two Farman 12-cylinder V engines, liquid-cooled,

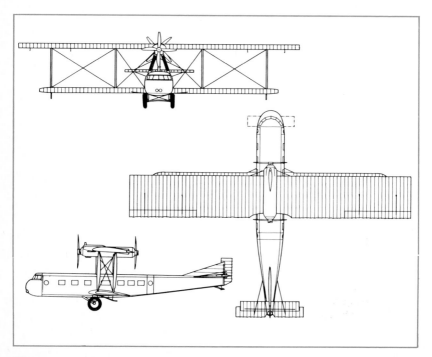

were mounted in tandem over the fuselage and just below the upper wing. The propellers, each with four blades, were well pitched and supported by four metal structures that also housed the two radiators. This arrangement of the engines had excellent aerodynamic results and also made it possible to increase the comfort of passengers and crew, who were sufficiently insulated from engine and propellor noise. The undercarriage, simple and neatly trimmed to the fuselage, also made its contribution to the plane's elegance of line.

Passenger accommodation also received careful attention. The cabin was light and spacious, thanks to seven square windows on each side, and the interior was decorated in excellent taste. A bar was also provided. The plane could carry between twelve and twenty-four passengers, depending on the distance and type of flight. With a full load of passengers, the plane's range was reduced to about 310 miles (500 km), but with only

Aircraft: **Farman F.180**
Manufacturer: **Avions H. & M. Farman**
Type: **Civil transport**
Year: **1928**
Engine: **Two Farman 12We, 12-cylinder V, liquid-cooled, 500 hp each**
Wingspan: **85 ft 4 in (26 m)**
Length: **59 ft (17.98 m)**
Height: **—**
Weight: **17,610 lb (7,990 kg)**
Cruising speed: **106 mph (170 km/h)**
Ceiling: **13,000 ft (4,000 m)**
Range: **620 mile (1,000 km)**
Crew: **2**
Passengers: **24**

twelve aboard the range was almost doubled. On night flights, between twelve and seventeen passengers could be accommodated in couchette seats. Another guarantee of the plane's safety was its ability to maintain altitude with only one engine carrying a total weight of 15,400 pounds (7,000 kg).

The first F.180, the Oiseau Bleu, regstered F-AIMX, went into service with the Lignes Farman in February 1928. It was followed by two other planes, registered F-AIRZ and F-AIVR.

Lioré et Olivier 213

Adapted from the LeO 20 heavy bomber, the Lioré et Olivier 213 became one of the most luxurious passenger planes of its time. It was called the Rayon d'Or (Ray of Gold) and painted red, gold, and white. It saw service on two of the most prestigious European routes, Paris–London and Paris–Lyons– Marseilles. The Air Union counted chiefly on the plane's elegance and on high-quality service to attract passengers. One of the Rayons d'Or, transformed into a kind of flying restaurant, offered meals that could compete with the most famous French restaurants of the period. The plane's success was confirmed by long years of service. When the Air Union company was absorbed by the new Air France in 1933, eleven LeO 213s were still in service. By 1934 they had logged a total of 20,000 hours in the air.

The version that was directly adapted from the LeO 20 bomber was called LeO 21 and made its appearance in 1926. It was a biplane driven by two 420 hp Gnome–Rhône Jupiter radial engines. The modified fuselage could accommodate eighteen passengers in two separate cabins. This prototype, which went into service with the Air Union in 1926, was followed the next year by a model that

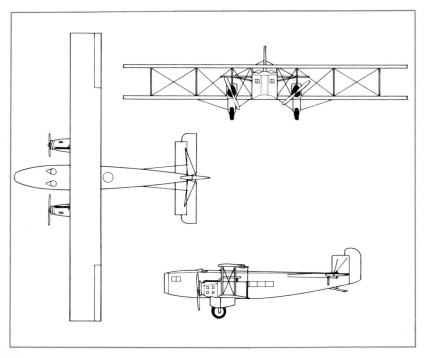

Lioré et Olivier 213 – 1928

was further modified, the LeO 212. This new model had two 450 hp liquid cooled, 12-cylinder V, Renault 12 Ja engines. The fuselage was altered, and a restaurant for twelve was installed. The LeO 212, together with the LeO 21, was used on the Paris–London run from July 30, 1927.

The next development was the LeO 213, which appeared in 1928. Although identical in concept with its predecessor, this plane was somewhat larger. The fuselage was longer and reinforced, and the cables and guidelines had been transferred from the passenger cabin to the outside of the plane. The passengers, reduced to twelve in number, were lodged in the centre cabin, while the forward cabin was set aside for baggage. A single row of seats ran down each side of the cabin. Three planes in service with the Air Union were equipped with bars, and the crew was increased to three by the addition of a steward.

Lioré et Olivier built a total of eleven LeO 213s. After the prototype,

Aircraft: **Lioré et Olivier 213**
Manufacturer: **Etablissements Lioré et Olivier**
Type: **Civil transport**
Year: **1928**
Engine: **Two Renault 12 Ja, 12-cylinder V, liquid-cooled, 450 hp each**
Wingspan: **76 ft 11 in (23.43 m)**
Length: **52 ft 4 in (15.95 m)**
Height: **14 ft 1 in (4.30 m)**
Weight: **12,548 lb (5,692 kg)**
Cruising speed: **108 mph at 3,200 ft (174 km/h at 1,000 m)**
Ceiling: **14,700 ft (4,500 m)**
Range: **350 mile (560 km)**
Crew: **2–3**
Passengers: **12**

three were finished in 1929 and 1930, and four more were delivered in 1931. These planes belonged to the Air Union, and saw service alongside the LeO 212 restaurant. This aircraft's interior was designed in collaboration with the Compagnie des Wagons-Lits. The tables were lined up on one side of the cabin, and four people could sit at each table, two on one side and two on the other. This plane, registered F-AIFE, ended its unusual career in 1931, when it was transformed into a cargo plane.

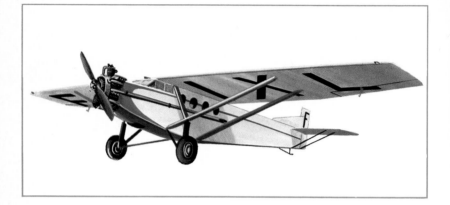

Farman F.190

Aircraft: **Farman F.190**
Manufacturer: **Avions H. & M. Farman**
Type: **Civil transport**
Year: **1928**
Engine: **Gnome-Rhône 5Ba, 5-cylinder radial, air-cooled, 230 hp**
Wingspan: **47 ft 3 in (14.40 m)**
Length: **34 ft 3 in (10.45 m)**
Height: —
Weight: **3,900 lb (1,800 kg)**
Cruising speed: **100 mph (160 km/h)**
Ceiling: **16,900 ft (5,150 m)**
Range: **530 mile (850 km)**
Crew: **1**
Passengers: **4**

The Farman F.190 was rather popular in the late 1920s and early 1930s. Of some hundred constructed, twenty-four saw service with various airlines. Farman Lignes had fourteen in regular service, and the Air Union acquired seven. When Air France was founded in 1933, it acquired fifteen F.190s, which saw service on medium-range flights for several years.

Designed in 1928, the F.190 was a high-wing monoplane. A small aircraft, it could accommodate a pilot and four passengers. The structure was of wood, the wings were fabric-covered, and the fuselage was covered in plywood. Propulsion was provided by a 230 hp, air-cooled, 5-cylinder, Gnome–Rhône Titan 5Ba radial engine. But later models were equipped with a variety of engines. The F.192 had a 230 hp Salmson 9Ab radial; the F.193 had a 230 hp Farman 9Ea engine; the F.194 had a 250 hp Hispano–Suiza 6Mb engine; the F.197 had a 240 hp Lorraine 7Me engine; the F.198 had a 250 hp Renault 9A engine; and the F.199 had a 325 hp Lorraine 9Na engine. About fifty planes in all had the original Ghome–Rhône Titan engine.

In addition to Farman Lignes and the Air Union, other airlines employed the Farman F.190, including CIDNA, Air Orient in Saigon, LARES in Romania, and two companies operating in Africa.

Cams 53-1

Derived from a naval reconnaissance hydroplane, the Cams 53 became one of the classic French transports in the Mediterranean and saw service well into the 1930s. This biplane was powered by two 500 hp Hispano–Suiza engines housed in tandem just under the upper wing. The type and force of propulsion were what chiefly distinguished it from its predecessor, the Cams 51 C, which had been adapted from the military aircraft the Cams 51 R3. The prototype of the 53 was built in 1928 and delivered to Aéropostale, which put it into service on October 22 of the same year on the Marseilles–Algiers run. The year 1929 saw the appearance of a new model, the 53-1, whose hull was considerably stronger and whose fuel capacity had been increased by 88 gallons (400 l). A more powerful Hispano–Suiza engine was introduced, a 580 hp model. The adoption of a radial engine led to a

Aircraft: **Cams 53-1**
Manufacturer: **Chantiers Aéro-Maritimes de la Seine**
Type: **Civil transport**
Year: **1929**
Engine: **Two Hispano-Suiza 12Lbr, 12-cylinder V, liquid-cooled, 580 hp each**
Wingspan: **66 ft 11 in (20.40 m)**
Length: **48 ft 7 in (14.82 m)**
Height: **—**
Weight: **14,308 lb (6,490 kg) (loaded)**
Cruising speed: **106 mph (170 km/h)**
Ceiling: **14,700 ft (4,500 m)**
Range: **650 mile (1,050 km)**
Crew: **2**
Passengers: **4**

further variation of the aircraft. This new model, of which only four were built, was known as the Cams 53–3. The engine was a 480 hp Gnome–Rhône Jupiter 9Akx.

The various types of Cams 53 were used by several French airlines. The Aéropostale had six; Air Orient had twelve; the Air Union had eight. In 1933 Air France took twenty-one and kept them in service until 1935. One, however, registered F-AIZB, remained in service until 1938.

Breguet XIX Super TR

A world record was set in September 1929: 4,912 miles (7,905 km) were flown in 51 hours and 19 minutes. Another world record was set in December 1929: 4,989 miles (8,029 km) were flown non-stop on a closed circuit. And in January and February 1930, still more world records were established: speed, distance, and endurance with a load of more than half a ton, as well as distance and endurance with more than a ton. But aside from these outstanding achievements, another sports undertaking made the Breguet XIX Super TR famous throughout Europe: the non-stop Atlantic crossing from Paris to New York. It was the reverse of the flight Charles Lindbergh had made three-and-a-half years earlier. The Breguet, piloted by Dieudonné Costes and Maurice Bellonte flew 3,699 miles (5,953 km) in 37 hours and 18 minutes at an average speed of 103.9 miles an hour (167.3 km/h). Notwithstanding the tragic flight of Nungesser and Coli, who went down in the Atlantic in their

Oiseau Bleu, France could consider itself one of the most prestigious nations in the world of flying.

The Point d'Interrogation (Question Mark), as the Breguet XIX Super TR was called was specially designed for competition flying. It was an adaptation of the Breguet XIX G.R., a French military long-range reconnaissance biplane, which was one of the three basic versions of the XIX type, which had been developed in 1921. More than a thousand XIXs were produced after 1925. The basic type was a two-seater biplane, with a metal skeleton and simple smooth lines.

When, in 1927, Breguet decided to produce a version of the plane for competition flying, the first goal was a plane that could cross the Atlantic, from Paris to New York, non-stop. The model that was chosen was extensively modified with a view to increasing fuel capacity. The fuselage tanks were enlarged, two tanks were added to the wings, and more fuel could be carried below the lower wing surfaces in detachable containers. The design and manufacturing expenses were

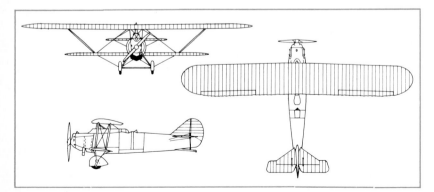

shared by Breguet, the Hispano–Suiza company, and a patron who asked to remain anonymous until the flight had taken place. He was the perfume manufacturer Francis Coty, who contributed about £10,000.

When the plane was ready, Breguet's chief test pilot, Dieudonné Costes, chose his navigator, Maurice Bellonte, and set the date for his first attempt. The Point d'Interrogation took off on July 13, 1929, but was driven back by bad weather. Two months later, Costes decided to abandon the crossing temporarily and to try to establish a new world distance record. On September 27 he took off from Le Bourget and flew until he ran out of fuel. The Breguet landed at Tsitsikar, Manchuria, having flown 4,912 miles (7,905 km). The Atlantic crossing took place after other records had been established. On September 1, 1930, the Point d'Interrogation took off from Le Bourget at 10.45 in the morning, and after 37 hours and 18 minutes in the air, it landed at Curtiss Field, New York. Among the twenty-

Aircraft: **Breguet XIX Super TR**
Manufacturer: **Société Anonyme des Ateliers d'Aviation Louis Breguet**
Type: **'Transatlantic' (or 'Competition')** aircraft
Year: **1929**
Engine: **Hispano-Suiza 12 Nb, 12-cylinder V, liquid-cooled, 650 hp**
Wingspan: **60 ft (18.30 m)**
Length: **35 ft 2 in (10.72 m)**
Height: **13 ft 4 in (4.06 m)**
Weight: **14,700 lb (6,700 kg)**
Cruising speed: **130 mph (210 km/h)**
Maximum speed: **150 mph at 2,900 ft (245 km/h at 900 m)**
Ceiling: **21,900 ft (6,700 m)**
Range: **5,900 mile (9,500 km)**
Crew: **2**

five thousand spectators who turned out to greet the fliers was Charles Lindbergh.

On September 4, Costes and Bellonte took off again, and twelve hours later they were in Dallas, Texas. The two pilots flew some 9,300 miles (15,000 km), paying courtesy visits to major American cities before flying back to Paris on October 25. On their return to France, the two airmen were decorated with the Legion of Honor. The Point d'Interrogation found a permanent home in the Musée de l'Air in Paris.

Couzinet 70 Arc-en-Ciel

Designed for transatlantic postal service, the Couzinet Arc-en-Ciel (Rainbow) went into service with Aéropostale, alongside the Latécoère 300 Croix du Sud (Southern Cross) hydroplane, on the long route between St. Louis, Senegal, and Natal, Brazil. Only one Arc-en-Ciel was ever built, and it was modified several times. In the last five months of 1934, it completed eight Atlantic crossings. But the most noteworthy flight took place on January 16, 1933, when the pilot Jean Mermoz and three crew members inaugurated the South American route by covering the distance between St. Louis and Natal in 14 hours and 27 minutes.

The Couzinet 70 was the result of a design that the twenty-three-year-old René Couzinet developed in 1928 in collaboration with Marcel Maurice Drouhin. Their plan was to construct an aeroplane that could make the Atlantic crossing from east to west. Drouhin and Couzinet were so enthusiastic that they launched a public collection throughout France to get the necessary funds to construct the plane. Two million francs were collected, and the first Arc-en-Ciel was built. In August 1928, the plane crashed during a test flight, and Marcel Maurice Drouhin was killed. A second model was destroyed by fire.

Couzinet could not be stopped.

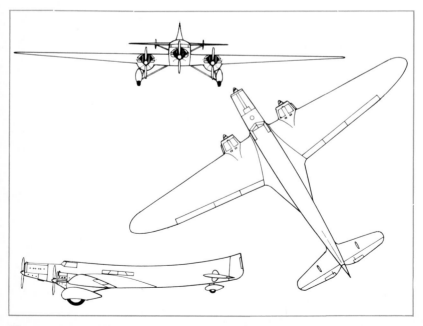

Though mourning the death of his friend, he continued to design planes modelled after his original project. The 70 type, also called Arc-en-Ciel, was built expressly for the trans-Atlantic service of Aéropostale. Just like its prototype, this plane was a low-wing monoplane powered by three 650 hp Hispano–Suiza engines. The hull was broad and the undercarriage was fixed. But the lines of the plane were rather unusual. In particular, the fuselage was altogether original in shape. Its continuous vertical tapering, including the rudder, acted as a drift board. The wings were very thick and they were made heavier by the large engine housing, and the undercarriage was almost as long as the wing was broad. The whole plane was covered in wood. There was accommodation for four crew members and a cabin for cargo, with three windows on each side.

After Mermoz's inaugural flight, the Couzinet 70 was extensively modified and renamed Couzinet 71. The

Aircraft: **Couzinet 70 Arc-en-Ciel**
Manufacturer: **Société des Avions René Couzinet**
Type: **Civil transport**
Year: **1929**
Engine: **Three Hispano-Suiza 12Nb, 12-cylinder V, liquid-cooled, 650 hp each**
Wingspan: **98 ft 5 in (30 m)**
Length: **53 ft (16.15 m)**
Height: **—**
Weight: **37,000 lb (16,790 kg)**
Cruising speed: **147 mph (236 km/h)**
Maximum speed: **174 mph (280 km/h)**
Range: **4,200 mile (6,800 km)**
Crew: **4**
Cargo: **1,300 lb (600 kg)**

fuselage was lengthened, the tail structure was altered, and the three-blade propellers were replaced by two-blade propellers. Both the 70 and 71 had metal propellers. Thus remodelled, the Arc-en-Ciel began its regular postal run to South America on May 28, 1934. Beginning in June of that year, there was a monthly Atlantic crossing. Early in 1935, the plane was overhauled once again. The undercarriage fairings were removed, and trimmer engine housings were introduced, while the radiators were moved.

Latécoère 28

About fifty Latécoère 28s were con-structed. Extensive use was made of the plane by Aéropostale on runs between France and Africa as well as on South American runs. During its intensive career, from 1929 to the middle 1930s, the Latécoère 28 established nine world records for speed, endurance and distance with loads of 1,100 pounds (500 kg), 2,200 pounds (1,000 kg), and 4,400 pounds (2,000 kg). The aircraft that set the records in 1930 was a naval version piloted by Lieutenant Paris. Another 28, christened Comte de la Vaulx and piloted by Jean Mermoz, inaugurated the postal service run between Toul-ouse, France, and Rio de Janeiro. It covered the St. Louis, Senegal, to Natal, Brazil, lap in twenty-one hours of flight. This Atlantic crossing took place on May 12–13, 1930.

The Latécoère 28 was a high-wing monoplane with smooth lines and was propelled by a 500 hp Hispano–Suiza engine. Two variant models were powered by a 600 hp and a 650 hp Hispano–Suiza engine. These two models were known respectively as the Latécoère 28-3 and 28-5. Both the land and sea models had a metal skeleton. The wings were fabric-covered, and the fuselage was covered

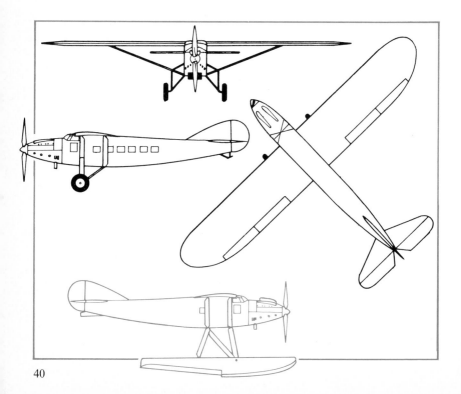

in metal and fabric. The commodious cabin housed a two-man crew, while the passenger model could accommodate eight passengers.

The original models, the Latécoère 28-0 and 28-1, were both land planes. The seaplane versions of these two aircraft, the 28-3 and the 28-5, which were equipped with more powerful Hispano–Suiza engines, were earmarked exclusively for postal transport. These two planes had two landing pontoons and a larger wing area. They could carry a load of between 660–1,320 pounds (300 and 600 kg) and had a significantly greater range than their predecessors. The 28-3 had a range of 1,900 miles (3,200 km), and the 28-5 had a range of 3,291 miles (5,297 km).

After long service with the Aéropostale company, the Latécoère 28s continued to fly for Air France. When Air France was founded in 1933, it took thirty 28s and two seaplanes. The Aeroposta Argentina took four 28s, while the Venezuelan LAV (Linea

Aircraft: **Latécoère 28-3**
Manufacturer: **Forges et Ateliers de Construction Latécoère**
Type: **Civil transport**
Year: **1929**
Engine: **Hispano-Suiza 12 Lbr, 12-cylinder V, liquid-cooled, 600 hp**
Wingspan: **63 ft 2 in (19.25 m)**
Length: **44 ft 9 in (13.64 m)**
Weight: **11,060 lb (5,017 kg)**
Cruising speed: **124 mph at 6,500 ft (200 km/h at 2,000 m)**
Ceiling: **18,000 ft (5,500 m)**
Range: **1,900 mile (3,200 km)**
Crew: **2**
Cargo: **659 lb (299 kg)**

Aeropostal Venezolana) took five. These planes were in regular service until the middle of the 1930s.

Experimental versions of the 28 were also developed in limited numbers. A version for the navy, the 290, was built in 1933. And a radically different model was designed later. This was the 350, a three-engine plane that could carry ten passengers. But it never got off the drawing board.

Farman F.220

In September 1935 the best time ever for an Atlantic crossing was thirteen hours and thirty-seven minutes, from Dakar to Natal. This record was established by a four-engine Farman F.220, a civil version of a bomber built early in 1930. Expressly adapted for South Atlantic runs by Air France, the commercial F.220, which was quite similar to the military version, entered service in 1935. The fundamental differences were in the rudder mechanism, the moving of the radiators, and the substitution of the bomber's four-blade propellers by three-blade propellers. Of course, all the armament was removed. It was a high-wing monoplane, with four Hispano–Suiza engines installed in tandem pairs, two on each side of the fuselage. The engine housings were supported by two small semi-wings that protruded from the sides of the plane.

The inaugural flight of Le Centaure

Aircraft: **Farman F.220**
Manufacturer: **Avions H. & M. Farman**
Type: **Civil transport**
Year: **1930**
Engine: **Four Hispano-Suiza 12 Lbr, 12-cylinder V, liquid-cooled, 600 hp each**
Wingspan: **118 ft 1 in (35.99 m)**
Length: **69 ft (21.03 m)**
Height: **—**
Weight: **35,000 lb (16,000 kg)**
Cruising speed: **136 mph at 11,400 ft (219 km/h at 3,500 m)**
Ceiling: **19,600 ft (6,000 m)**
Range: **2,700 mile (4,500 km)**
Crew: **2**
Cargo: **17,600 lb (8,000 kg) (including crew)**

(as Air France called this plane, registered F-ANLG) took place on June 3, 1935. Henri Guillaumet and Laurent Guerrero flew the plane from Dakar to Natal in fourteen hours and fifty-two minutes, not much more than the record time set in September of the same year. The plane made the Atlantic crossing several times, establishing various speed records. One of the more important records was established June 15–18, 1935, when a Farman F.220 flew from Paris to Buenos Aires in sixty-eight hours and forty-five minutes.

Farman F.300

After the success of the F.190, the Farman company decided to develop a family of planes that would continue the lines and structure of the earlier model, albeit on a larger scale. The F.300 prototype took to the air in 1930. The F.300s resembled the F.190s, but the new planes were equipped with three 230 hp Salmson radial engines. Two of the engines were housed on the wings, while the third was attached to the fuselage. They were high-wing planes with wooden skeletons and covered in wood and fabric. The cabin, which was relatively large, could accommodate eight passengers and two crew.

There were seven models of the F.300, their nomenclature varying according to engine type. The Farman F.302 was a single-engine plane; a 650 hp Hispano–Suiza was mounted on the fuselage. The Farman F.310 had two pontoons. A total of some

Aircraft: **Farman F.300**
Manufacturer: **Avions H. & M. Farman**
Type: **Civil transport**
Year: **1930**
Engine: **Three Salmson 9Ab, 9-cylinder radial, air-cooled, 230 hp each**
Wingspan: **62 ft 7 in (19.08 m)**
Length: **43 ft 9 in (13.35 m)**
Height: **11 ft 6 in (3.50 m)**
Weight: **9,987 lb (4,530 kg)**
Cruising speed: **118 mph at 6,500 ft (190 km/h at 2,000 m)**
Ceiling: **14,700 ft (4,500 m)**
Range: **530 mile (850 km)**
Crew: **2**
Passengers: **8**

twenty F.300s were built, but they were used intensively in their time. The Lignes Farman used them on the Paris–Berlin and the Paris–Brussels–Essen–Hamburg–Copenhagen–Malmö runs. Air Orient used them out of Damascus. And F.300s were in service with the Compagnie Transafricaine d'Aviation and the Yugoslavian line Aeroput. The F.300s in service with the Lignes Farman were called 'Etoile d'Argent (Silver Star). When fifteen F.300s were taken over by Air France, each plane was given the name of a different flower.

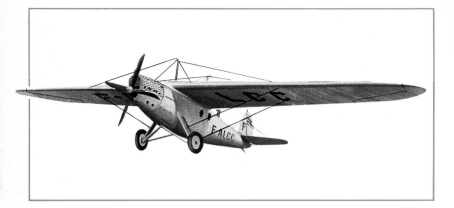

Blériot 110

In February 1931 Lucien Bossoutrot and Maurice Rossi set a world record for closed-circuit distance flying. They flew 5,482 miles 340 yards (8,822.325 km) in seventy-five hours and twenty-three minutes. A year later, on March 26, 1931, the record was increased to 6,587 miles 1,337 yards (10,601.480 km) in seventy-six hours and thirty-four minutes. On August 5, 1933, Maurice Rossi and Paul Codos established a new world record in long-distance flying. They flew 5,657 miles (9,104 km) from New York to Rayak, Syria, in fifty-five hours and thirty minutes. These are some of the major achievements of the Blériot 110, a plane designed for competition flying. For almost five years it dominated the flying world. Zappata's design was begun in 1929, construction got under way in April and was finished by May 9, 1930. The plane took to the air a week later.

Aircraft: **Blériot 110**
Manufacturer: **Blériot Aéronautique**
Type: **—**
Year: **1930**
Engine: **Hispano-Suiza, 12-cylinder V, liquid-cooled, 600 hp**
Wingspan: **86 ft 11 in (26.50 m)**
Length: **47 ft 9 in (14.57 m)**
Height: **16 ft 1 in (4.90 m)**
Weight (empty): **6,570 lb (2,980 kg)**
Weight (loaded): **15,980 lb (7.250 kg)**
Maximum speed: **130 mph (210 km/h)**
Range: **6,588 mile (10,601 km) (record)**
Crew: **2**
Cargo: **10,730 lb (4,870 kg)**

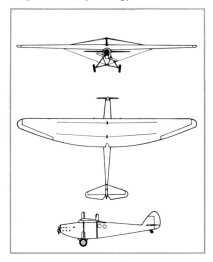

F

Blériot 125

The design of the Blériot 125 was one
of the most original and advanced of
those that marked the development of
civil aviation in the 1930s. Although
this aircraft never got beyond the
prototype stage, it attracted a great
deal of attention at the 12th Salon de
l'Aviation in Paris, where it was
shown in November 1930. What distinguished the Blériot 125 was its
configuration. It was especially designed to provide the maximum of
comfort to its twelve passengers.
There were two separate fuselages
below the wings. Each fuselage ended
in a tail piece supporting the tail unit.
The three-man crew were housed in a
small central cabin over the wing. One
of the two Hispano–Suiza engines,
500 hp each, had a tractor propeller
and the other a pusher propeller. The
Blériot 125 made several test flights in
1931, and a hydroplane version was
also contemplated.

Aircraft: **Blériot 125**
Manufacturer: **Blériot Aéronautique**
Type: **Civil transport**
Year: **1931**
Engine: **Two Hispano-Suiza 12Hbr, 12-
cylinder V, liquid-cooled, 500 hp each**
Wingspan: **96 ft 5 in (29.40 m)**
Length: **45 ft 3 in (13.80 m)**
Height: **13 ft 1 in (4 m)**
Weight: **15,740 lb (7,140 kg)**
Cruising speed: **112 mph (180 km/h)**
Ceiling: **14,700 ft (4,500 m)**
Range: **500 mile (800 km)**
Crew: **3**
Cargo: **4,230 lb (1,920 kg) (12 passengers)**

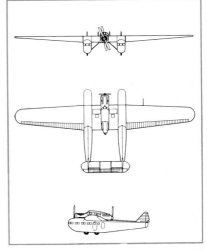

45

Latécoère 300

Specially designed aeroplanes were built for Atlantic crossings. One such plane, the Latécoère 300, was one of the most famous aircraft of its day. On its first appearance this large four-engine flying boat, called the Croix du Sud (Southern Cross), established a record by flying 2,286 miles (3,678 km) from Marseilles to St. Louis, Senegal, in just under twenty-four hours. The Latécoère 300 made several Atlantic crossings on the Dakar–Natal route, but it was lost at sea on December 7, 1936, with all its crew. The captain of the Croix du Sud was Jean Mermoz,

one of the most famous French pilots of the 1930s.

The Latécoère 300 was designed at the request of the French government, which wanted a postal plane that could carry a load of one ton across the ocean. The prototype took to the air in 1931 but went down in the sea off Marseilles a few months later. The aircraft was badly damaged. It was salvaged and repaired, and almost a year later it was again aloft. It was this reconstructed plane that was given the name of Croix du Sud.

The configuration of aircraft fol-

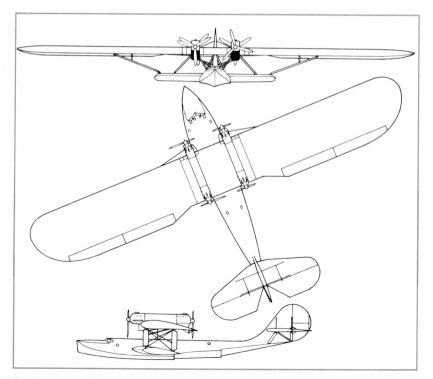

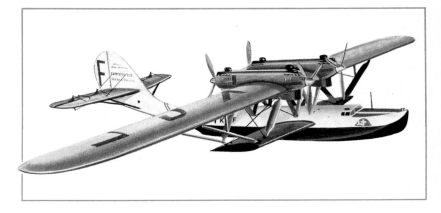

lowed one of the most successful flying boat plans of the time. There was a large central hull and two large floats on the sides of the fuselage. The high-winged Latécoère 300 had four, 650 hp, Hispano–Suiza engines. These were arranged in pairs, and mounted in pods just over the fuselage. Each pair had one pusher propeller and one tractor propeller. The plane was all-metal, both in skeleton and covering, but the wings remained cloth-covered. Everything about the plane was designed with trans-oceanic flight in mind, including a sleeping compartment for the crew and a hold containing fuel and oil tanks with a capacity of more than ten-tons.

From the time it went into service, December 31, 1933, until its disappearance, the Croix du Sud completed some fifteen flights across the Atlantic. Its achievements led to orders for six more planes, three for Air France and three for the French navy. These planes, which were known as Latécoère 301s and 302s respectively,

Aircraft: **Latécoère 300**
Manufacturer: **Forges et Ateliers de Construction Latécoère**
Type: **Civil transport**
Year: **1932**
Engine: **Four Hispano-Suiza 12 Nbr, 12-cylinder V, liquid-cooled, 650 hp each**
Wingspan: **145 ft (44.19 m)**
Length: **85 ft 11 in (26.18 m)**
Height: **—**
Weight: **50,700 lb (23,000 kg)**
Cruising speed: **100 mph (160 km/h)**
Ceiling: **15,000 ft (4,600 m)**
Range: **2,900 mile (4,800 km)**
Crew: **4**
Cargo: **2,200 lb (1,000 kg)**

were slightly modified versions of the original 300. The wings had a greater dihedral, and the tail surface was larger. The Air France planes were delivered early in 1936 and named Ville de Buenos Aires, Ville de Rio de Janeiro, and Ville de Santiago du Chile. Two of these planes were in service for several years, but the Ville de Buenos Aires was lost at sea only a month after it went into service, on the Natal–Dakar run.

Wibault 283.T

Between 1933 and 1938, Air France served the major European routes with a fast three-engine plane, the Wibault of the 280.T series. The variations of this model that appeared beginning in 1930 made it an all-round short-and medium-range transport. This extremely strong and reliable plane was very modern in design. All-metal in skeleton and covering, it was a low-wing plane. The quality of design was confirmed by its adaptability to modification in the four series of Wibaults that were built. The chief modifications included the addition of more powerful engines and, in the case of the 283.T, the addition of stronger propellers and increased fuel capacity. The rest was fundamentally unchanged.

The three-engine Wibault made its debut at the Paris Salon de l'Aviation in 1930, the same year the Blériot 125 prototype was shown. Like Louis Blériot's design, that of the Wibault was impressive because of the new technical innovations and because of the original configuration of the plane. Men in the profession as well as the general public were struck by the plane's modern look. But the Blériot and the Wibault were totally different concepts in aircraft. The Blériot was totally untraditional and represented a dramatic departure from the reality of contemporary flight. Indeed the plane never went into production. The Wibault, on the other hand, was based on a formula that had been successful in the past, but it improved on past

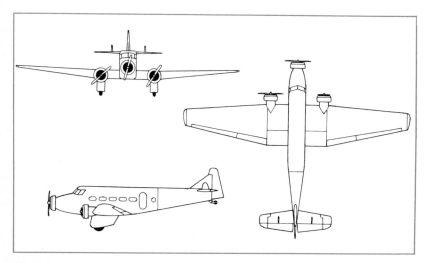

experience and became what one might call a classic.

The Wibault 280.T was a low-wing monoplane covered in duralumin. It was originally powered by three 300 hp Hispano–Suiza radial engines. The large, square-sectioned fuselage could accommodate ten passengers and two crew, who sat side by side in the cockpit. The undercarriage was fixed and later equipped with fairings to reduce drag. The second prototype had 350 hp Gnome–Rhône engines and came to be known as the 281.T. The next model, the 282.T, differed only in the fairings of two outside engines. The 283.T model had new propellers, Ratiers instead of the original Gnome–Rhônes, and larger fuel tanks.

The first 282.Ts produced were delivered to the CIDNA and Air Union companies for the Paris–Prague–Istanbul and Paris–London routes. All of the planes were transferred to the newly established Air France in

Aircraft: **Wibault 283.T**
Manufacturer: **Chantiers Aéronautiques Wibault**
Type: **Civil transport**
Year: **1934**
Engine: **Three Gnome-Rhône Titan Major 7kd, 7-cylinder radial, air-cooled, 350 hp each**
Wingspan: **74 ft 2 in (22.60 m)**
Length: **55 ft 9 in (16.99 m)**
Height: **—**
Weight: **13,981 lb (6,342 kg)**
Cruising speed: **143 mph (230 km/h)**
Ceiling: **17,000 ft (5,200 m)**
Range: **620 mile (1,000 km)**
Crew: **2**
Passengers: **10**

1933. The new airline acquired ten 283.Ts in 1934. The Wibaults were kept in service until 1938. Some of them were modified, and an experimental model, registered F-AKEL, was equipped with a retractable undercarriage.

Blériot 5190
Santos-Dumont

Like so many other French transport planes, the Blériot 5190 was especially designed and constructed for trans-Atlantic flights. Designed in response to specifications issued by the French government in 1928, this four-engine flying boat was not actually built until 1933. After its inaugural flight on the South Atlantic route, the Blériot 5190, which was christened the Santos–Dumont (after Alberto Santos–Dumont, the Brazilian aviation pioneer who had died in 1932), completed twenty-two crossings, notably reduc-ing the flying time between Toulouse and Buenos Aires.

The first test flight of this plane took place on August 11, 1933, after the construction of the prototype had been delayed because of Blériot's financial difficulties. Tests were carried out for several months. On January 6, 1934, all the tests were positive. The 5190 was a large central-hull flying-boat with a metal skeleton; the wings and instrument housings were covered in fabric, while the fuselage and tail were metal-covered. The semi-circular sectioned central hull had two levels. The high wing rested on a superstructure that was installed in the centre of the fuselage, where the pilot and flight

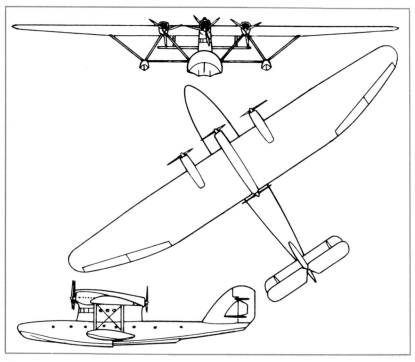

engineer sat. Two lateral floats were attached to the wings and central hull by metal struts. The four 650 hp Hispano–Suiza engines were installed on the wings. The outer engines had tractor propellers. The other two engines were mounted as a pair over the cockpit. The three-bladed metal propellers had adjustable pitch, and the engines could be adjusted in flight.

From the first test flights it was already clear that the Blériot 5190 was an extremely efficient plane. During a test take-off, the Santos–Dumont succeeded in lifting sixteen tons off the water in seventeen seconds with the forward central engine off. Although the trans-oceanic model could accommodate only 1,300 pounds (600 kg) of cargo, the difference between the plane's weight loaded and unloaded was accounted for by more than 18,700 pounds (8,500 kg) of fuel and the eight-man crew required by long-distance flights. With these facts in mind, the designers calculated that with more powerful engines, the Blér-

Aircraft: **Blériot 5190 Santos-Dumont**
Manufacturer: **Blériot Aéronautique**
Type: **Civil transport**
Year: **1934**
Engine: **Four Hispano-Suiza 12 Nbr, 12-cylinder V, liquid-cooled, 650 hp each**
Wingspan: **141 ft 1 in (43.00 m)**
Length: **85 ft 3 in (26 m)**
Height: **—**
Weight: **48,500 lb (22,000 kg)**
Cruising speed: **118 mph (190 km/h)**
Ceiling: **—**
Range: **1,900 mile (3,200 km)**
Crew: **8**
Cargo: **1,300 lb (600 kg)**

iot 5190 could accommodate up to sixty passengers on the short Mediterranean runs. The lighter load of fuel and the smaller crew needed on these flights would increase the plane's capacity for paying customers. However, this model was never constructed, and the Santos–Dumont remained the only 5190 ever built.

After its first trans-Atlantic flight, between Dakar and Natal, which was captained by Lucien Bossoutrot on November 27, 1934, the Blériot entered regular service with Air France. It was registered with the authorities as F-ANLE.

Bloch 120

The Bloch 120 saw almost six years of service in the years just before the outbreak of World War II. A particularly hardy and robust, all metal plane, the Bloch 120 did service from Algeria, across the Sahara, to Nigeria, and from the Congo to Madagascar. It was picked by the government for service on the routes of the new Régie Air Afrique, which was founded in 1934. The plane's inaugural flight, on September 7, 1934, was from Algiers to Niamey, Nigeria. The following year two Bloch 120s were taken by the Service de Navigation Aérienne de Madagascar and were put on runs to the heart of Africa. In 1937 all the African routes were assigned to the Régie Air Afrique, which took over the seven Bloch 120s then in commercial use. As a passenger craft, the 120 could carry up to ten passengers as well as the crew, and was therefore, extremely adaptable.

Aircraft: **Bloch 120**
Manufacturer: **Avions Marcel Bloch**
Type: **Civil transport**
Year: **1934**
Engine: **Three Lorraine Algol 9Na, 9-cylinder radial, air-cooled, 300 hp each**
Wingspan: **67 ft 5 in (20.54 m)**
Length: **50 ft 2 in (15.30 m)**
Height: **—**
Weight: **13,200 lb (6,000 kg)**
Cruising speed: **143 mph (230 km/h)**
Ceiling: **20,600 ft (6,300 m)**
Range: **—**
Crew: **3**
Cargo: **(3-4 passengers) 1,700 lb (800 kg)**

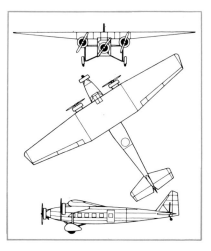

Breguet 530 Saigon

The Breguet 530 Saigon was an improved and enlarged version of the British Short Calcutta. The Breguet company had been licensed in 1931 to build a French version of this flying boat. Two 530 Saigons were constructed in 1934 for Air France and were used on Mediterranean flights for several years. Five Calcuttas were built in France, and a larger version was begun in 1932. This plane was built in two models. One of these was the 521 Bizerte, of which about 30 aircraft were built for the French navy. The other was manufactured for the Air Union, which wanted a commercial plane. This was the 530 Saigon. It was a large, all-metal, central hull biplane. The plane had three 785 hp Hispano–Suiza engines mounted between the wings. There were three classes on board: eleven passengers in second class; six in first class; and two or three in deluxe.

Aircraft: **Breguet 530 Saigon**
Manufacturer: **Société Anonyme des Ateliers d'Aviation Louis Breguet**
Type: **Civil transport**
Year: **1934**
Engine: **Three Hispano-Suiza 12 Ybr, 12-cylinder V, liquid-cooled, 785 hp each**
Wingspan: **115 ft (35.06 m)**
Length: **66 ft 7 in (20.30 m)**
Height: **24 ft 7 in (7.51 m)**
Weight: **33,000 lb (15,000 kg)**
Cruising speed: **124 mph (200 km/h)**
Ceiling: **16,400 ft (5,000 m)**
Range: **680 mile (1,100 km)**
Crew: **2**
Passengers: **20**

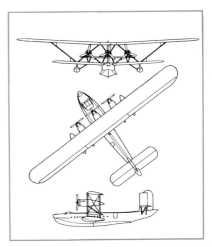

Dewoitine D.338

The Dewoitine D.338, a slender elegant three-engine plane, was perhaps the finest transport plane built in France before World War II. A development of the D.332, which had been built in 1933, the D.338 was used exclusively by Air France. Thirty-one D.338s were built, and they saw service on such prestige routes as Paris–Marseilles–Cannes, Paris–Dakar, Paris–Hong Kong, and Paris–Damascus–Hanoi. The culmination of the three-engine formula, the D.338 continued to be used commercially even after the end of World War II. Of the nine planes that survived the war,

eight were used for some time on the Paris–Nice run, before being replaced by new planes of the postwar generation.

The first of the series that culminated in the D.338 was built in 1933 by the Société Aéronautique Française, which was simply the new name of the Constructions Aéronautique E. Dewoitine. The original design was the D.332, a low-wing, all-metal, three-engine transport plane. This aircraft's slender line was broken only by the fixed undercarriage. Baptized Émeraude (Emerald), the plane was delivered to Air France, which used it to try out new short-and medium-range routes. These experimental flights came to a tragic end. After reaching Saigon in 48 hours, the

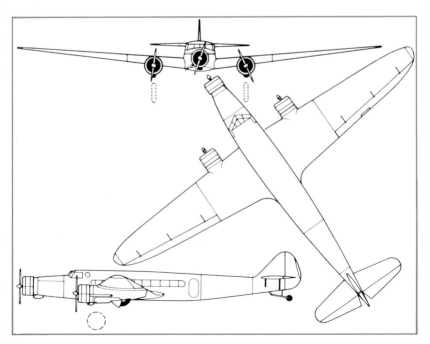

D.332, piloted by Maurice Noguès, crashed into a mountain during a storm on its return flight.

Three D.333s were built for Air France in 1935. One of these crashed, and the other two saw service on the South American run until 1938. The D.333 was very similar to the D.332, but it could carry up to ten passengers instead of eight. While the D.333 was in construction, the Société Aéronautique Française had already begun design of a later model, the D.338. The prototype took to the air in 1935 and was delivered to Air France the following year. The tests showed that it was well suited for European, South American, and Far Eastern routes. Twenty-one D.338s were originally ordered, but the number was soon increased to thirty. Although the D.338 had the same general lines as the D.332 and the D.333, it was notably larger. But it had a retractable undercarriage. The portion that protruded below the fuselage when the wheels were up was covered by aero-

Aircraft: **Dewoitine D.338**
Manufacturer: **Société Aéronautique Française**
Type: **Civil transport**
Year: **1935**
Engine: **Three Hispano-Suiza 9V 16/17, 9-cylinder radial, air-cooled, 650 hp each**
Wingspan: **96 ft 3 in (29.35 m)**
Length: **72 ft 7 in (22.13 m)**
Height: **—**
Weight: **24,500 lb (11,150 kg)**
Cruising speed: **162 mph (260 km/h)**
Ceiling: **16,000 ft (4,900 m)**
Range: **1,200 mile (1,950 km)**
Crew: **3**
Passengers: **22**

dynamic fairings. And the 575 hp engines of the earlier models were replaced by 650 hp engines. With this increase in power, the plane could carry up to twenty-two passengers, except on African flights (fifteen passengers) and Far Eastern runs (twelve passengers). On Far Eastern flights, six passengers were accommodated in couchette-seats.

Potez 62

The work horse of Air France, the Potez 62 saw service around the world in the years before the outbreak of World War II. It was used on European lines as far as Scandinavia, on Far Eastern runs, on South American routes, to cross the Andes, and between Buenos Aires and Santiago. A strong and sturdy plane, the 62 was a variation of the Potez 54 bomber, but without the ugly bulky lines of the military plane. The fuselage of the 62 was smooth and neat, and in profile it had the shape of a wing section.

The project was begun in 1934, and the prototype first took to the air on January 28, 1935. The test flights continued until April, and the plane was delivered to Air France, which assigned it to the Paris–Marseilles–Rome route. Air France ordered eleven more 62s.

A high-wing, two-engine monoplane, the 62 had fabric-covered wings and tail, while the fuselage was wood-covered. The two engines were Gnome–Rhône 14-cylinder radials of 870 hp each. Like those of the bomber, the engines were housed between the fuselage and wings. The engine housings also accommodated the wheels of the main undercarriage, operated hydraulically. The spacious cabin could accommodate between fourteen and

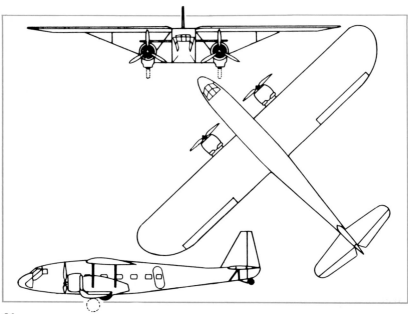

sixteen passengers in two compartments, one of which was a smoking
compartment. The cabin was hand-
somely decorated; it was soundproof
and had heating and air conditioning
systems. Baggage was stowed in two
holds, one in the tail and one in the
nose of the plane, where the two
restrooms were located.

The original model, the 62-0, was
joined by a modified model in 1935.
This 62-1 had different ` engines:
720 hp Hispano–Suizas, which were
liquid-cooled. Ten 62-1s were ordered
by Air France, which put them into
service the following year on domestic
South American routes. In 1936, the
year Air France received its Potez
fleet, the company extended and increased its routes. The Potezs were
used on several European runs and in
the Far East as well. The planes proved themselves robust, comfortable,
and safe. Almost all of them remained
in service until the outbreak of World
War II, although newer aircraft were

Aircraft: **Potez 62**
Manufacturer: **Société des Aéroplanes Henry Potez**
Type: **Civil transport**
Year: **1935**
Engine: **Two Ghome-Rhône 14 Kirs Mistral Major, 14-cylinder radial, air-cooled, 870 hp each**
Wingspan: **73 ft 7 in (22.44 m)**
Length: **56 ft 10 in (17.32 m)**
Height: **—**
Weight: **16,500 lb (7,500 kg)**
Cruising speed: **174 mph at 6,500 ft (280 km/h at 2,000 m)**
Ceiling: **24,600 ft (7,500 m)**
Range: **620 mile (1,000 km)**
Crew: **2**
Cargo: **(14-16 passengers) 660 lb (300 kg)**

also introduced. One 62-0 was assigned as a special transport craft to the
air ministry. Another, the plane registered FC-AYM and called the
Dunquerque, saw service in wartime
as a military transport with the Free
French.

Latécoère 521

The gigantic Latécoère 521, a veritable Jumbo of the 1930s, could carry thirty passengers across the Atlantic or seventy passengers on Mediterranean routes. When its design was begun, in 1933, this large flying boat represented the first of its type in the world. Its use on routes to North America was prevented by the outbreak of World War II and the subsequent rapid development of land planes. The Latécoère 521 was, in a way, France's last and most advanced creation in the chapter of aviation's history that saw the flying boat as the commercial transport craft *par excellence*.

As early as 1930 the Latécoère factory had projected a large trans-Atlantic aircraft, a plane to be pow-ered by four of the 1,000 hp engines that Hispano–Suiza was then develop-ing. This plane, the 520, was abandoned on the drawing board when Hispano–Suiza gave up the engine project. The original plane design was modified to accommodate six less powerful Hispano–Suiza engines. The construction of this new plane, the 521, began in 1933. It was an all-metal aircraft. A two-decked aircraft, it had separate compartments for service areas, crew and captain's quarters, passenger cabins, and baggage holds. The high wing rested on the upper part of the fuselage, while the lower wing had two floats. The six engines were accommodated in four housings. Each of the inner housings held two engines, one with a pusher propeller, the other with a tractor propeller. The two outer engines were equipped with tractor

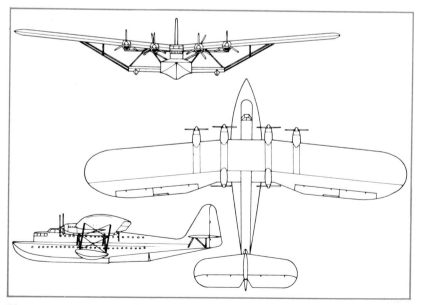

propellers. The plane's technical features and its range made the 521 seaplane able to run a passenger service across the Atlantic. The 521 was named Lieutenant de Vaisseaux Paris ('Lieutenant Paris').

The plane's first flight came to an unhappy end. After setting out from Biscarosse, it set down at Dakar, Natal, Martinique, and Pensacola. On January 4, 1936, it was caught in a hurricane and crashed at sea. A year went by before the 521 could fly again. It was rebuilt after the accident and equipped with less powerful engines (650 hp Hispano–Suizas). In 1937 the plane set several records: on October 25 for distance, flying 3,586 miles 503 yards (5,771.3 km) from Morocco to Brazil; on December 27 for speed (131.13 mph; 211.02 km/h) for some 620 miles (1,000 km) with a load of approximately 22,000 pounds (10,000 kg); on December 29 for speed (117.9 mph; 189.741 km/h), for some 620 miles (1,000 km) with a load of about 33,000 pounds (15,000 kg); on

Aircraft: **Latécoère 521**
Manufacturer: **Forges et Ateliers de Construction Latécoère**
Type: **Civil transport**
Year: **1935**
Engine: **Six Hispano-Suiza 12 Ybrs, 12-cylinder V, liquid-cooled, 860 hp each**
Wingspan: **161 ft 9 in (49.31 m)**
Length: **103 ft 9 in (31.62 m)**
Height: **29 ft 9 in (9.07 m)**
Weight: **83,627 lb (37,933 kg)**
Cruising speed: **130 mph (210 km/h)**
Ceiling: **20,600 ft (6,300 m)**
Range: **2,500 mile (4,100 km)**
Crew: **8**
Passengers: **30–70**

December 30, the plane carried 33,000 pounds (15,000 kg) to an altitude of 11,509 feet (3,508 m) and 39,771 pounds (18,040 kg) to an altitude of 6,561 feet (2,000 m). The first flight to New York was completed on August 31, 1938, by way of Lisbon and the Azores. In 1939 the 521 was joined by an altered model, the Latécoère 522, which was called the Ville de Saint-Pierre. Because of World War II, these two planes did not enter regular commercial service. They were assigned to the French navy along with three other Latécoères.

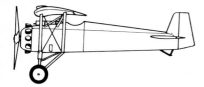

1926 Wibault 72. Wingspan: 35 ft 11 in (10.95 m). Length: 24 ft 9 in (7.55 m). Maximum speed: 138 mph (222 km/h). Engine: 420 hp Gnome-Rhône Jupiter 9 Ac radial. The prototype was the winner of the fighter competition of 1925, and this plane was impressive for the speed with which it reached high altitudes. In less than eleven minutes it could reach 13,000 feet (4,000 m). The following year it was adopted by the air force as a high-altitude interceptor and remained on front-line duty until 1932.

1927 Loire-Gourdou-Leseurre LGL 32. Wingspan: 40 ft (12.20 m). Length: 24 ft 9 in (7.55 m). Maximum speed: 155 mph (250 km/h). Engine: 420 hp Gnome-Rhône Jupiter 9 Ac radial. Three hundred and fifty of these monoplane fighters were built for the French air force. The first aircraft were delivered towards the end of 1927 and, together with the Wibault 72 and the Nieuport-Delage 62, constituted the front-line aircraft for many years.

1928 Nieuport-Delage 62b. Wingspan: 39 ft 4 in (12.00 m). Length: 25 ft (7.64 m). Maximum speed: 168 mph (270 km/h). Engine: 500 hp Hispano-Suiza 12 Md. One of the three basic fighter aircraft of the French air force in the 1930s. A total of 345 62bs were built, while 330 more were built in model 622, which had more powerful engines and metal

propellers. The plane's official operational life ended in 1932, although a few aircraft saw service in 1940, when Germany invaded France.

1930 Dewoitine D.27 C.1. Wingspan: 32 ft 2 in (9.80 m). Length: 21 ft 4 in (6.50 m). Maximum speed: 194 mph (312 km/h). Engine: 500 hp Hispano-Suiza 12 Mc. Designed in Switzerland by Emile Dewoitine (after his French company went out of business), the D.27 C.1. was an excellent combat plane. About seventy aircraft were built for the Swiss air force.

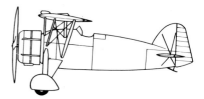

1933 Morane-Saulnier 225. Wingspan: 34 ft 7 in (10.55 m). Length: 23 ft 9 in (7.25 m). Maximum speed: 207 mph (333 km/h). Engine 500 hp Gnome-Rhône 9 radial. Seventy-two of these small tough fighter planes were built. Delivery to air force units began in 1933. The Morane-Saulnier 225 was an extremely aerobatic aeroplane. In 1934 Michel Detroyat piloted a 225 to second place in the world championship aerobatics contest.

1934 Caudron C.460. Wingspan: 22 ft 1 in (6.73 m). Length: 23 ft 4 in (7.11 m). Maximum speed: 314 mph (505 km/h). Engine: 340 hp Renault. One of the most famous French racing planes, the C.460 was designed by Marcel Riffard for the Deutsche de la Meurthe Trophy race.

1934 Bloch 200. Wingspan: 73 ft 7 in (22.43 m). Length: 52 ft 10 in (16.10 m). Maximum speed: 143 mph (230 km/h). Engines: Two 870 hp Gnome–Rhône 14 radials. The plane was designed to specifications issued in 1932 for a plane to replace the LeO 20 bomber. The Bloch 200 made its maiden flight in the summer of 1933 and within two years was in service with twelve air force units. The bomber was also very popular outside France. Czechoslovakia alone built 124 Bloch 200s under licence.

1934 Potez 540. Wingspan: 72 ft 6 in (22.10 m). Length: 53 ft 1 in (16.18 m). Maximum speed: 193 mph (310 km/h). Engines: Two 690 hp Hispano–Suiza 12. This plane was designed and built in a little less than three months. A total of 185 540s were built, as well as later versions.

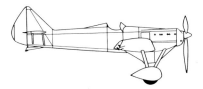

1934 Dewoitine D.510. Wingspan: 39 ft 8 in (12.09 m). Length: 26 ft (7.94 m). Maximum speed: 244 mph (393 km/h). Engine: 860 hp Hispano–Suiza 12. Developed from the D.500 series, this aircraft was built to replace the Nieuport-Delage 62 fighter biplanes. The Dewoitine D.510 was the first French fighter aircraft to break the 400 km/h barrier (about 240 mph) in horizontal flight. A total of 120 were built, many of which were still in service in 1940.

1934 Farman F.221. Wingspan: 118 ft (36.00 m). Length: 70 ft 4 in (21.45 m). Maximum speed: 202 mph (325 km/h). Engines: Four 860 hp Gnome–Rhône 14 radials. This was the French air force's first four-engine bomber. The 221 prototype first took to the air in the spring of 1932. The second prototype set a world altitude record on June 16, 1934, with a 5-ton payload.

1935 Spad 510. Wingspan: 28 ft 11 in (8.81 m). Length: 23 ft 3 in (7.08 m). Maximum speed: 231 mph (372 km/h). Engine: 690 hp Hispano–Suiza 12. This was the French air force's last biplane fighter. The prototype made its first flight early in 1933, and sixty aircraft were ordered. But the plane did not enjoy a brilliant career. Its fuel system caused frequent difficulty, and the undercarriage was too weak.

1935 Amiot 143. Wingspan: 80 ft 6 in (24.55 m). Length: 59 ft 10 in (18.24 m). Maximum speed: 183 mph (295 km/h). Engines: Two 760 hp Gnome–Rhône 14 radials. A total of 178 of these two-engine bombers were built for the French air force. The plane saw active duty during the German invasion. The Amiot 143 was heavily armed. It had four machine guns and could carry a maximum of 1.7 tons of bombs.

Great Britain

British civil aviation got off to a slow start after World War I. The history-making British trans-Atlantic flights of 1919 (the R.34 dirigible's round-trip crossing and the Alcock and Brown non-stop flight in the Vimy IV) did not provide immediate impetus for the development of civil transport. They remained isolated episodes of heroism and daring. Unlike France, where the government gave official support to the development of air lines and made a great contribution to the consolidation and expansion of commercial flying, Britain's civil aviation pioneers were left to their own devices in the first difficult years after the end of the war. And there were many problems: the aircraft, the engines, maintenance, operating costs, and above all the need to offer a service that was sufficiently safe and inviting to overcome the instinctive hesitation that the idea of transport aircraft evoked. Since the government did not

help the private companies and because of fierce competition from the nearest rivals (Germany and France), the first British commercial operators lagged behind other countries, and British aviation lost its earlier pre-eminence in the field.

Civil aviation was authorized only in April 1919, and A. V. Roe and Company, one of the first aeroplane companies in Britain, made the first attempt to set up regular air transport service. The first route was established on May 10 between Alexander Park, Southport, and Blackpool, a distance of about 50 miles (80 km). The aircraft were Avro three-seater biplanes. On September 30, the company decided to suspend the service, after 194 flights had been completed. Meanwhile another air transport company had been founded, Aircraft Transport and Travel. This line was the first in the world to establish daily international flights. The company started with some War-surplus bombers, de Havilland D.H.4As. The company carried out a series of test flights in the summer of 1919 with a view to setting up a London–Paris service. The first regular commercial flight took place on August 25. The flight from Hendon airport to Le Bourget lasted two and a half hours. The flights continued for some time, and the company made a name for itself for punctuality and safety. Without government help, however, the company ran into difficulties. It made efforts at expansion with the acquisition of a mail contract and with the opening of a route between London and Amsterdam. The company's financial difficulties increased, and it finally went out of business on December 15, 1920.

At the same time another airline was established by the aeroplane manufacturer Handley Page. Adapting the 0/400 heavy bombers that had been built towards the end of World War I, the Handley Page Transport company began test flights in the summer of 1919, and on September 2 inaugurated regular flights to Paris in direct competition with Aircraft Transport and Travel (ATT). Handley Page had the advantage. Its planes were larger, safer, and more comfortable, and they could carry more passengers. Morever, the company had vast financial resources, because the parent company had become one of Great Britain's leading industries during World War I. Within two months, the transport company had carried 554 passengers and a total cargo of well over four tons. Service improved in the following months,

when Handley Page introduced the first plane expressly designed and built for civil aviation, the W8. This outstanding aircraft put the company in the forefront, and not only in Great Britain. Handley Page's success, however, did not lead the government to take any more active interest in civil aviation. For some time the government continued to turn a deaf ear to appeals from the new industry. And several companies went out of business. The British Aerial Transport Company (BAT) had been founded in 1917, and after the war it established routes between London and Birmingham and London and Amsterdam. But the company's fortunes declined, and it went out of business in January 1920. Financial difficulties also led to the closure of other short-lived companies, the Supermarine Aviation Company, the North Sea Aerial and General Transport, and the Air Post of Banks.

In 1921 even the more important airlines (Handley Page and Instone Air Lines, founded on May 15, 1920) found themselves in serious trouble. On February 28, 1921, the Handley Page company and Instone terminated all flights to France as a form of protest.

This drastic decision had unexpectedly dramatic results. The government was attacked in the newspapers and in parliament. The nation's prestige was at stake. The government then established a committee to examine the problems of the airlines. After heated debate, it was decided that each company be given a contribution of £25,000. It was the first official recognition of commercial aviation in Great Britain and the first step in a new aviation policy.

Handley Page and Instone resumed their services to France (on March 19 and 21 respectively). New undertakings were begun, and new air transport companies were founded. While local competition increased, Britain's air presence generally increased. Daimler Airways was founded in 1922, and British Marine Air Navigation was created the following year. In order to make routes as efficient as possible, the four companies divided up their areas of activity. Handley Page concentrated its efforts, and put its best planes on the prestigious London–Paris route. Instone took over the Brussels route, and Daimler had the Dutch route with the Amsterdam run. British Marine Navigation had its own routes between the coasts of Britain and France. The year 1923 was fundamental in the development of commercial aviation in Britain. Although progress had been made since 1921, the government realized that long-term planning was necessary if civil aviation was to survive. On December 3 an agreement was signed to join the four major companies in a single organization. The new company would take over all routes and all operational aircraft. It would employ only British-built planes and engines. And if it maintained a certain annual mileage, it would receive government subsidies amounting to one million pounds over ten years. On March 31, 1924, the union became operative, and the new company, Imperial Airways, Ltd., officially went into business the next day.

For a while Imperial Airways concentrated its efforts on consolidating its main European routes. Initially, it was less interested in extending its routes than in improving the quality of its service. Then it began extending its routes to Africa and the Far East, inaugurating new intercontinental lines to the rest of the empire. In the 1930s there was a new flurry of activity, and several more companies were established. Thus the aeroplane became an even more popular form of transport. Hillman's Airways was founded in 1932, Spartan Airlines made its debut in 1933, and United Airways and British Continental Airways were both established in 1935. These companies joined together in 1935 to form British Airways. The union of Highland Airways and Northern & Scottish Airways in 1937 gave birth to Scottish Airways. And several other smaller companies also entered the field. Thus Great Britain reached a thoroughly competitive position with respect to the major countries of Europe.

The years just before World War II saw the completion of Imperial Airways' expansion programme. The company's routes reached the outermost limits of the British Empire: Capetown in Africa, Hong Kong and Singapore in the Far East, and Brisbane and Sidney in Australia. These prestige routes were highly competitive, for Air France, KLM, and Deutsche Lufthansa also flew them. The outbreak of World War II put a halt to further immediate expansion.

de Havilland D.H.10
Amiens III

Like the Vickers Vimy and the Handley Page V/1500, the D.H.10 was constructed too late for service in World War I. Like the other two planes, it was designed as a bomber with the specific aim of developing a plane that could deliver a payload to Germany. But this aim was not to be achieved. Aside from action in India between 1921 and 1923, during the Moplah rebellion, the aeroplane saw no military service. In the years immediately following World War I, the plane was used only for transport,

particularly of mail. In 1919 the D.H.10s of No. 120 Squadron R.A.F. began a regular postal run between England and Germany, delivering mail to British troops on the Rhine. The Amiens (as the plane was called) became the first to make a night run on postal service. Two years later the D.H.10s on duty in Egypt set up another, more difficult postal route – across the desert, between Cairo and Karachi.

The project for the D.H.10 was begun in 1917 by the Aircraft Man-

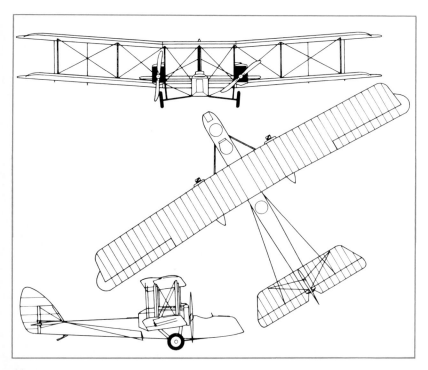

ufacturing Company, where Geoffrey de Havilland was chief designer and test pilot. This plane was a larger and more powerful version of the D.H.3, which had been tested in 1916 but never entered production. The plan of the first prototype was identical with that of its predecessor: a two-engine biplane with pusher propellers. The second prototype, instead, had two 360 hp Rolls-Royce Eagle engines with tractor propellers, and this was the model that was finally decided on. The test flights confirmed the plane's efficiency as a day bomber, and the British Air Ministry ordered 1,295 planes of the third prototype, which was equipped with 400 hp American Liberty engines. But these engines were scarce, and mass production of the aircraft was delayed. By the time of the armistice, there were only eight planes of this type in service with the R.A.F. The end of the war automatically cancelled mass-production of this aircraft, and only about two hundred D.H.10s were completed.

Aircraft: **de Havilland D.H.10 Amiens III**
Manufacturer: **Aircraft Manufacturing Co.**
Type: **Day bomber**
Year: **1919**
Engine: **Two Liberty 12, 12-cylinder V, liquid-cooled, 400 hp each**
Wingspan: **65 ft 6 in (19.96 m)**
Length: **39 ft 7 in (12.06 m)**
Hm: **14 ft 6 in (4.41 m)**
Weight: **9,000 lb (4,100 kg)**
Maximum speed: **112 mph at 10,000 ft (180 km/h at 3,000 m)**
Ceiling: **16,400 ft (5,000 m)**
Endurance: **6 hr**
Armament: **2–4 machine guns; 850 lb (400 kg) of bombs**
Crew: **3–4**

The Amiens saw service in only four R.A.F. squadrons: No. 120, stationed at Hawkinge, Great Britain, which inaugurated the postal service to troops in Germany; No. 104, also in the United Kingdom; No. 60, stationed in India; and No. 216, stationed in Egypt. It was No. 216 that saw the end of the D.H.10's career. The last D.H.10s were replaced in 1923 by the Vickers Vimy.

Tarrant Tabor

Bomb Berlin! This strategic plan had enormous influence on the development of aviation during World War I. Thus several aircraft were developed that would be remembered in history as large and efficient war machines. The Tarrant Tabor was intended as such a plane. But this enormous triplane, which theoretically could deliver a payload of two tons of bombs to the German capital, turned out to be a failure in practice. The limitations and naivety of the Tarrant Tabor's design were dramatically exposed the first time the aircraft took to the air, several months after the end of the war. The bomber crashed on take-off, and the two test pilots, F. G. Dunn and P. T. Rawlings, were killed. The project was abandoned.

The Tabor was the first and only aircraft manufactured by W. G. Tarrant, Ltd., a small woodworking company in Surrey that had produced wooden aeroplane parts during the war. The design was the work of Captain T. M. Wilson of the technical section of the British air ministry. The specifications asked for a plane that could reach Berlin from bases in Great Britain, and an aircraft that could be manufactured by women workers using local timber. In this sense, the triplane's structure was a masterpiece of ingenuity. An all-wood plane was constructed that was very strong. The slender circular-sectioned fuselage

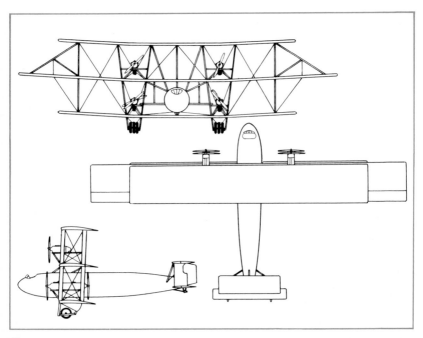

was connected to the three wings (the central one being wider than the others) by a complicated set of struts and supports. The choice of engines fell to the 500 hp Napier Lion. Two pairs of engines were installed on the lower wing, while two engines were also installed on the middle wing. The undercarriage consisted of six wheels mounted in two groups of three. Because the plane was so large, only the parts were manufactured at the Tarrant plant. The plane was put together inside a dirigible hangar at the Royal Aircraft Establishment in Farnborough. The fuselage was delivered on a special truck on November 22, 1918, and the other parts followed later. Since the war had ended, the assembly was put off, and it was May 26, 1919 before the giant triplane was ready for its first test flight.

At 6.10 a.m., the pilot, F. G. Dunn, after revving the engines, decided to take off. Six other people were aboard, including the second officer, Rawl-

Aircraft: **Tarrant Tabor**
Manufacturer: **W. G. Tarrant Ltd.**
Type: **Heavy bomber**
Year: **1919**
Engine: **Six Napier Lion, 12-cylinder V, liquid-cooled, 500 hp each**
Wingspan: **131 ft 3 in (40 m)**
Length: **73 ft 2 in (22.30 m)**
Height: **37 ft 3 in (11.35 m)**
Weight: **45,000 lb (20,400 kg)**
Maximum speed: **108 mph (175 km/h)**
Ceiling: **13,000 ft (5,000 m)**
Range: **900–1,200 mile (1,500–1,900 km)**
Armament: **4,600 lb (2,100 kg) of bombs**
Crew: **5**

ings, and the plane's designer. Dunn tried to take off on only four engines, but there was insufficient power. He turned on the other two engines and began his take-off again. It was the disproportion of the thrust of the engines that caused the crash. Halfway down the runway, the big triplane suddenly lifted its tail and lurched forward. The two pilots were hurled from the cockpit and killed instantly. The other five people aboard were uninjured.

Handley-Page W8b

In 1920 the Handley-Page W8 was considered the finest commercial aeroplane for safety, comfort, and speed. It was the first aircraft in Great Britain expressly constructed for civil transport. It had recently established a national record by carrying a payload of 3,690 pounds (1,674 kg) to an altitude of 14,000 feet (4,270 m). This aircraft was the product of Handley-Page's far-seeing policy in the years after World War I. The company set out to meet the future needs of civil transport. Because of the technical progress made in aviation during the war, it seemed clear that civil aviation was to have an important future.

The Handley-Page company had been founded for a market that was originally military, but its experience during the war awakened the company to future possibilities. Several Handley-Page 0/400 heavy bombers were used in the closing months of the war to carry R.A.F. personnel back from France to England. And the 0/400 was drafted into regular transport service between London and Paris during the negotiations for the 1919 peace treaty. Some disarmed 0/400s provided the original backbone of Handley-Page Transport Ltd., the transport company founded on June 14, 1919. And it was these reconverted bombers that were the first registered civil aircraft after the war, when they were put in regular service to France, Holland, and Belgium.

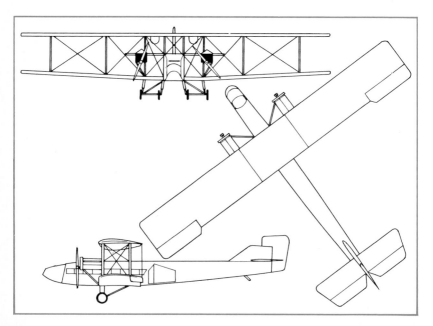

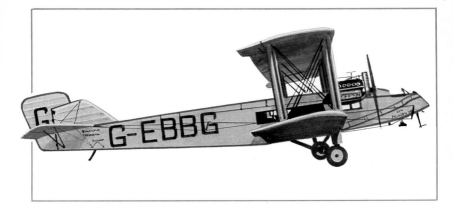

It was no surprise, then, when early in 1920 Handley-Page announced that it had produced an exclusively commercial plane, the W8. It was entirely without rivals at the time, and it won a prize of £7,500 for its advanced design. After a series of demonstration flights, which ended with the crash landing of the prototype (because of bad weather), Handley Page produced a new model of the plane, the W8b; three of these aircraft were put in regular service by Handley-Page Transport Ltd. in 1922, on London–Paris–Brussels flights. The W8b was substantially the same as the W8, but the W8b had less powerful engines (two 360 hp Rolls-Royce Eagles replaced the 450 hp Napier Lions), carried twelve instead of fifteen passengers, and had modified fuel tanks and supply. These three planes were christened Princess Mary, Prince George, and Prince Henry and saw service with Handley-Page Transport Ltd. until 1924. In that year the company was absorbed by Imperial

Aircraft: **Handley-Page W8b**
Manufacturer: **Handley-Page Ltd.**
Type: **Civil transport**
Year: **1922**
Engines: **Two Rolls-Royce Eagle VIII, 12-cylinder V, liquid-cooled, 360 hp each**
Wingspan: **75 ft (22.86 m)**
Length: **60 ft 1 in (18.31 m)**
Height: **17 ft (5.18 m)**
Weight: **12,500 lb (5,650 kg)**
Cruising speed: **90 mph (145 km/h)**
Ceiling: **10,000 ft (3,000 m)**
Range: **400 mile (640 km)**
Crew: **2**
Passengers: **12**

Airways, which was founded on April 1, six years after the Royal Air Force had been founded (by amalgamating the Royal Naval Air Service and the Royal Flying Corps). The new national airline used the W8b well into the 1930s, except for the Princess Mary, which was destroyed in 1928. During the 1920s and 1930s other variations of the original model were subsequently introduced, including the Handley-Page W9 and W10.

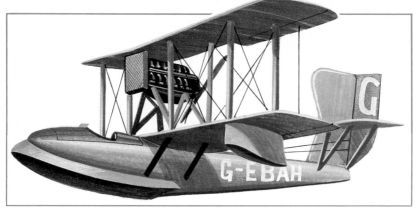

Supermarine Sea Lion

Aircraft: **Supermarine Sea Lion**
Manufacturer: **The Supermarine Aviation Works Ltd.**
Type: **Competition**
Year: **1922**
Engine: **Napier Lion, 12-cylinder V, liquid-cooled, 450 hp**
Wingspan: **32 ft (9.75 m)**
Length: **24 ft 9 in (7.54 m)**
Height: —
Weight (empty): **2,115 lb (960 kg)**
Weight (loaded): **2,840 lb (1,290 kg)**
Maximum speed: **162 mph (260 km/h)**
Ceiling: —
Endurance: **3 hr**
Crew: **1**

After two successive Italian victories in 1920 and 1921, the prestigious Schneider Trophy was won back by the English in 1922, who had last won the cup in 1914 with the Sopwith Tabloid. The 1922 winner, which was to repeat its success in later years, was a biplane, a seaplane driven by one of the finest British engines of the period, the 450 hp Napier Lion. The plane was flown by Captain Henry C. Biard. He was the only Englishman in the race, and his victory was hotly contested by three Italian competitors. Indeed, had the Italians won a third year in a row, they would have retained the cup permanently, and so it would have been lost to England forever.

It was a thrilling race. It took place in Naples, on August 12, 1922, the final day of an aviation week that had drawn hosts of enthusiastic spectators. The course was triangular, and the competitors had to fly thirteen laps

for a total distance of 200 nautical miles (370 km). Biard was the first to take off, followed by three Italian seaplanes, a Macchi M.17, a Savoia S.51, and a Macchi M.7. The English pilot put on the pressure from the start. For the first six laps he maintained an average speed of about 160 mph (260 km/h) and overtook the other planes, which had taken off after he did. He lost speed on the final laps and won the cup with an average of 145.67 mph (234.43 km/h) after 1 hour 34 minutes and 57.6 seconds of flight.

Gloster Grebe

Aircraft: **Gloster Grebe**
Manufacturer: **Gloucestershire Aircraft Co.**
Type: **Fighter**
Year: **1923**
Engine: **Armstrong Siddeley Jaguar IV, 14-cylinder radial, air-cooled, 400 hp**
Wingspan: **29 ft 4 in (8.94 m)**
Length: **20 ft 3 in (6.17 m)**
Height: **9 ft 3 in (2.82 m)**
Weight: **2,614 lb (1,185 kg)**
Maximum speed: **152 mph (245 km/h)**
Ceiling: **22,900 ft (7,000 m)**
Endurance: **2 hr 45 min**
Armament: **2 machine guns**
Crew: **1**

Designed by H. P. Folland, this small and highly manoeuverable fighter saw service in the R.A.F. for five years and proved itself to be one of the best fighter planes of the post-war generation. The Grebe Mk. I made its first appearance at Hendon in 1923, at the annual Royal Air Force review. The plane was a variation on another biplane designed by Folland in 1922, the two-seater Grouse trainer. The Grebe had the same configuration and general structure as its predecessor. The prototype was powered by a 325 hp Armstrong Siddeley Jaguar III radial engine, but when the plane went into general production the engine was replaced by a 400 hp Jaguar IV. The plane was an immediate success because of its manoeuverability and was ordered for R.A.F. squadrons during the general reorganization of the air force after World War I. The one hundred and twenty-nine Grebe

Mk. IIs were assigned to six units and remained in service until 1929, when they were replaced by Armstrong Whitworth Siskins. The Grebe had many chances to display its acrobatic prowess, especially with No. 25 Squadron, which gave a spectacular display at the Hendon show in 1925. The plane was also remarkable for endurance, as was demonstrated in tests conducted by the R.A.F. One of these tests was the first terminal velocity by a British fighter during which the aeroplane reached a speed of 240 mph (386 km/h) without difficulty.

73

Fairey Flycatcher

For eleven years, from 1923 to 1934, the Fairey Flycatcher was the frontline fighter of British naval aviation, and for eight years, from 1924 to 1932, it was the only one in service. Small, tough, fast, and extremely manoeuverable, it was the most popular plane in the world of carrier aircraft. The plane was designed in 1922 in answer to a request by the Air Ministry for a single-seat polyvalent fighter, that is, an aircraft for land and sea duty, with undercarriage and hook suitable for take-off and landing on carrier flight decks. F. Duncanson designed the variant models for Fairey Aviation. The tests and test flights were all successful, and 195 Flycatchers were produced between 1922 and 1930. The Flycatcher saw service on several aircraft carriers, while amphibious and seaplane models were based along the coast of Great Britain and in the Mediterranean.

Aircraft: **Fairey Flycatcher**
Manufacturer: **Fairey Aviation Ltd.**
Type: **Fighter (landplane)**
Year: **1923**
Engine: **Armstrong Siddeley Jaguar III, 14-cylinder radial, air-cooled, 400 hp**
Wingspan: **29 ft (8.84 m)**
Length: **23 ft (7.01 m)**
Height: **12 ft (3.65 m)**
Weight: **3,028 lb (1,373 kg)**
Maximum speed: **134 mph at 5,000 ft (215 km/h at 1,500 m)**
Ceiling: **20,600 ft (6,200 m)**
Range: **260 mile (420 km)**
Armament: **2 machine guns; 80 lb (36 kg) of bombs**
Crew: **1**

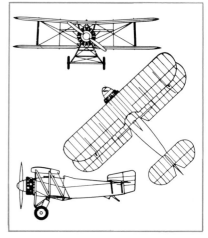

Gloster Gamecock

A successor of the Grebe in the series of aircraft designed by H. P. Folland, the Gloster Gamecock was the last wood-structured fighter biplane to see service in the R.A.F. The Gamecock maintained the general structure and high manoeuvreability of its predecessor. The design was begun in answer to specifications issued in 1923, and the prototype took to the air for the first time in February 1925. When the tests were completed, orders began coming in. A total of 82 of these aircraft (Mk. I) were built. They were equipped with 425 hp Jupiter VIs, which were lighter and more trustworthy than the Armstrong Siddeley Jaguars that powered the Gloster Grebe. The fighter saw service with five units of the R.A.F., beginning in March 1926, though it was not kept in service long. The only Squadron to keep the Gamecock in service until 1931 was No. 23.

Aircraft: **Gloster Gamecock I**
Manufacturer: **Gloucestershire Aircraft Co.**
Type: **Fighter**
Year: **1925**
Engine: **Bristol Jupiter VI, 9-cylinder radial, air-cooled, 425 hp**
Wingspan: **29 ft 9 in (9.08 m)**
Length: **19 ft 8 in (5.99 m)**
Height: **9 ft 8 in (2.94 m)**
Weight: **2,863 lb (1,299 kg)**
Maximum speed: **155 mph at 5,000 ft (250 km/h at 1,500 m)**
Ceiling: **22,000 ft (6,700 m)**
Range: **365 mile (587 km)**
Armament: **2 machine guns**
Crew: **1**

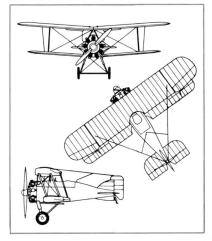

Armstrong Whitworth
A.W.155 Argosy I

From its foundation, Imperial Airways Ltd. was aware of the need for multi-engine aircraft to guarantee passenger safety. Such planes as the Armstrong Whitworth Argosy and the de Havilland Hercules were designed to meet this need, and they assured the company's early success.

The Argosy was also Armstrong Whitworth's first attempt at creating a commercial transport plane. The design fully exploited the company's experience in the construction of military aircraft. The Argosy was a large three-engine biplane with tubular steel structure and powered by three 385 hp Armstrong Siddeley Jaguar engines. One of the engines was installed at the squared-off nose of the plane, just in front of the open cockpit, while the other two engines were housed laterally between the upper and lower wings. There was room for twenty passengers, and the baggage was stowed in a separate compartment in the tail.

The prototype took to the air at Hendon on July 3, 1926, and two other planes followed a few months later, also on order to Imperial Airways. After a series of tests and trial flights on future lines (including a

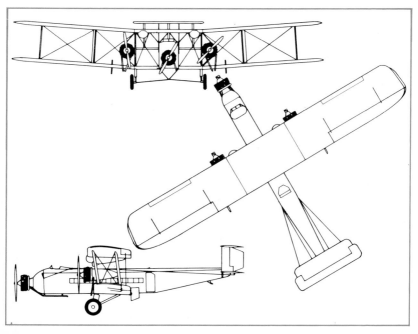

flight to Paris on August 5, 1926), the three planes were put into service on the London–Paris, London–Brussels, and London–Cologne lines and named after cities in Britain. G-EBLF was called the City of Glasgow; G-EBLO was called the City of Birmingham; and the third plane G-EBOZ, was called the City of Wellington, later renamed City of Arundel. In its attempt to offer the best in comfort and service, Imperial Airways managed to outdo its direct and most important rival, the French Air Union, which early in 1927 was readying its LeO 212 'restaurant-plane' for deluxe flights between Paris and London. On May 1, 1927, the Argosy prototype made its maiden voyage with a luxury flight to Paris. The Lioré et Olivier 212 was put into service on the same run by Air Union three months later. The Imperial Airways flight was called the Silver Wing, and the Argosy had a bar installed in place of two passenger seats. Although the Argosy did not provide restaurant

Aircraft: **Armstrong Whitworth A.W. 155 Argosy I**
Manufacturer: **Armstrong Whitworth Aircraft Ltd.**
Type: **Civil transport**
Year: **1926**
Engine: **Three Armstrong Siddeley Jaguar III, 14-cylinder radial, air-cooled, 385 hp each**
Wingspan: **90 ft (27.43 m)**
Length: **64 ft 6 in (19.66 m)**
Height: **19 ft (5.79 m)**
Weight: **18,000 lb (8,150 kg)**
Cruising speed: **90 mph (145 km/h)**
Ceiling: **—**
Range: **400 mile (650 km)**
Crew: **2**
Passengers: **20**

service, two stewards served food and drink during the two-and-a-half-hour flight between Paris and London.

In 1929, with the addition of four Argosy IIs, the fleet of Imperial Airways boasted a total of seven Argosy aircraft. The airline kept the planes in service well into the 1930s. The four Argosys that were not destroyed in crashes were withdrawn from service in 1934.

de Havilland D.H.66 Hercules

As the Armstrong Whitworth Argosy was created to meet the demand for comfortable and efficient passenger transport, so the de Havilland D.H.66 Hercules was developed to satisfy an equally ambitious requirement of Imperial Airways: to provide postal and cargo transport throughout the British Empire. Previously, this service had been assigned to the R.A.F. Thanks to its resilience and reliability, the Hercules was so successful on tropical routes, that West Australian Airways also ordered the aircraft for its postal and passenger runs between Perth and Adelaide.

The Hercules project got under way in 1925. Imperial Airways wanted a very robust aircraft with energy to spare in order to reduce to a minimum the particular hazards of flying in tropical climates. The Hercules was a large three-engine biplane, powered by three 420 hp Bristol Jupiter VI engines. The plane's skeleton was in wood and metal, and the skin was fabric. The plane could accommodate seven passengers as well as the three-man crew, and there was ample room for mail and cargo: over 460 cubic feet (13 m³) at the rear of the passenger cabin and almost 160 cubic feet (4.5 m³) in a separate compartment toward the tail, the prototype first took to the air on September 30, 1926, and on December 27 it was transferred to Cairo, to inaugurate the new route

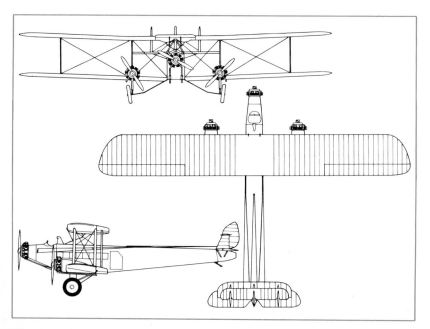

to India. On January 8, 1927, the first of two Hercules in service with Imperial Airways reached Karachi. It was christened the City of Delhi. The second Hercules, called the City of Cairo, took off on January 12 on the inaugural flight from Heliopolis across the desert to Basra. Three more Hercules were delivered that spring. The route to Karachi was only officially opened two years later and was extended to Delhi in the last months of 1929.

Meanwhile another airline had decided to use the Hercules on its more difficult routes. The West Australian Airways wanted to provide a mail and passenger service between Perth and Adelaide. Four planes were ordered and delivered in early 1929. They were modified versions of the planes in service with Imperial Airways. The cockpit was completely enclosed, and the passenger capacity was doubled to fourteen. The West Australian Airways put the planes into service at once, and the inaugural flight between

Aircraft: **de Havilland D.H.66 Hercules**
Manufacturer: **The de Havilland Aircraft Co. Ltd.**
Type: **Civil transport**
Year: **1926**
Engine: **Three Bristol Jupiter VI, 9-cylinder radial, air-cooled, 420 hp each**
Wingspan: **79 ft 6 in (24.23 m)**
Length: **55 ft 6 in (16.91 m)**
Height: **18 ft 3 in (5.56 m)**
Weight: **15,500 lb (7,000 kg)**
Cruising speed: **108 mph (175 km/h)**
Ceiling: **13,000 ft (4,000 m)**
Range: **—**
Crew: **3**
Passengers: **7**

Perth and Adelaide took place on June 2, 1929. Later the cockpit was also enclosed on the Hercules in service with Imperial Airways, where the last planes of this type were retired only in 1935. Over a period of time Imperial Airways lost four Hercules in accidents, and to maintain the airline's routes, two planes were ordered from de Havilland and two were acquired from the West Australian Airways between 1930 and 1931.

Vickers Victoria V

The first large-scale airlift in history was carried out in Afghanistan to evacuate the city of Kabul, which had been devastated by rebels. Eight Vickers Victorias assigned to No. 70 Squadron stationed in Iraq made a large contribution to this action between December 12, 1928, and February 25, 1929. This relief operation carried 586 civilians and about 24,000 pounds (11,000 kg) of belongings out of the city.

As the Vickers Vimy bomber was modified to create two transport planes, the civilian Commercial and the military Vernon, so the Vimy's successor, the Vickers Virginia, led to the development of a two-engine military transport plane, the Victoria. The Virginia had been designed in 1922, and a total of 126 aircraft were manufactured in a variety of models. The Virginia was a large two-engine biplane, driven by two 570 hp Napier Lion engines. The configuration and structure were similar in concept to that of the Vickers Vimy. Alongside the bomber, however, a military transport model was also developed. The experimental prototype of this aircraft took to the air for the first time in October 1922. Although the Victoria maintained the general lines of the bomber, it had a large elliptical-section fuselage; the structure was wood and metal; and the surface was wood and fabric. The same engines were used by the transport plane and

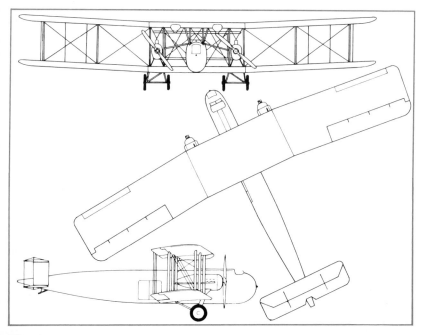

by the bomber and were installed laterally between the upper and lower wings. The transport could carry twenty-two passengers and several hundred pounds of baggage.

A total of 94 Victorias were manufactured The wings of Mk. III model were slightly different to those of the two prototypes. They were dihedral and slightly slanted back. The Mk. V, with a wood and metal skeleton, had a modified rudder system. And the Mk. VI had two 622 hp Bristol Pegasus radial engines, instead of the Mk. V's 570 hp Napier Lion engines. In 1933 production of these planes came to an end.

Like many other military transports used by the R.A.F., the Victorias saw most of their service in the Middle East and in India. The first units to be assigned the Victoria were No. 70 Squadron, stationed in Iraq, and No. 216, in Egypt, which received delivery in August 1926. Only a few Victorias saw service in Great Britain. One of these aircraft was given a rather

Aircraft: **Vickers Victoria V**
Manufacturer: **Vickers (Aviation) Ltd.**
Type: **Military transport**
Year: **1926**
Engine: **Two Napier Lion XI, 12-cylinder V, liquid-cooled, 570 hp each**
Wingspan: **87 ft 4 in (26.62 m)**
Length: **59 ft 6 in (18.13 m)**
Height: **17 ft 9 in (5.41 m)**
Weight: **17,736 lb (8,045 kg)**
Maximum speed: **108 mph (175 km/h)**
Ceiling: **16,000 ft (4,900 m)**
Range: **770 mile (1,240 km)**
Crew: **2**
Passengers: **22**

unusual assignment. From March 1932 it was assigned to the Central Flying School of the Royal Air Force for training in blind flying techniques. The main cabin was filled with all the instruments needed for blind flying.

The Vickers Victoria was in service abroad until 1935, and it accomplished many remarkable flights. Victorias were used to transport military personnel from Cairo to Aden, to Capetown, and to Somalia between 1926 and early 1932. And during 1932 Victorias flew troops from Egypt to Cyprus, during the disorders there.

Armstrong Whitworth Atlas

The Armstrong Whitworth Atlas was the first aircraft expressly designed for the support of ground troops to be used by the Royal Air Force. The prototype took to the air on May 10, 1925, and the first unit to be supplied with this small and robust two-seater became operational in October 1927. The duties of the Atlas were varied and complicated: photographic reconnaissance, artillery observation, dropping supplies, carrying messages, and ground attack with bombs and machine guns. The plane was a great success in all these activities and remained in service until 1933–34. A total of 446 aircraft were constructed. This extremely robust and reliable plane was also used in the Middle East, and a few aircraft were equipped with floats for landing on water. A dual-control model was built for training.

Aircraft: **Armstrong Whitworth Atlas**
Manufacturer: **Armstrong Whitworth Aircraft Ltd.**
Type: **Army co-operation**
Year: **1927**
Engine: **Armstrong Siddeley Jaguar IV C, 14-cylinder radial, air-cooled, 450 hp**
Wingspan: **39 ft 6 in (12.04 m)**
Length: **28 ft 6 in (8.68 m)**
Height: **10 ft 6 in (3.20 m)**
Weight: **4,018 lb (1.823 kg)**
Maximum speed: **142 mph (228 km/h)**
Ceiling: **16,800 ft (5,120 m)**
Range: **480 mile (770 km)**
Armament: **2 machine guns; 448 lb (203 kg) of bombs**
Crew: **2**

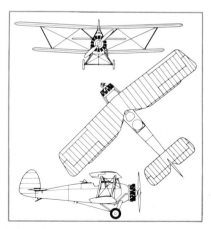

Supermarine S.5/25
Supermarine S.6
Supermarine S.6B

The place was Lee on Solent, England. The date was September 13, 1931. Nineteen years of annual competition had come to an end. The Schneider Trophy was permanently retained by Great Britain. An epoch of self-sacrifice and technical ingenuity had come to an end. The Supermarine S.6B, piloted by John H. Boothman had flown the race all by itself. The leading contenders, Italians and Frenchmen, had not succeeded in getting their aircraft ready on time, so the Supermarine flight ended by

being a simple flight against the clock. Its performance established a new world record: 340.04 mph (547.22 km/h).

The Supermarine S.6B was the last member of the family of competition flying planes designed by Reginald J. Mitchell, the man who was later to design the immortal Spitfire. And it would be fair to say that the experience Mitchell acquired in so many years of designing aircraft for Schneider Trophy competitions all went into his most famous plane. The fame and success of the Spitfire also owed a great deal to another outstanding figure in British aviation during the years of the Schneider Trophy. This man was Henry Royce, who had

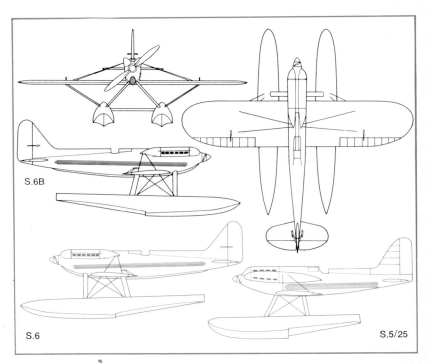

S.6B

S.6

S.5/25

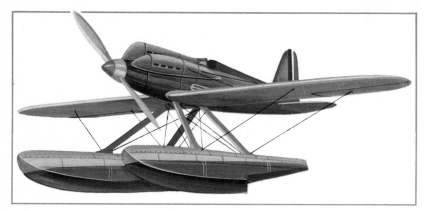

developed for the last two rounds of the Schneider Trophy the splendid engine from which the Rolls-Royce Merlin was to be derived during the Second World War.

The first of the S series was the Supermarine S.4, which was designed for the 1925 Schneider Trophy competition. This was a revolutionary aircraft. It was the first time since 1913 (the year the Deperdussin monoplane won the race) that the monoplane formula was revived in a competition seaplane version. But the S.4 project came to an unhappy end. Because of a sudden structural weakness in the wing, the plane crashed during a trial run before the race in Baltimore. The winner that year was James Doolittle, in an army hydroplane, the Curtiss R3C-2, with an average speed of 232.57 mph (374.27 km/h).

Mitchell was not disheartened. It was shown indirectly that his fundamental idea of reviving the monoplane was sound when another monoplane became the winner of the 1926 event. The Italian Macchi M.39 won the

trophy that year with an average speed of 246.49 mph (396.68 km/h). Great Britain did not take part that year, because the new Supermarine, the S.5 was still under construction. Mitchell applied the latest technology in his design and created an almost perfect aircraft with extremely sophisticated aerodynamics, the result of extensive research carried out in the laboratories and wind tunnels of the Royal Aircraft Establishment and the National Physical Laboratory. The plane had an all-metal fuselage with covered wings. Everything was designed to accommodate the engine, the powerful 876 hp, Napier Lion VII B. The liquid-cooling radiators were housed on the wing, while oil radiators were housed along the fuselage. The engine housing had three rows of protruding cylinders, but the designer still managed to reduce the section of the aircraft to the minimum, 5.90 ft^2 (0.548 m^2). The Supermarine S.5/25 won the 1927 edition of the Schneider Trophy in Venice. The pilot was Sidney N. Webster with a final average

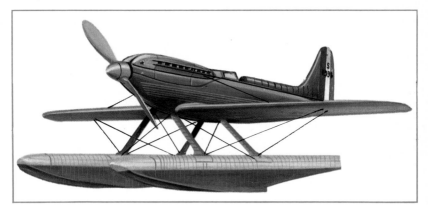

speed of 281.64 mph (453.25 km/h). Another Supermarine, the S.5/21, took second place in the same race, with an average speed of 273.04 mph (439.41 km/h) and confirmed the importance of the aircraft.

The success of the S.5 made it possible for Mitchell to continue his work, and he designed two more aircraft, the S.6 and the S.6B, in which the advanced qualities of the earlier model were even more highly developed. The new aircraft had specially adapted Rolls-Royce R engines. The S.6's engine had 1,900 horse power, while the S.6B's engine furnished 2,350 horse power. Aside from the greater power, these later models were slightly larger than the S.5. The last two competitions for the Schneider Trophy (which were held at two-year intervals after 1927) were won by the Supermarine S.6 (average speed 328.63 mph; 528.86 km/h) in 1929 and by the S.6B in 1931. The 1929 race was held at the Isle of Wight, and the pilot of the Supermarine was H. R. D. Waghorn.

Aircraft: **Supermarine S.5/25**
Manufacturer: **The Supermarine Aviation Works Ltd.**
Type: **Competition**
Year: **1927**
Engine: **Napier Lion VII B, 12-cylinder V, liquid-cooled, 875 hp**
Wingspan: **26 ft 9 in (8.15 m)**
Length: **24 ft 2 in (7.36 m)**
Height: **12 ft (3.65 m)**
Weight (empty): **2,710 lb (1,229 kg)**
Weight (loaded): **3,250 lb (1,474 kg)**
Maximum speed: **310 mph (499 km/h); 319.57 mph (514.28 km/h) in 1928**

Aircraft: **Supermarine S.6**
Manufacturer: **The Supermarine Aviation Works Ltd.**
Type: **Competition**
Year: **1929**
Engine: **Rolls-Royce R, 12-cylinder V, liquid-cooled, 1,900 hp**
Wingspan: **30 ft (9.14 m)**
Length: **28 ft 10 in (8.78 m)**
Height: **12 ft 3 in (3.73 m)**
Weight (empty): **4,471 lb (2,028 kg)**
Weight (loaded): **5,771 lb (2,618 kg)**
Maximum speed: **358 mph (576 km/h)**

Aircraft: **Supermarine S.6B**
Manufacturer: **The Supermarine Aviation Works Ltd.**
Type: **Competition**
Year: **1931**
Engine: **Rolls-Royce R, 12-cylinder V, liquid-cooled, 2,350 hp**
Wingspan: **30 ft (9.14 m)**
Length: **28 ft 10 in (8.78 m)**
Height: **12 ft 3 in (3.73 m)**
Weight (empty): **4,590 lb (2,082 kg)**
Weight (loaded): **6,086 lb (2,761 kg)**
Maximum speed: **408 mph (656 km/h)**

Short S.8 Calcutta
Short S.17 Kent

The introduction of the Short S.8. Calcutta seaplanes on the Mediterranean runs made it possible for Imperial Airways to achieve an ambitious goal: plane connections between London and Karachi. Extending the existing route, the trip took seven days: from London to the coast by train, and then to Genoa aboard an Armstrong Whitworth Argosy; from Genoa to Alexandria, Egypt, aboard a Calcutta seaplane; and on to Karachi aboard the de Havilland Hercules.

A total of five Short S.8 Calcuttas were constructed on order from Imperial Airways for the Mediterranean run. The Calcutta was a three-engined biplane with an all-metal hull. Fifteen passengers could be accommodated and hot meals were served during the flight. The plane also carried mail and goods. The prototype took to the air on February 14, 1928, and after various trials and flight tests, a series of publicity and demonstration flights were undertaken. Members of the British Parliament also inspected the aircraft. And on April 16, 1929, the Mediterranean service was launched.

Meanwhile the Short Bros. had prepared a larger version of its S.8 seaplane. This was the S.17 Kent. The new aircraft maintained the same configuration and structure as its

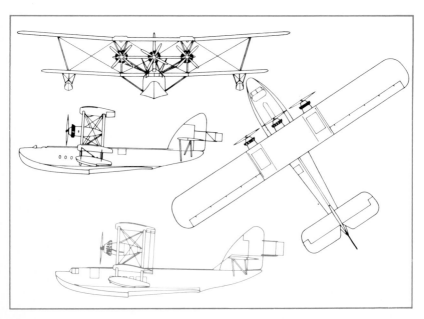

predecessor, but was powered by four engines instead of three. This represented a marked increase in comfort for the passengers. Although the cabin was enlarged, the passenger capacity was only increased by one. The Kent was rightly considered the most comfortable air transport of its period. The passengers were seated in four rows with plenty of leg room and folding tables. Hot meals were prepared and served in flight. The third Kent was put at the disposal of the Prince of Wales, who made a series of trips in 1931.

Kents were put in service on Mediterranean routes and made it possible for the Calcuttas to be transferred to South African runs. The planes were flown intensively. In August 1932 the three Kents had flown a total of 98,253 miles (158,116 km), 90,549 miles (145,719 km), and 77,470 miles (124,671 km) respectively without any mechanical difficulties. By this time the Calcuttas had flown about 494,000 miles (795,000 km).

Aircraft: **Short S.8 Calcutta**
Manufacturer: **Short Bros.**
Type: **Civil transport**
Year: **1928**
Engine: **Three Bristol Jupiter XIF, 9-cylinder radial, air-cooled, 540 hp each**
Wingspan: **93 ft (28.34 m)**
Length: **66 ft 9 in (20.34 m)**
Height: **23 ft 9 in (7.24 m)**
Weight: **22,460 lb (10,190 kg)**
Cruising speed: **92 mph (148 km/h)**
Ceiling: **13,500 ft (4,100 m)**
Range: **650 mile (1,050 km)**
Crew: **3**
Passengers: **15**

Aircraft: **Short S.17 Kent**
Manufacturer: **Short Bros.**
Type: **Civil transport**
Year: **1931**
Engine: **Four Bristol Jupiter XFBM, 9-cylinder radial, air-cooled, 555 hp each**
Wingspan: **113 ft (34.44 m)**
Length: **78 ft 5 in (23.90 m)**
Height: **28 ft (8.53 m)**
Weight: **32,000 lb (14,500 kg)**
Cruising speed: **105 mph (169 km/h)**
Ceiling: **19,500 ft (5,900 m)**
Range: **450 mile (720 km)**
Crew: **4**
Passengers: **16**

Hawker Hart

One of the most important of the classical military aircraft of the years around 1930 was the Hawker Hart light bomber. It was designed by Sydney Camm, who was later to create another classic, the Hurricane of World War II. The Hart marked a new dimension in the concept of bombing planes. Earlier bombers had been slow and awkward, easy prey to enemy fighters. But the highly manoeuvreable biplane that Camm designed marked the beginning of a new era. The Hawker Hart was extremely manoeuvreable and could match in performance, and sometimes outdo, the best fighters of its day.

The project was undertaken to meet specifications advanced by the British Air Ministry in 1926. What was required was a highly efficient day bomber. The Hart prototype took to the air in June 1928. It was subjected to rigid tests and compared with two competitors, the Avro Antelope and the Fairey Fox. The Hart won the competition, and a first order for fifteen aircraft was placed with the Hawker company. The plane was put on public view at the Olympia Air Show in July 1929. Sydney Camm's design owed its success chiefly to the careful choice of engine and the attention paid to the plane's aerodynamics. In fact, the Hart was an extremely elegant plane with its tapering rounded lines. The engine was a new model Rolls-Royce, the 525 hp Kestrel. The skeleton of the plane was all-metal, and the skin was fabric. The plane was both robust and light in weight.

Delivery of the first aircraft began in January 1930, with the re-equipping of No. 33 Squadron stationed at Eastchurch. A total of 151 Hawker bombers were ordered, and planes were also constructed under licence by other manufacturers. Armstrong Whitworth produced 149, Vickers

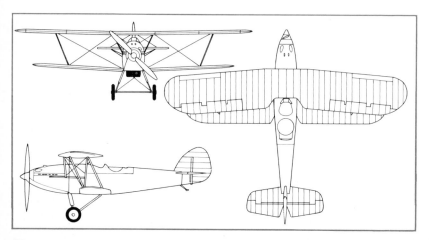

constructed 112, and Gloster turned out 40 of these bombers. In addition to these 452 aircraft, another 507 were turned out in training models. They were used throughout the air force. To meet the requirements of various theatres of operation, modified versions were produced, including the Hart C, the Hart India, and the Hart Special. The India and the Special were equipped for heavy duty in tropical climates. They had desert equipment, a larger radiator, stronger tyres, brakes on the two main wheels of the landing gear, and a lighter Kestrel engine (515 hp). The Hart saw duty with seven squadrons based in Great Britain and with five more in India and the Middle East. Its replacement began in 1936 with the arrival of the more modern Hawker Hind. Gradually the planes were shifted to Auxiliary Air Force squadrons, where they saw duty until 1938.

The Hawker Hart also saw duty in the Estonian and the Swedish air forces. Estonia bought eight aircraft in

Aircraft: **Hawker Hart**
Manufacturer: **H. G. Hawker Engineering Co. Ltd.**
Type: **Day bomber**
Year: **1929**
Engine: **Rolls-Royce Kestrel IB, 12-cylinder V, liquid-cooled, 525 hp**
Wingspan: **37 ft 3 in (11.35 m)**
Length: **29 ft 4 in (8.94 m)**
Height: **10 ft 5 in (3.17 m)**
Weight: **4,554 lb (2,065 kg)**
Maximum speed: **184 mph (296 km/h)**
Ceiling: **21,300 ft (6,500 m)**
Range: **470 mile (760 km)**
Armament: **2 machine guns: 500 lb (226 kg) of bombs**
Crew: **1**

1932, and two years later Sweden bought four. Between 1935 and 1936 the Swedish state aircraft manufacturing company built twenty-four Harts under licence. These aircraft were equipped with Bristol Pegasus engines, and were the only Harts ever to see combat duty: during the Russo–Finnish War of 1939–40, Swedish volunteers flew them alongside the Finnish forces.

Handley-Page H.P.36 Hinaidi
Handley-Page H.P.24 Hyderabad

Between 1926 and 1933 the Royal Air Force was equipped with two heavy bombers manufactured by Handley-Page, the Hyderabad and the Hinaidi. The two aircraft were similar in concept and development. They were the last large British bombers to emerge from the designs that had begun with the Handley-Page 0/400 and the Vickers Vimy, airplanes that had appeared during World War I. A transition aircraft, the Handley-Page Heyford, appeared in 1933. Although it was a biplane, it represented a marked advance over its predecessors and anticipated the monoplane bombers that would enter service during the years 1937–39.

The Handley-Page Hyderabad, which entered squadron service in 1935, was developed from the Handley Page W8, a commercial transport plane developed in 1920. The prototype of the Hyderabad made its maiden flight in October 1923 and was not very different from the civil aircraft, although it was generally stronger and heavier. The Hyderabad was an all-wood aircraft, the last bomber of this kind in the Royal Air Force. After the tail structure had been modified, fourteen aircraft were ordered initially, and thirty more were ordered later. The first R.A.F. unit to be equipped with the new bomber was No. 99 Squadron, which received its Hyderabads in December 1925.

Production was fairly slow, and another two years went by before a second squadron became operative.

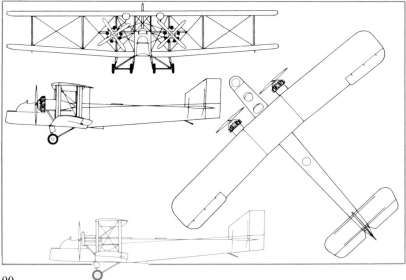

Meanwhile, Handley-Page had already begun working on an improved model of the plane, the Hinaidi. The new bomber followed the general configuration of the Hyderabad, but it was faster and was equipped with a pair of 440 hp Bristol Jupiter radial engines. The Hinaidi prototype, which took to the air for the first time on March 26, 1927, was an all-wood plane, but when it went into production, the wood was replaced by metal, and the plane was made much stronger. Thirty-three metal Hinaidis were manufactured, and they began to replace the Hyderabads in 1929. The new plane could carry about 440 pounds (200 kg) more bombs, flew 13 mph (22 km/h) faster, and had a greater range and slightly higher ceiling. The Hinaidi remained on duty in four bomber squadrons until 1933. A troop transport version of the Hinaidi was also developed. Called the Clive, this aircraft could carry twenty-three servicemen.

Aircraft: **Handley-Page H.P. 36 Hinaidi**
Manufacturer: **Handley-Page Ltd.**
Type: **Heavy night bomber**
Year: **1929**
Engine: **Two Bristol Jupiter VIII, 9-cylinder radial, air-cooled, 440 hp each**
Wingspan: **75 ft (22.86 m)**
Length: **59 ft 2 in (18.03 m)**
Height: **17 ft (5.18 m)**
Weight: **14,400 lb (6,500 kg)**
Maximum speed: **122 mph (197 km/h)**
Ceiling: **14,500 ft (4,400 m)**
Range: **850 mile (1,370 km)**
Armament: **3 machine guns; 1,440 lb (650 kg) of bombs**
Crew: **4**

Aircraft: **Handley-Page H.P. 24 Hyderabad**
Manufacturer: **Handley-Page Ltd.**
Type: **Heavy night bomber**
Year: **1926**
Engine: **Two Napier Lion, 12-cylinder V, liquid-cooled, 454 hp each**
Wingspan: **75 ft (22.86 m)**
Length: **59 ft 2 in (18.03 m)**
Height: **16 ft 9 in (4.95 m)**
Weight: **13,590 lb (6,160 kg)**
Maximum speed: **108 mph (175 km/h) at sea level**
Ceiling: **14,000 ft (4,200 m)**
Range: **—**
Armament: **3 machine guns; 1,100 lb (500 kg) of bombs**
Crew: **4**

Bristol Bulldog Mk. IIA

One of the most popular peacetime fighters in the Royal Air Force, the Bristol Bulldog was a typical combat plane of the second generation after World War I. Fast, powerful, and extremely manoeuverable, it was one of the last open-cockpit fighter biplanes to see mass front-line duty with the R.A.F., until the introduction of the Gloster Gladiator in 1937. The Bulldog was a long-lived plane. It entered service in May 1929 and saw duty in ten fighter squadrons until it was replaced by the Gladiator, the last combat biplane in British aviation.

The Bulldog was designed by Frank S. Barnwell, who had designed the F.2A and F.2B, which won fame in World War I. The Air Ministry wanted a fighter to replace the Gloster Gamecock and the Armstrong Whitworth Siskin. The Bristol company built two prototypes. The first took to

the air on May 17, 1927, and the other on January 21, 1928. The two aircraft differed slightly in structure and fuselage length. Otherwise they were substantially identical. An all-metal structure, it was fabric-covered except for the nose. The second prototype, called Bulldog Mk. II, was preferred. A first order of twenty-five aircraft was placed, and then another twenty-three. But the most popular model was the Mk. IIA, which had structural modifications and a more powerful Bristol Jupiter engine. The undercarriage was stronger, the tyres were larger, and the wheels were equipped with brakes. The oil-circulation system was redesigned, the drift was modified, and a rear wheel was added in place of the landing skid. Two hundred and fifty-four Mk. IIAs were delivered to the R.A.F.

The first unit to receive the new

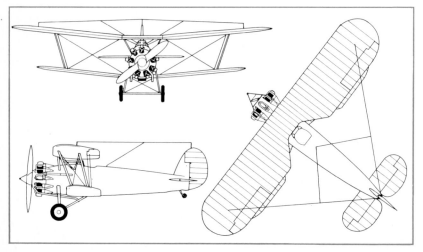

GB – Bristol Bulldog Mk.IIA

fighters was No. 3 Squadron, in June 1929. And in the next few months, as production continued, nine other front-line units were equipped with this aircraft. The Bristol Bulldog became the spearhead of national defence. At its peak, the Bristol Bulldog constituted seventy per cent of Britain's fighter force.

Other versions of the Bulldog were developed later. Among these was the training plane known as the Bulldog II M. It was a dual-control two-seater and represented a variation of the Mk. IIA with modified wings and rudder surface. Fifty-eight of these aircraft were constructed and saw service at the R.A.F.'s Central Flying School and in other training units. Another important version was the Mk. IVA, which was popular in Finland. This aircraft was powered by a stronger engine, the Bristol Mercury VIS.2; its 645 hp made it considerably more powerful than the Jupiter. Finland ordered seventeen planes for its air force. Some of them even saw service

Aircraft: **Bristol Bulldog Mk.IIA**
Manufacturer: **Bristol Aeroplane Co.**
Type: **Fighter**
Year: **1929**
Engine: **Bristol Jupiter VII F, 9-cylinder radial, air-cooled, 490 hp**
Wingspan: **33 ft 11 in (10.33 m)**
Length: **25 ft 2 in (7.67 m)**
Height: **9 ft 10 in (2.99 m)**
Weight: **3,503 lb (1,589 kg)**
Maximum speed: **174 mph at 10,000 ft (280 km/h at 3,000 m)**
Ceiling: **27,000 ft (8,200 m)**
Range: **—**
Armament: **2 machine guns; 80 lb (35 kg) of bombs**
Crew: **1**

during the Russo–Finnish War in 1939–40. Sweden also acquired eleven Bulldog Mk. IIAs. Denmark, Estonia, and Latvia also ordered Bulldogs. Siam and Japan were the farthest customers to buy Bulldogs; each bought two aircraft.

Handley-Page H.P.42E

For almost ten years, from 1931 to 1939, the Handley-Page H.P.42 was the veritable trademark of Imperial Airways. Slow, majestic, and safe, these big four-engine biplanes continued to fly when newer and more sophisticated aircraft were already crowding Britain's airports. They represented the best of a transport philosophy that put passenger comfort and safety before everything else. A total of eight H.P.42s were built and assigned to the European and Eastern sectors of Imperial Airways. These aircraft established an unimpeachable record for efficiency, flying millions of miles and carrying hundreds of thousands of passengers throughout the world. The first H.P.42W, the Heracles, which was assigned to European runs, had by September 11, 1938 (seven years after its first regular flight), flown over a million miles and carried 95,000 passengers.

The Handley-Page design was developed to meet specific demands of Imperial Airways, which wanted a commercial transport vehicle that was suited for European as well as Eastern routes. This big biplane had an all-metal structure, and the fuselage was mostly covered with corrugated duralumin. The plane was powered by four 550 hp Bristol Jupiter radial engines housed laterally, two on the upper wing and two on the lower. A special control was installed to prevent the upper engines from being started before the lower engines were

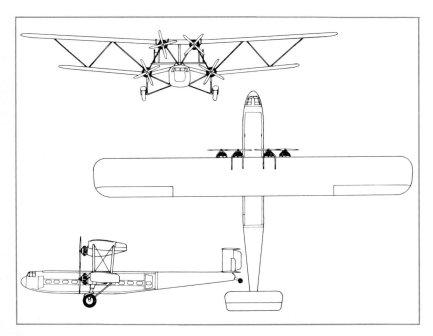

working. Otherwise an imbalance of power might make the plane nose over during take-off. This was only one of the special devices adopted to guarantee the maximum safety and the greatest passenger comfort. The central section of the lower wing was curved up the fuselage so as not to penetrate the cabin and reduce interior space. The noisiest part of the cabin, the section next to the engines, was set aside as a baggage hold and restroom. The decoration of the interior was elegant, and the service was considered 'excellent', thanks in large part to the high quality of the meals that were served in flight. In the E model of the H.P.42 (East), the two passenger cabins each accommodated twelve people, while the W model (West) housed eighteen and twenty passengers, respectively, in the two cabins.

The prototype E model, named the Hannibal, made its maiden flight on November 17, 1930, and a trial flight on the London–Paris route was made

Aircraft: **Handley-Page H.P.42 E**
Manufacturer: **Handley-Page Ltd.**
Type: **Civil transport**
Year: **1931**
Engine: **Four Bristol Jupiter XIF, 9-cylinder radial, air-cooled, 550 hp each**
Wingspan: **130 ft (39.62 m)**
Length: **89 ft 9 in (27.36 m)**
Height: **27 ft (8.23 m)**
Weight: **28,000 lb (12,700 kg)**
Cruising speed: **100 mph (160 km/h)**
Ceiling: **—**
Range: **—**
Crew: **2**
Passengers: **24**

on June 9, 1931. The other planes in the series were constructed in the following months, and the last H.P.42 W was delivered in February 1932. All eight aircraft were given names from mythology and history, both classical and northern. The four H.P.42 Es were named Hannibal, Horsa, Hanno, and Hadrian. The H.P.42 Ws were named Heracles, Horatius, Hengist, and Helena. The Helena outlived her sister ships and was only dismantled by royal navy personnel in 1941. The plane's fuselage was saved and for some time served as an operations office for a Royal Navy Squadron.

de Havilland D.H.82A Tiger Moth

The Tiger Moth is probably the most famous training plane in the history of aviation. A total of 7,300 Tiger Moths were built, and the plane saw fifteen years of continuous service with the R.A.F. In the years preceding the Second World War this small biplane was used by most of the civilian flying schools in Great Britain, and it was the standard trainer during the early years of the war for military flying in England, Canada, Australia, and New Zealand. Tens of thousands of pilots around the world learned to fly in this famous aircraft. After the war, in 1947, the Royal Air Force declared the Tiger Moth obsolete, but most of the planes ended up on the civil market. Flying clubs rushed to buy Tiger Moths, because aircraft manufacturers were not immediately able to satisfy the peacetime demand for light planes. So the Tiger Moth had a second lease of life, and many British flying clubs still take great care of their still airworthy planes.

The Tiger Moth was the culmination of a series of light aircraft designs begun in 1924 with the D.H.51. The original idea was to develop a touring plane that was extremely simple and, more important, very economical. But the D.H.51 was not a great success. It was the D.H.60 Moth that was to catch on in 1925. The D.H.60 is rightly considered the legitimate founder of the line of biplanes that was ultimately to produce the Tiger Moth. Almost five hundred and fifty D.H.60s were built in a version that was equipped with a Renault engine; and more than six hundred were built in model G, which was powered by a new engine, the Gipsy, designed and built by the de Havilland company itself. It was F. B. Halford who designed this engine for the de Havilland company. Originally intended as a record-flight engine for competition flying, it became one of the most popular engines in the history of touring planes. Its simplicity, resilience, safety, and low cost made it the ideal engine for light aircraft.

The Tiger Moth made its maiden

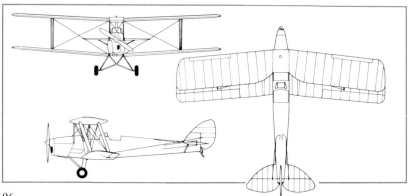

flight on October 26, 1931, and large-scale production began almost at once. The small two-seater biplane was built with a skeleton in wood and metal, while, except for the nose, it was entirely covered in fabric. The two wings were rectangular and equal in span and width and so angled that access to the forward cockpit was easy, and in case of emergency the pilot would have no trouble bailing out. Over the years, the Gipsy engine was increased in horse power. The gas tank was installed in the middle of the upper wing, and a subsidiary tank could be installed in the forward cockpit.

Although most of the initial production was earmarked for the Royal Air Force, up until 1939 the de Havilland company managed to manufacture a number of aircraft for civil flying schools. By the time World War II broke out, some 1,400 aircraft had already been constructed. The war stimulated greater production, and Tiger Moths were built in Canada,

Aircraft: **de Havilland D.H. 82A Tiger Moth**
Manufacturer: **The de Havilland Aircraft Co.**
Type: **Trainer**
Year: **1931**
Engine: **de Havilland Gipsy Major, 4-cylinder in-line, air-cooled, 130 hp**
Wingspan: **29 ft 4 in (8.94 m)**
Length: **23 ft 11 in (7.29 m)**
Height: **8 ft 9 in (2.66 m)**
Weight: **1,825 lb (828 kg)**
Maximum speed: **104 mph (167 km/h)**
Ceiling: **14,000 ft (4,200 m)**
Range: **300 mile (480 km)**
Crew: **2**

Australia, and New Zealand by local affiliates of the de Havilland company. In Great Britain, the production of Tiger Moths was entrusted to Morris Motors Ltd., in order to make it possible for the de Havilland company to dedicate all its efforts to the development of combat planes, including the famous Mosquito.

The Tiger Moth found one unusual use during the war. It was used as a radio-controlled target for anti-aircraft artillery training.

Hawker Fury I
Hawker Demon

In the years between the two world wars two competing schools of technology formed around the in-line and radial engines respectively, and each school maintained that its engine was the better one. The result of this continued rivalry was the creation of ever better aircraft, and the great technological development that was to be responsible for the finest aircraft created in the Second World War. Among planes that were developed with the in-line engine, the Hawker Fury deserves special distinction. It has been described as the most elegant biplane ever constructed. A distinguished radial-engine counterpart of the Fury was the Bristol Bulldog.

The designer of the Fury was Sidney Camm, the man who had designed the Hawker Hart. The prototype of the Fury took to the air for the first time on March 25, 1931. Observers were impressed by its speed, its ease in reaching high altitudes, and its general flying performance, not to mention the purity of its lines. This aircraft continued in general outline the technical characteristics and aerodynamics of the 1928 Hawker Hart: all-metal structure covered with fabric, except for the nose; Rolls-Royce engine with careful cowling; generally rounded and slender lines. The Fury was chosen as the standard fighter for the Royal Air Force, and production got under way. A total of 117 aircraft had been built by 1935. The first unit to be equipped with the new plane was No. 43 Squadron, in May 1931. The next two Squadrons in which the Fury became operational were Nos 1 and 25. Throughout their years of service (until 1939), Furys were on regular display at every air show held in Great

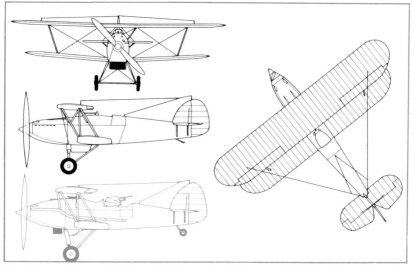

Britain and were admired for their aerobatic qualities.

Almost simultaneously with the Fury, Sydney Camm developed another fighter aircraft, the Hawker Demon. Although this plane was part of the same family, it was different in concept. The Hawker Demon was basically a variation on the Hawker Hart bomber. The Demon was developed to meet a specific need of the Air Ministry: the creation of a fighter capable of intercepting the Hart itself, that is, a plane that could match the Hart's exceptional performance. Sydney Camm found the simplest solution: he converted the bomber into a two-seater fighter, gave it more armament, and equipped it with a 584 hp Kestrel engine. The aircraft had its operational trials in March 1931, and production began at once. A total of 234 Hawker Demons were constructed, and the aircraft remained in service until 1939. One of the more interesting modifications that was made to the aircraft in the course of its

Aircraft: **Hawker Fury I**
Manufacturer: **Hawker Aircraft Ltd.**
Type: **Fighter**
Year: **1931**
Engine: **Rolls-Royce Kestrel IIS, 12-cylinder V, liquid-cooled, 525 hp**
Wingspan: **30 ft (9.14 m)**
Length: **26 ft 8 in (8.12 m)**
Height: **10 ft 2 in (3.09 m)**
Weight: **3,490 lb (1,580 kg)**
Maximum speed: **207 mph at 14,000 ft (333 km/h at 4,200 m)**
Ceiling: **28,000 ft (8,500 m)**
Range: **305 mile (490 km)**
Armament: **2 machine guns**
Crew: **1**

Aircraft: **Hawker Demon**
Manufacturer: **Hawker Aircraft Ltd.**
Type: **Fighter**
Year: **1931**
Engine: **Rolls-Royce Kestrel V, 12-cylinder V, liquid-cooled, 584 hp**
Wingspan: **37 ft 3 in (11.35 m)**
Length: **29 ft 7 in (9.01 m)**
Height: **10 ft 5 in (3.17 m)**
Weight: **4,464 lb (2,025 kg)**
Maximum speed: **182 mph at 16,400 ft (293 km/h at 5,000 m)**
Ceiling: **27,500 ft (8,300 m)**
Endurance: **2 hr 30 min**
Armament: **3 machine guns**
Crew: **2**

career was the installation in the rear cockpit of a hydraulic machine gun turret. This new variation was known as the Turret Demon.

Armstrong Whitworth
A.W.15 Atalanta

The Armstrong Whitworth Company had safety and efficiency in mind when it developed the A.W.15, and this aircraft had an enviable and fairly long career (almost 12 years). Only one of the eight Atalantas constructed after 1932 was lost in a crash. Of the other seven, three continued to fly until 1942 and two remained in the air until 1944.

The plane had been ordered in 1931 by Imperial Airways, which wanted the aircraft for two of the most difficult runs on its lines: the Nairobi–Capetown route and the Karachi–Singapore line. Since these flights were carried out in tropical climates and passed over inhospitable terrain, an especially comfortable and safe plane was required. What was needed was a plane that would reduce passenger discomfort to a minimum, and limit as far as possible the chances of accident. The Armstrong Whitworth design offered an elegant, high-wing, four-engine plane with slender aerodynamic lines and ample space

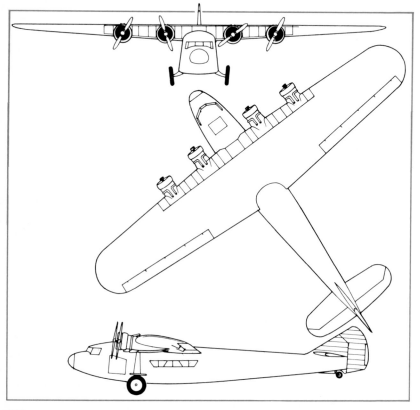

for passengers and baggage. The four engines offered a margin of power sufficient for overall safety. And the aerodynamics of the plane contributed much to increase its cruising speed and thereby shorten the time of flights. For strength the plane had an all-metal skeleton and a plywood skin. All this went to make the Atalanta one of the first high-wing monoplanes without wind-resistant-elements.

The prototype made its first flight on June 20, 1932, and in September of the same year it completed its performance trials. Other aircraft were produced in the following months, and in December the first trial run was made on the Capetown route. The plane took off from Croydon on December 31 and reached Capetown on February 14, 1933, after several delays due to engine trouble. In May a similar test flight was made to Australia. This was the seventh A.W.15, the Astraea, and it was equipped with long-range auxiliary fuel tanks. The flight to Melbourne (13,900 miles;

Aircraft: **Armstrong Whitworth A.W.15 Atalanta**
Manufacturer: **W. G. Armstrong Whitworth Ltd.**
Type: **Civil transport**
Year: **1932**
Engine: **Four Armstrong Siddeley Serval III, 10-cylinder radial, air-cooled, 340 hp each**
Wingspan: **90 ft (27.43 m)**
Length: **71 ft 6 in (21.79 m)**
Height: **15 ft (4.57 m)**
Weight: **21,000 lb (9,500 kg)**
Cruising speed: **130 mph (210 km/h)**
Ceiling: **13,000 ft (3,900 m)**
Range: **400 mile (640 km)**
Crew: **3**
Passengers: **17**

22,500 km) was not without mishap, including a forced landing in a forest when fuel ran out. This flight took a month, but in actual flight the plane made an average speed of about 100 mph (165 km/h). The Karachi –Singapore route was opened on July 7, 1933, and stayed in service until 1939. The five Atlantas that were still in service in 1941 were turned over to the Indian Air Force, which employed the aircraft during the war on antisubmarine patrol duty.

101

Handley-Page H.P.50 Heyford

The Handley-Page Heyford marked the end of an era in the Royal Air Force. This unusual and not very attractive aircraft was the last biplane heavy bomber to see duty in R.A.F. Squadrons. The unusual feature of the Heyford was what made it successful. The fuselage of the plane was attached to the upper, rather than the lower, wing system. This innovation on the part of the designers was not accidental. It was intended to make ground maintenance easier. The high fuselage of the bomber made it easy for ground personnel to work around the aircraft,

as they did not have to bend down. It was equally easy to load the bombs, which were housed in the middle of the lower wing. The high positioning of the fuselage also gave the nose and ventral gunners ample firing space.

The Heyford was designed in 1927 to meet the Air Ministry's specification for a heavy bomber to replace the Virginia and the Hinaidi. The prototype took to the air in June 1930 and made its official debut two years later. It was an extremely robust aircraft, with its all-metal, fabric-covered structure. It was well-armed, fast, and had a relatively long range. The plane was powered by a pair of 525 hp Rolls-Royce Kestrel IIIS engines, which were housed in pods

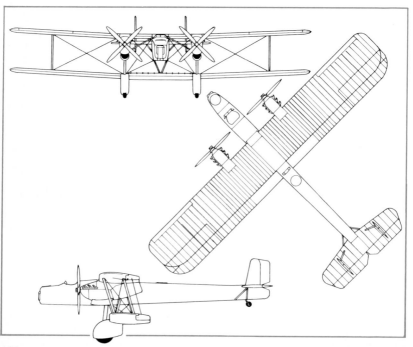

suspended from the upper wing. Large numbers were ordered, and production continued until July 1936, by which time 124 aircraft had been constructed. In the same year the first monoplane bombers made their appearance, the Armstrong Whitworth Whitleys and from 1937 the Heyford was gradually withdrawn from frontline duty and assigned to training units, where it saw service through the first years of World War II.

Several variations on the Heyford were manufactured, each with technical improvements and increased engine power. The Mk.I, the original version, was followed by the Mk.IA, of which 38 were built, and by the Mk. II. The latter was equipped with Rolls-Royce Kestrel VI engines, in which the original power of 640 hp was intentionally reduced. But power was again increased in the last production model, the Mk.III, of which seventy aircraft were produced. The first unit to be equipped with the Heyford was No. 99. Squadron, in November 1933,

Aircraft: **Handley-Page H.P.50 Heyford**
Manufacturer: **Handley-Page Ltd.**
Type: **Heavy night bomber**
Year: **1933**
Engine: **Two Rolls-Royce Kestrel IIIS, 12-cylinder V, liquid-cooled, 575 hp each**
Wingspan: **75 ft (22.86 m)**
Length: **58 ft (17.67 m)**
Height: **17 ft 6 in (5.33 m)**
Weight: **16,900 lb (7,700 kg)**
Maximum speed: **142 mph at 13,000 ft (228 km/h at 3,900 m)**
Ceiling: **21,000 ft (6,400 m)**
Range: **900 mile (1,500 km)**
Armament: **3 machine guns; 2,800 lb (1,300 kg) of bombs**
Crew: **4**

and as production gathered momentum other units received the bomber. At the height of its popularity, this aircraft was employed by eleven bomber units stationed in Great Britain. The first signs of war and the R.A.F.'s expansion programme (which resulted in the first generation of World War II bombers) put an end to the Heyford's career, and a two-decade period in aviation came to an end.

Fairey Gordon II

The Gordon was designed to replace the Fairey III F as a daylight bomber and reconnaissance aircraft. Although the concept of the Gordon was similar to that of its predecessor, it represented a development and improvement on the older plane. The basic difference was the adoption of a radial engine, the Armstrong Siddeley Panther, in place of the Napier Lion V engine. The Gordon was a faster plane and a generally better performer. It was so successful that the Fleet Air Arm also ordered Gordons in a slightly varied form. This aircraft was known as the Seal. The Gordon Mk. II was the final variation of the plane and went into manufacture in 1933. This model was a two-seater biplane, all metal in structure and covered with fabric. The plane saw service in several bomber units stationed in Great Britain and in the Middle East until 1939.

Aircraft: **Fairey Gordon II**
Manufacturer: **Fairey Aviation Co. Ltd.**
Type: **Bomber**
Year: **1933**
Engine: **Armstrong Siddeley Panther II A, 14-cylinder radial, air-cooled, 525 hp**
Wingspan: **45 ft 9 in (13.94 m)**
Length: **36 ft 8 in (11.17 m)**
Height: **14 ft 2 in (4.31 m)**
Weight: **5,900 lb (2,670 kg)**
Maximum speed: **143 mph at 3,000 ft (230 km/h at 900 m)**
Ceiling: **22,000 ft (6,700 m)**
Range: **600 mile (950 km)**
Armament: **2 machine guns; 460 lb (200 kg) of bombs**
Crew: **2**

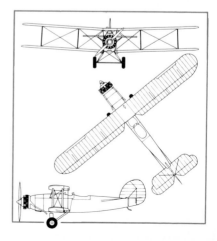

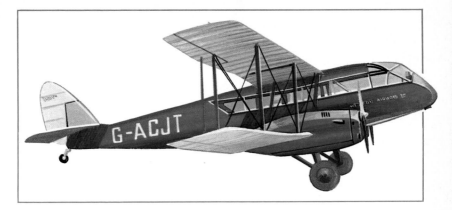

de Havilland D.H.84 Dragon Mk. I

After several successful single-engine planes, de Havilland turned to the manufacture of a larger aircraft that would incorporate the qualities of its earlier planes. Model D.H.84, which made its maiden flight in 1932, was the first of a series of light, multi-engine aircraft that were to become famous in the history of aviation. Called the Dragon, the D.H.84 had been specially ordered from de Havilland for commercial transport to Paris. It was an elegant two-engine biplane powered by two 130 hp Gipsy Major engines, and could carry six passengers and 220 pounds (100 kg) of baggage at a cruising speed of 109 mph (175 km/h). The Dragon became very popular and was soon on order by several small airlines. The de Havilland company manufactured a total of 115 Dragons, which were used around the world by a host of small air transport companies.

Aircraft: **de Havilland D.H.84 Dragon Mk.I**
Manufacturer: **The de Havilland Aircraft Ltd.**
Type: **Civil transport**
Year: **1933**
Engine: **Two de Havilland Gipsy Major, 4-cylinder in-line, air-cooled, 130 hp each**
Wingspan: **47 ft 4 in (14.42 m)**
Length: **34 ft 6 in (10.51 m)**
Height: **10 ft 1 in (3.07 m)**
Weight: **4,200 lb (1,900 kg)**
Cruising speed: **108 mph (175 km/h)**
Ceiling: **12,500 ft (3,800 m)**
Range: **460 mile (740 km)**
Crew: **1**
Cargo: **270 lb (120 kg) (6 passengers)**

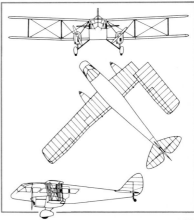

de Havilland D.H.86

The first type of de Havilland four engine aeroplane the D.H.86, was especially designed at the request of the Australian government. Australia wanted a commercial aircraft that could fly passengers along the Singapore–Brisbane route. Like the D.H.66 Hercules and the A.W.15 Atalanta and many other aircraft, the D.H.86 was designed to provide high levels of comfort and safety for passengers and to withstand the difficulties presented by tropical climates and long flying over open water. de Havilland produced a standard company type with four engines, and the new aircraft, the D.H.86, met all of these requirements. Indeed, it was

unofficially referred to as the Express.

The prototype first took to the air on January 14, 1934, only four months after the design had been undertaken. In general configuration, the plane resembled the D.H.84, although several structural improvements were made. The new aircraft was powered by two pairs of Gipsy Six engines, a new 6-cylinder version of the famous light-aircraft Gipsy engine. The D.H.86 could carry ten passengers, four more than the D.H.84, and its cruising speed was increased to 145 mph (230 km/h). After a series of trial flights, the prototype was named Diana and painted with the colors of the Railway Air Service Ltd., which

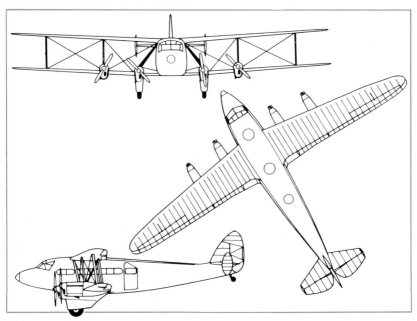

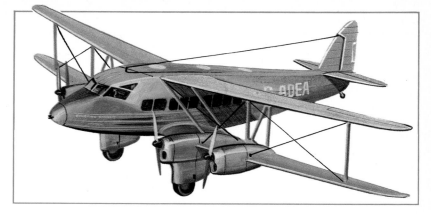

inaugurated a new domestic route on August 20, 1934, a route connecting Croydon, Castle Bromwich, Barton, Belfast, and Renfrew. But at the Australian company's request, the plane was modified by the installation of a double cockpit and the addition of fuel tanks. This aircraft was called the D.H.86 A. From the exterior of the plane these alterations could be seen from the slight elongation of the nose.

The aircraft was also used by Imperial Airways, which bought a dozen planes for European, African, and Far Eastern routes, and these runs were kept open even after the outbreak of World War II. The D.H.86 was as popular as its predecessor and was soon in service in several airlines, including the Qantas and Holyman lines in Australia. A new version appeared in 1936, the D.H.86 B, which had modifications to the structure of both fuselage and tailplane. But only a few of these aircraft were ever constructed. Production stopped in 1937. The plane continued to be used after

Aircraft: **de Havilland D.H. 86**
Manufacturer: **The de Havilland Aircraft Ltd.**
Type: **Civil transport**
Year: **1934**
Engine: **Four de Havilland Gipsy Six I, 6-cylinder in-line, air-cooled, 200 hp each**
Wingspan: **64 ft 6 in (19.66 m)**
Length: **43 ft 11 in (13.38 m)**
Height: **13 ft (3.96 m)**
Weight: **9,200 lb (4,100 kg)**
Cruising speed: **143 mph (230 km/h)**
Ceiling: **20,500 ft (6,250 kg)**
Range: **760 mile (1,220 km)**
Crew: **2**
Passengers: **10**

the beginning of the war. About half of the D.H.86s saw service in the British and Australian air forces. After the war, some of them returned to civilian life in service with small charter companies. Only one Express survived until the late 1950s, the aircraft registered G-ACZP, which was kept at Eastleigh, the home base of Jersey Airways, a company that had acquired six D.H.86s in 1935.

de Havilland D.H.89 Dragon Rapide

The role played in the history of aviation by the D.H.89 Dragon Rapide has often been considered 'almost' as important as that of the Douglas DC-3. But, to tell the truth, the de Havilland transport biplane did not have the versatility or variety of employment that characterized the Douglas. Nevertheless the Dragon Rapide was a veritable classic in the field of commercial aviation. Seven hundred and twenty-eight Dragon Rapides were built in a decade, and these aircraft made a remarkable contribution to the spread of light-weight transport. There are still a great many Dragon Rapides in service in several parts of the world, offering a striking contrast to the ultramodern jets of the present.

Although the Rapide was intended as an improved version of the D.H.84 Dragon, it turned out to be a smaller model of the D.H.86 instead. The structure of the D.H.86 was improved, and the Rapide was equipped with the powerful six-cylinder Gipsy engines. The prototype made its first flight on April 17, 1934, and made its public debut on July 13, at the King's Cup Race in Hatfield. During the race, the plane made a forced landing during a violent hail storm.

Hillman's Airways was the first

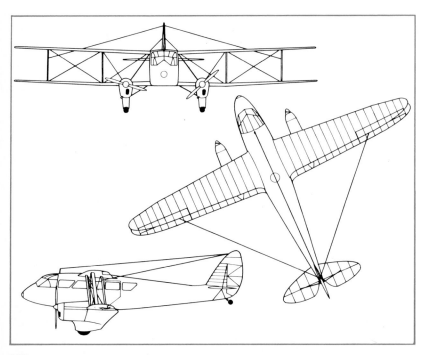

commercial line to use the new aircraft. Seven planes were ordered by Hillman's, and soon the aircraft was an enormous success. A dozen British airlines ordered the plane, especially for short-distance flights. Thirteen foreign airlines bought the plane, including one sold to the Italian line Ala Littoria. Besides these companies, there were many private purchasers of the aircraft in England and throughout the world.

After becoming famous as a commercial plane, the Dragon Rapide won distinction during the Second World War. The plane was considered excellent for training and for transport and communication, so a military version, known as the Dominie, was produced. A total of 532 Dominies were produced, 186 by the de Havilland company and the rest by Brush Coachworks Ltd. A great many aircraft survived the war; they were declared surplus and put on the civilian market. This third period in the Dragon Rapide's career repre-

Aircraft: **de Havilland D.H.89 Dragon Rapide**
Manufacturer: **The de Havilland Aircraft Ltd.**
Type: **Civil transport**
Year: **1934**
Engine: **Two de Havilland Gipsy Six I, 6-cylinder in-line, air-cooled, 200 hp each**
Wingspan: **48 ft (14.63 m)**
Length: **34 ft 6 in (10.52 m)**
Height: **10 ft 3 in (3.12 m)**
Weight: **5,500 lb (2,500 kg)**
Cruising speed: **133 mph (214 km/h)**
Ceiling: **19,500 ft (6,000 m)**
Range: **580 mile (930 km)**
Crew: **1**
Passengers: **6–8**

sented an extension of its commercial career. The R.A.F. planes were re-adapted and modified to the specifications of various buyers. In addition to private owners and small companies that used the plane for charter and short flights, the British European Airways Corporation employed a whole fleet of these biplanes for flights to Scotland and the Channel Islands. A number of Dragon Rapides were also sold abroad.

de Havilland D.H.88 Comet

One of the finest racing planes ever built, the de Havilland D.H.88 Comet was created for one of the most important races of the 1930s. However, not only did the Comet win the England–Australia race (in 70 hours and 54 minutes flying time) but also it continued to establish a series of outstanding records for distance and endurance. One of its record-making flights took it from Gravesend, England, to Sydney, Australia, then on to Blenheim, New Zealand, and back again to England. The Comet flew over 25,000 miles in ten days, twenty-one hours and twenty-two minutes.

The Comet's history began in 1933, when Sir Macpherson Robertson put up a cash prize for the Victorian Centenary air race from England to Australia. At the time the only planes

capable of competing were American, and de Havilland decided to build an aircraft that could uphold the prestige of British aviation. Four amateur fliers ordered the plane: Jim and Amy Mollison, a couple devoted to flying, Bernard Rubin, and A. O. Edwards, the managing director of the Grosvenor House Hotel. The first of the three aircraft took off on September 8, 1934, and the other two followed a few weeks later.

The Comet was an elegant two-engine monoplane, all wood in construction and powered by two 230 hp, Gipsy Six R engines. Each engine powered a two-blade propeller. The undercarriage was retractable, manually controlled, and the two crew members were housed in a long cabin with adjacent seats. It was a very fast aircraft and had a long range. The three Comets – registered G-ACSP

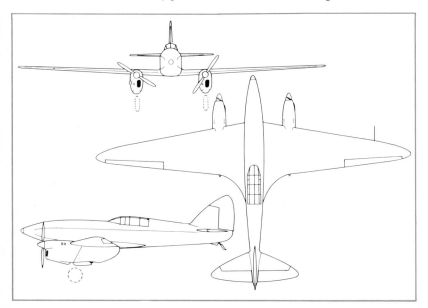

(Mr and Mrs Mollison), G-ACSR (Bernard Rubin), and G-ACSS (A. O. Edwards) – set out for the race on October 20, 1934, from Mildenhall.

The race had several dramatic moments. Rubin's Comet (piloted by Owen Cathcart-Jones and Ken Waller) had to make a forced landing in Persia, while the D.H.88 flown by Jim and Amy Mollison (painted black and gold and called 'Black Magic') and the red Comet, 'Grosvenor House' (flown by C. W. A. Scott and Tom Campbell-Black) managed to reach Baghdad without a stop. Subsequently the Mollisons had engine trouble and had to withdraw from the race. Rubin's green Comet, at first reported missing, set out again and made up for some of the time lost. But it was the 'Grosvenor House' that finally won the race, after fierce competition from the Americans. The second Comet arrived in fourth place. This latter aircraft was sold to the French government in April 1935, and another was ordered from the manufacturer. The Mollison's D.H.88 was sold to Por-

Aircraft: **de Havilland D.H.88 Comet**
Manufacturer: **The de Havilland Aircraft Ltd.**
Type: **Competition**
Year: **1934**
Engine: **Two de Havilland Gipsy Six R, 6-cylinder in-line, air-cooled, 230 hp each**
Wingspan: **44 ft (13.41 m)**
Length: **29 ft (8.83 m)**
Height: **10 ft (3.05 m)**
Weight: **5,550 lb (2,510 kg)**
Cruising speed: **220 mph (350 km/h)**
Maximum speed: **237 mph (381 km/h)**
Ceiling: **19,000 ft (5,800 m)**
Range: **2,900 mile (4,700 km)**
Crew: **2**

tugal for a flight from Lisbon to Rio de Janeiro. The fifth and last Comet to come off the production line was named 'Boomerang'. It was ordered by a private citizen but was declared missing during an attempt to set a record time on a flight to Capetown. The last achievement of the 'Grosvenor House' dates from March 15, 1938. Piloted by Clouston and Ricketts, it flew to Australia and back in ten days, twenty-one hours, and twenty-two minutes. This aircraft has been saved, and is being refurbished to flying condition by the Shuttleworth Trust.

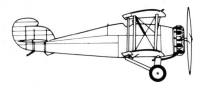

1924 Hawker Woodcock. Wingspan: 32 ft 6 in (9.91 m). Length: 26 ft 2 in (7.98 m). Maximum speed: 138 mph (222 km/h). Engine: 420 hp Bristol Jupiter IV radial. This was the first fighter aircraft built in Great Britain after the First World War. It was built to replace those designed toward the end of the war. A biplane with conventional lines and structure, the Woodcock remained in service until the appearance of the Gloster Gamecock.

1924 Avro Andover. Wingspan: 68 ft (20.72 m). Length: 51 ft 3 in (15.62 m). Maximum speed: 110 mph (177 km/h). Engine: 650 p Rolls-Royce Condor III. This plane was built by Avro for the Royal Air Force as a replacement for the de Havilland D.H.10 over desert routes between Cairo and Baghdad. Three military models were built for passenger and ambulance service, while a commercial model was built for Imperial Airways.

1924 Armstrong Whitworth Siskin III A. Wingspan: 33 ft 2 in (10.11 m). Length: 25 ft 4 in (7.72 m). Maximum speed: 156 mph (251 km/h). Engine: 425 hp Armstrong Siddeley Jaguar IVS. Of more than 400 fighter aircraft built until 1931, most were in the variant model IIIA. The plane saw service in the Canadian and Swedish air forces as well as in the R.A.F.

1926 Blackburn Iris. Wingspan: 97 ft (29.56 m). Length: 67 ft 4 in (20.52 m. Maximum speed: 118 mph (190 km/h). Engines: Three 675 hp Rolls-Royce Condor IIIB. The design for this large reconnaissance seaplane was begun in 1924, and the first plane was delivered two years later. Five versions were built, with different engines and variations in construction detail. They made a number of long-distance flights.

1927 Hawker Horsley. Wingspan: 56 ft 6 in (17.22 m). Length: 38 ft 10 in (11.83 m). Maximum speed: 126 mph (202 km/h). Engine: 665 hp Rolls-Royce Condor IIIA. This torpedo-bomber was designed in 1923 and remained operational for twelve years. A total of 128 aircraft were built, but the most famous Horsley was the one that established a world distance record in May 1927 by flying from Cranwell to the Persian Gulf, a distance of 3,420 miles (5,504 km).

1928 Westland Wapiti. Wingspan: 46 ft 5 in (14.15 m). Length: 31 ft 8 in (9.65 m). Maximum speed: 135 mph (217 km/h). Engine: 480 hp Bristol Jupiter VIIIF radial. Designed as a replacement for de Havilland's war-time bomber, the D.H.9A, the Wapiti was built by Westland in 1927. The plane had the same cabin and landing gear as its predecessor. A total of 517 aircraft were built in various versions and saw several years of service.

1929 Boulton Paul Sidestrand. Wingspan: 71 ft 3 in (21.71 m). Length: 45 ft 7 in (13.89 m). Maximum speed: 147 mph (237 km/h). Engines: Two 425 hp Bristol Jupiter VI radials. Several years passed between the retirement of the de Havilland D.H.10 and the appearance of a new multi-engined daylight bomber in the R.A.F. This plane was the Boulton Paul Sidestrand. The large twin-engine biplane carried three machine guns and had a bomb capacity of more than 1,000 lb (450 kg).

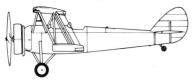

1932 Avro Tutor. Wingspan: 34 ft (10.36 m). Length: 26 ft 6 in (8.07 m). Maximum speed: 122 mph (196 km/h). Engine: 240 hp Armstrong Siddeley Lynx radial. Chosen to replace the Avro 504 N as a basic training plane, the Avro 621 (which soon came to be known as the Tutor) saw service in the Irish, Danish, Canadian, Greek, and South African air forces as well as in the R.A.F. A total of 795 aircraft were built, and many ended up on the civilian market.

1932 Vickers Vildebeest IV. Wingspan: 48 ft 6 in (14.93 m). Length: 37 ft 8 in (11.48 m). Maximum speed: 156 mph (251 km/h. Engine: 825 hp Bristol Perseus VIII radial. Designed in 1928 as a replacement for the Hawker Horsley torpedo-bomber, the first Vickers Vildebeest entered squadron service only in 1933. It saw several years of intensive service. A total of 181 aircraft were built, many of which were still in service in 1939.

1935 Hawker Hind. Wingspan: 37 ft 3 in (11.35 m). Length: 29 ft 7 in (9.01 m). Maximum speed: 186 mph (299 km/h). Engine: 640 hp Rolls-Royce Kestrel V. The Hind was a transitional model between its predecessor, the Hawker Hart, and the more modern monoplane bombers the R.A.F. was later to adopt. A total of 528 planes were built. They served in 30 bomber squadrons until 1939, when they were assigned to training duty.

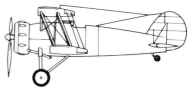

1935 Gloster Gauntlet. Wingspan: 32 ft 9 in (9.99 m). Length: 26 ft 2 in (7.97 m). Maximum speed: 230 mph (370 km/h). Engine: 645 hp Bristol Mercury VI S2 radial. This was the R.A.F.'s last fighter biplane with an open cockpit. It was considered the fastest combat plane in R.A.F. service at the time. A total of 228 aircraft were built, not including the prototypes. At the peak of its career, it equipped fifteen fighter squadrons. The Gauntlet remained in service until 1939.

1935 Blackburn Shark IIA. Wingspan: 46 ft (14.02 m). Length: 38 ft 5 in (11.71 m). Maximum speed: 138 mph (222 km/h). Engine: 700 hp Armstrong Siddeley Tiger VIC radial. The Shark was the last torpedo biplane used for naval service. The design was begun in 1933, and the prototype took to the air the following year. More than 200 aircraft were built in a variety of models. They remained in service until 1938.

Germany

Two hours and eighteen minutes was the time it took to fly the 120 miles (193 km) from Berlin to Weimar in Wartime surplus A.E.G. biplanes. This was the time logged for the first regular air passenger service in the world. This daily flight was inaugurated in 1919 by the Deutsche Luft-Reederei, barely a month and a half before the French commenced a regular passenger flight. This may be considered the first step in the evolution of German civil aviation and the beginning of the rapid expansion of civil aviation throughout the world.

Soon the Deutsche Luft-Reederei introduced a service between Berlin and Frankfurt and Berlin and Hamburg. By the spring there were commercial lines throughout Germany, and other airlines had been established. Among these were the Lloyd Luftverkeher Sablatnig, the Saechsische Luft Reederei, the Bayerischer Luft Lloyd, and the Albatros. It was some sort of world 'first', for Germany led the way in civil aviation as early as

1919 and demonstrated at once an enormous interest in the transport future of the aeroplane.

By the terms of the peace treaty Germany was forbidden to build large aeroplanes, but these restrictions only stimulated German ingenuity. While observing the treaty to the letter, the German aviation industry explored new areas of technology and produced high-performance aircraft. Thus such an advanced plane as the Junkers F 13 could not be used in Germany, although it was sold to airlines in dozens of countries.

The year 1924 marked the unification of several smaller airlines into two major companies. Among the smaller airlines to be absorbed were the Danziger Luft-Reederei (the first company to run Baltic routes), the Junkers Luftverkehr, the Deutscher Luft Lloyd, and the Danziger Lloyd Luftdienst. Junkers Luftverkehr, which had been established by one of Germany's most important aircraft manufacturers, now absorbed several of the smaller lines. The other major company was Deutscher Aero Lloyd, which was formed by the amalgamation of the Aero Union companies and the Lloyd Luftdienst. The two major companies served all of Germany and much of the rest of Europe, thanks to agreements with the leading companies in other countries. As early as 1921 the Air Union had made an agreement with the Soviet authorities to found the Deruluft company (Deutsche–Russische Luftverkehr). This was the first air transport company in Russia and one of the first attempts at international expansion. On January 6, 1926, Junkers and Aero Lloyd were consolidated in a new company that was heavily backed by the government. This was the Deutsche Lufthansa. Lufthansa was to make a name for itself as the busiest and most enterprising company in Europe, and played a fundamental role in the rebirth of German air power.

Deutsche Lufthansa's first flight was made on April 6, and within a few months the company's routes extended well beyond Germany's borders and outside Europe. And it was soon Europe's leader for efficiency and regularity. In 1927 Lufthansa had a fleet of about 120 planes, including some of the most advanced aircraft of the time. The company's continuous expansion and the consequent demand for newer and better planes was a constant stimulus to the German aircraft industry. And during these years Junkers and Dornier, especially, built some outstanding planes and led the world in aircraft development. In

the early 1930s the Deutsche Lufthansa was well ahead of other European companies in number of passengers carried. In 1930 Lufthansa carried almost 110,000 passengers, while another 14,000 were carried by the Deutsche Verkehrsflug, a company that included various small airlines serving domestic routes. Lufthansa had cooperative agreements at the time with twelve other European companies and jointly operated an extensive international flight network.

In the years before World War II Lufthansa reached the peak of its expansion, thanks in part to the development of large aircraft that were more suitable for military than for civil purposes. They were the embryo of the future German Luftwaffe. The Junkers Ju 52/3m, the workhorse of the future German air force made its appearance in 1932. The Heinkel He 70, the fastest civil plane of its time, was put in service in 1933. The Junkers Ju 86 appeared in 1936 and the Heinkel He 111 in 1936, both exceptional aircraft that were to become famous as Luftwaffe bombers. Another new aircraft, the four-engine Focke Wulf Fw 20, entered Lufthansa service in 1938. This plane was the Condor, which later ravaged North Sea convoys and British submarines. Although these aircraft made a contribution to civil aviation in the 1930s (Lufthansa carried its millionth passenger on September 28, 1934, during the period when its routes covered four continents), they soon saw military service, first in the Spanish Civil War and then in World War II.

A.E.G. J II

As in other countries so in Germany, the end of World War I and the birth of civil aviation saw military aircraft roughly transformd into commercial vehicles. And, as elsewhere, the primary impetus to create a network of commercial routes, both national and international, came from the need for postal transport. As early as 1918 Germany had begun to organize an air mail service, and by February 1919, the Deutsche Luft-Reederei (as the new company was called) began regular service. The greater part of the company's fleet consisted of A.E.G. J IIs, military planes that still bore their wartime insignia. These aircraft played a fundamental role in developing a domestic service, especially on the Berlin–Leipzig–Weimar route.

The A.E.G. J II was a direct development of the J I, which was a ground-attack version of the A.E.G. C IV reconnaissance plane that had

Aircraft: **A.E.G. JII**
Manufacturer: **Allgemeine Elektrizitäts Gesellschaft**
Type: **Civil transport**
Year: **1919**
Engine: **Benz Bz.IV, 6-cylinder in-line, liquid-cooled, 200 hp**
Wingspan: **44 ft 2 in (13.46 m)**
Length: **25 ft 11 in (7.90 m)**
Height: **—**
Weight: **3,570 lb (1,620 kg)**
Maximum speed: **93 mph (150 km/h)**
Ceiling: **14,700 ft (4,500 m)**
Range: **350 mile (565 km)**
Crew: **1**
Passengers: **2**

entered service in 1916. The J II was a two-seat biplane, all-metal in construction. Deutsche Luft-Reederei stripped the plane of its military armament and put it into domestic service. Subsequently some J IIs had a cabin installed in place of the rear cockpit, which made it possible to carry two passengers as well as the pilot. These planes were kept in service for several years, and four of them survived until 1926, when they were turned over to the Deutsche Lufthansa company.

Junkers F 13

A total of three hundred and twenty-two Junkers F 13s were constructed in thirteen years. The Junkers saw service throughout the period between the two World Wars with some thirty airlines in a dozen countries. The small Junkers F 13 made an outstanding contribution to the development of commercial aviation. Much of this success was due to the great strength and durability of the aircraft, which was an all-metal plane. Credit for the plane's success is also due to the Junkers company's policy in encouraging the creation and development of commercial flying. The company offered easy terms for purchase and even lent, rented, and gave away aircraft.

The Junkers F 13 was a later development of the first all-metal aircraft ever built, the J 1, a military plane introduced in 1915. After building the J 1, Hugo Junkers created a series of planes, introducing technical improvements with each new model. Among his more famous creations was the D I and the CL I of 1918. The aircraft was structured entirely of metal and covered with sheet of corrugated duralumin. Thus the plane was extremely hardy and particularly immune to the elements. After his success with military aircraft, Hugo Junkers applied the same structural techniques and the same materials to the production of civil aircraft after World War I. The actual design of the first civil aircraft was entrusted to the chief engineer at Junkers, Otto Reuter.

Two planes were designed. The first, known as the J 12, was simply a modified version of the attack plane J 10. The second, first known as the J 13 and then renamed F 13, was an entirely new aircraft and one that represented an extremely advanced concept for its time. It was a low-wing monoplane with a four-passenger closed cabin and an open two-man cockpit. The entire plane was covered with duralumin including the control

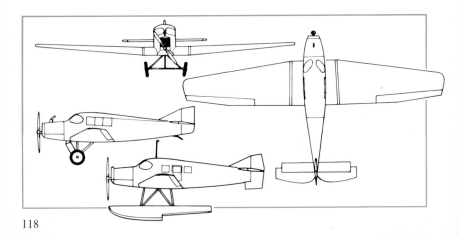

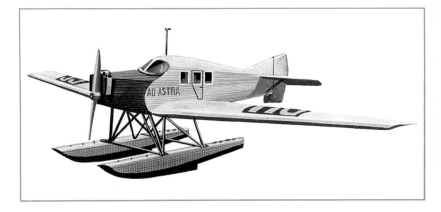

panel. The original engine was a 170 hp Mercedes that drove a two-blade propeller. But the production models were powered by 185 hp B.M.W. engines.

The prototype made its first flight on June 25, 1919. On September 13 of the same year the plane established an international record by carrying eight persons to an altitude of 22,150 ft (6,750 m). The record was never made official, because Germany had not been admitted to the International Aeronautics Federation. Despite its early achievements, the F 13 was not an immediate success. The main reason for this was that the market was flooded with surplus military aircraft at bargain prices. To remedy the situation, Junkers established its own air transport company in 1921, the Junkers–Luftverkehr, and established a series of routes between Germany, Hungary, Switzerland, and Austria. Some sixty F 13s were put in service.

When the Deutsche Lufthansa was founded in 1926, the F 13s had

Aircraft: **Junkers F 13**
Manufacturer: **Junkers Flugzeuge und Motorenwerke A.G.**
Type: **Civil transport (landplane)**
Year: **1919**
Engine: **B.M.W. IIIa, 6-cylinder in-line, liquid-cooled, 185 hp**
Wingspan: **58 ft 2 in (17.75 m)**
Length: **31 ft 6 in (9.60 m)**
Height: **14 ft 9 in (4.50 m)**
Weight: **3,810 lb (1,730 kg)**
Cruising speed: **87 mph (140 km/h)**
Ceiling: **13,000 ft (4,000 m)**
Range: **350 mile (560 km)**
Crew: **2**
Passengers: **4**

clocked 9 million miles (15 million kilometres) and boarded 281,748 passengers. The new national airline took over almost all the Luftverkehr F 13s and kept them in service until 1938 on 43 domestic passenger routes and two cargo lines. In the meantime the F 13 had caught on elsewhere as well. It was used by almost all the European airlines, and Brazil, Colombia, Canada, and South Africa also acquired the F 13. A variety of models were produced. Perhaps the most interesting variations were the ones that had snow skis or pontoons instead of a normal undercarriage.

Zeppelin–Staaken E.4/20

After the end of World War I an Allied commission was set up to repress any German attempt to revive aviation, and one of the innocent victims of this programme was the Zeppelin–Staaken E.4/20. It was a large, four-engine civil transport plane constructed in metal throughout. If the Allies had permitted production of this aircraft, commercial aviation's development might have been advanced by ten years. By order of the control commission, the plane was destroyed in 1922, two years after its construction and first, promising test flights. Its one sin was that it was the offspring of a series of military planes that had sown death and terror in the last years of the war, the R-type giant bombers. The Allies were afraid that the Germans might secretly develop another fearful bomber from such an advanced aeroplane and thus achieve a new supremacy in arms.

Thus Adolf Rohrbach's design for the Zeppelin–Staaken did not enjoy the same success as the Junkers F 13. The control commission also had a look at the F 13, and that aircraft's production was only authorized in 1920, when the commission acknowledged that it was a civil aircraft that could not be developed for military purposes. But the Zeppelin–Staaken E.4/20 was not so lucky. Construction began in May 1919. It was an extremely advanced aircraft, and a host

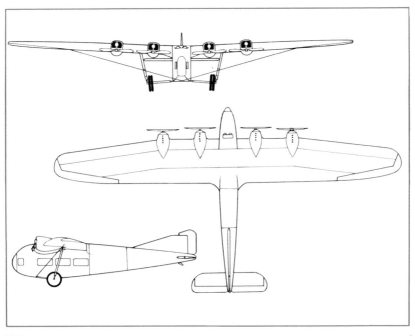

of structural procedures were employed in its construction that would not be used again for many years. Although the Zeppelin company took advantage of its experience with giant bombers, the E.4/20 was radically different. It was a large high-wing monoplane, all-metal in skeleton and skin, and powered by four 245 hp Maybach engines. It could accommodate 12 to 18 passengers in a spacious cabin inside the large rectangular fuselage. Zeppelin intended to use the plane commercially between Friedrichshafen and Berlin.

The first test flights were made with the prototype in September 1920 and showed the high quality of the plane's design. Despite its great size (a wingspan of 101 feet 8 inches (30.98 metres) and over 54 feet (16 metres) in length) and notwithstanding its weight (13,386 lb; 6,072 kg unloaded; about 18,700 lb; 8,500 kg loaded), the plane had a maximum speed of about 140 mph (230 km/h) and could maintain a cruising speed of 124 mph

Aircraft: **Zeppelin-Staaken E.4/20**
Manufacturer: **Zeppelin-Werke GmbH**
Type: **Civil transport**
Year: **1920**
Engine: **Four Maybach Mb.IVa, 6-cylinder in-line, liquid-cooled, 245 hp each**
Wingspan: **101 ft 8 in (30.98 m)**
Length: **54 ft 1 in (16.49 m)**
Height: **—**
Weight: **18,700 lb (8,500 kg)**
Cruising speed: **124 mph (200 km/h)**
Range: **740 mile (1,200 km)**
Crew: **3**
Passengers: **12–18**

(200 km/h) with a range of about 745 miles (1,200 km), between five and six hours in the air. The Allied commission, however, ordered the suspension of the test flights. And two years went by as the Zeppelin company tried unsuccessfully to convince the members of the commission to approve the project. But the E.4/20 was destroyed in November 1922.

Dornier Do L2 Delphin II

Aircraft: **Dornier Do L2 Delphin II**
Manufacturer: **Dornier Werke GmbH**
Type: **Civil transport**
Year: **1924**
Engine: **B.M.W. IV, 6-cylinder in-line, liquid-cooled, 300 hp**
Wingspan: **56 ft 1 in (17.10 m)**
Length: **39 ft 4 in (11.99 m)**
Height: —
Weight: **5,566 lb (2,525 kg)**
Cruising speed: **78 mph (125 km/h)**
Ceiling: **9,800 ft (3,000 m)**
Range: —
Crew: **1**
Passengers: **6–7**

The Delphin family, built by the Dornier company between 1920 and 1928, was a particularly interesting series of planes because of the originality of its construction rather than its commercial success. Only a few models of each of the four series were manufactured, and they were chiefly employed on domestic German routes. (The first of the Delphins was the L1, produced in 1920.) The prototype of the series was also the basic model, and the others were improved and more powerful variations on the same theme. An all-metal aircraft, the Delphin was a central-hull flying boat. The single engine of this monoplane was installed in the nose, with the cockpit just behind. The cabin of the first versions could accommodate six or seven passengers, while the final version, the 1928 Delphin III provided room for twelve or thirteen passengers. The Delphin II was the third model of the four produced in the series. It made its appearance in 1924. It had a longer hull than its predecessors and a more powerful engine; the 185 hp B.M.W. engine was replaced by a 300 hp version of the same engine. And the cockpit was transferred to the passenger cabin. The Delphin II, like the L1 and L1a models, was used by some smaller airlines, including the Ad Astra Aero and the Bodensee Aerolloyd, on short domestic runs.

Dornier Komet III

About the same time that Dornier built the Delphin, it manufactured a land plane that, except for the elimination of the central hull, was structurally identical with the earlier version. The Komet III, the last of the Komets, appeared in 1924. It was substantially new, much larger than its predecessors and more powerful as well, thanks to its 360 hp Rolls-Royce engine. It could accommodate six passengers and a two-man crew. The aircraft was manufactured for the Deutscher Aero Lloyd, which put several planes into service on European routes, including the Hamburg–Copenhagen–Zurich line. In 1925 the Komet III was improved and given a more powerful engine; this new aircraft was called the Merkur. Aside from the B.M.W. VI engine, which generated 600 hp, and some minor alterations, the Merkur was almost identical to the Komet.

Aircraft: **Dornier Komet III**
Manufacturer: **Dornier Werke GmbH**
Type: **Civil transport**
Year: **1925**
Engine: **Rolls-Royce Eagle IX, 12-cylinder V, liquid-cooled, 360 hp**
Wingspan: **62 ft 4 in (18.99 m)**
Length: **39 ft 4 in (11.98 m)**
Height: **11 ft 4 in (3.45 m)**
Weight: **6,600 lb (3,000 kg)**
Cruising speed: **96 mph (155 km/h)**
Ceiling: **11,500 ft (3,500 m)**
Range: **650 mile (1,050 km)**
Crew: **2**
Passengers: **6**

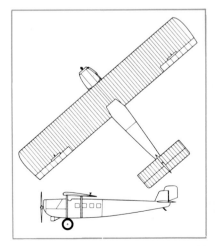

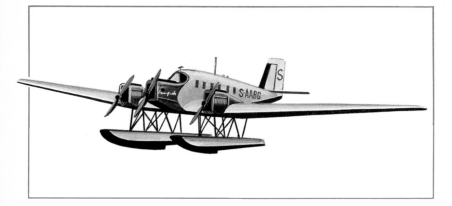

Junkers G24

After its success with the F 13, Junkers decided to build a larger and more powerful aircraft powered by three engines instead of one. This design was called the G23, a three-engine transport that in 1924 became the first multi-engine, all-metal monoplane in civil aviation. Because of limitations imposed by the peace treaty, several false starts were made before the problem of adequate power could be solved. Several engine groupings were tested until, in 1925, the optimum solution was found by making the plane bigger. This model was known as the G24. This aircraft was an immediate success, and some sixty G24s joined the G23 in commercial flights. The G24 also took part in some races. In July–August 1926, the G24 flew about 12,000 miles (20,000 km) from Berlin to Peking; and the following year, March 1927, the aircraft set a total of eleven world records for endurance and distance.

Aircraft: **Junkers G24**
Manufacturer: **Junkers Flugzeuge und Motorenwerke A.G.**
Type: **Civil transport**
Year: **1925**
Engine: **Three Junkers L.5, 6-cylinder in-line, liquid-cooled, 310 hp each**
Wingspan: **98 ft 1 in (29.90 m)**
Length: **51 ft 6 in (15.69 m)**
Height: **—**
Weight: **14,300 lb (6,500 kg)**
Cruising speed: **113 mph (182 km/h)**
Ceiling: **15,400 ft (4,700 m)**
Range: **800 mile (1,300 km)**
Crew: **3**
Passengers: **9**

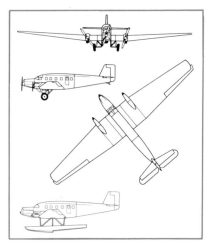

Albatros L 73

In answer to Deutsche Lufthansa's request for a passenger carrier capable of night flying, the Albatros–Flugzeugwerke designed and constructed a large two-engine biplane, the L 73, in 1926. Two aircraft were delivered in 1926 and were assigned to the airline's Berlin–Lübeck–Copenhagen–Malmö run until 1928. It was a conventionally-built plane with metal skeleton and fabric skin. The eight passengers were accommodated quite comfortably in a spacious cabin with seats that could be transformed into couchettes. The two-man crew occupied adjacent seats in a half-open cockpit without side windows.

The two aircraft, called the Preussen and the Brandenburg, went into service with Deutsche Lufthansa in 1926. They occasionally flew the Berlin–Vienna run besides their regular Berlin–Malmö route, and proved to be very successful.

In 1928, after the Brandenburg had been destroyed in a crash, the Lufthansa company ordered two more L 73s. The first L 73, the Preussen, had its engines modified and was still in service with Deutsche Lufthansa in 1932.

Aircraft: **Albatros L 73**
Manufacturer: **Albatros-Flugzeugwerke GmbH**
Type: **Civil transport**
Year: **1926**
Engine: **Two B.M.W. IV, 6-cylinder in line, liquid-cooled 240 hp each**
Wingspan: **64 ft 7 in (19.69 m)**
Length: **47 ft 11 in (14.61 m)**
Height: **15 ft 4 in (4.67 m)**
Weight: **10,160 lb (4,610 kg)**
Cruising speed: **90 mph (145 km/h)**
Ceiling: **9,800 ft (3,000 m)**
Range: **355 mile (570 km)**
Crew: **2**
Passengers: **8**

Focke Wulf A 17a

The A 17 was the first in a successful line of single-engine monoplanes that Focke Wulf produced between 1927 and 1931. The A 17, like all its successors, was nicknamed Möwe (Seagull). The A 17 was the second commercial airplane designed by Focke Wulf Flugzeugbau GmbH, the aircraft company that was to become world-famous during World War II for its combat planes.

The company was founded on January 1, 1924, by a group of Bremen businessmen who wanted to put to advantage the great aeronautic talents of two young men, Heinrich Focke and Georg Wulf. One became technical director, and the other assumed responsibility for flying and testing. Their first design was the A 16, a small transport plane. Although it was powered by only a 75 hp engine, it was able to carry three passengers and the pilot at a speed of 80 mph (135 km/h)

at an altitude of 5,200 feet (1,600 m). The second plane they designed appeared three years later, the first Möwe, the A 17. The fuselage structure of this high-wing monoplane was built of metal tubes, and the wing structure was in wood. The aircraft was covered in fabric and plywood. The aircraft was very simple and robust, and the wide V-shaped undercarriage was equipped with shock-absorbers. The prototype had a 420 hp Jupiter 9Ab, 9-cylinder radial engine that powered a two-blade propeller. The spacious cabin could accommodate eight while the two-man crew was housed in a closed cockpit.

The first test flights demonstrated the high-quality of the aircraft, and Deutsche Lufthansa ordered ten A 17s. Some of these were equipped with a 480 hp Siemens Jupiter VI engine, and this variation was known as the A 17a. The aircraft were employed on various domestic and international runs and saw service until 1935, the

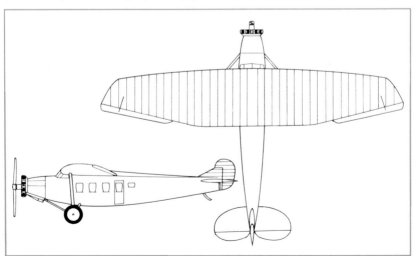

year Lufthansa transferred them to cargo transport on the Cologne–Frankfurt–Munich–Nuremberg and Berlin–Cologne lines.

The second Möwe, the A 20, was not particularly successful, but the third Focke Wulf Möwe design, the A 29, which appeared in 1929, was a fine aircraft. It was a direct descendent of the A 17 and had the same fuselage and wings. This time the engine was a 12-cylinder 600 hp B.M.W., liquid-cooled. Five aircraft were constructed, and four of them were purchased by Deutsche Lufthansa. The fifth plane went to the Deutsche Verkehrsfliegerschule, the German civil aviation school. The Lufthansa planes flew several routes, including runs to France and Switzerland, and were kept in service until 1934.

The last Möwe was the Focke Wulf A 38. This model was designed in 1930, and the next year four aircraft were constructed for Deutsche Lufthansa. The general structure was the same as that of its three predecessors, although it was somewhat larger.

Aircraft: **Focke Wulf A 17a**
Manufacturer: **Focke Wulf Flugzeugbau GmbH**
Type: **Civil transport**
Year: **1927**
Engine: **Siemens Jupiter VI, 9-cylinder radial, air-cooled, 480 hp**
Wingspan: **65 ft 7 in (19.99 m)**
Length: **48 ft (14.63 m)**
Height: **13 ft 1 in (3.99 m)**
Weight: **8,800 lb (4,000 kg)**
Cruising speed: **104 mph (167 km/h)**
Ceiling: **14,700 ft (4,500 m)**
Range: **500 mile (800 km)**
Crew: **2**
Passengers: **8**

Nevertheless, the wing was the same as that of the A 17 and the A 29. The fuselage had smoother lines and could house ten passengers and three crew members (including the radio operator). The engine was a 500 hp Siemens Sh 20u radial. The four planes that Lufthansa bought were named Bückeburg, Hessen, Lipper, and Thüringen and were kept in service until 1933. Their main routes were Berlin–Paris, Berlin–Berne, Berlin–Munich, and Berlin–Vienna. In 1931 the A 38s were also used on the Berlin–Lubeck–Copenhagen–Gothenburg–Oslo route.

Junkers W 33
Junkers W 34

After Charles Lindbergh's solo flight from Mineola to Paris, only one Atlantic barrier to aviation remained, the east–west crossing. This final barrier fell on April 12–13, 1928. It was a small single-engine monoplane, the Junkers W 33 (called the Bremen), that flew over 2,000 miles from Baldonnel, outside Dublin, to Greenly Island, Labrador. The flight, organized by Hermann Koehl, Gunther von Huenfeld, and an Irishman, James Fitzmaurice, took thirty-seven hours.

The east–west crossing of the Atlantic created a great deal of excellent publicity for the Junkers W 33, and the plane was a commercial success. The aircraft had been designed in 1926, along with the W 34 model. Both planes were a development of the F 13 model, and maintained their predecessor's structure and general concept. But they were improved models, especially where aerodynamics was concerned, and they had larger fuselages. The only difference between the W 33 and the W 34 was the engine. The former had a liquid-cooled, in-line engine, while the latter had an air-cooled radial engine. Both aircraft were produced in land and seaplane versions.

The W 33 was produced first. The prototype was nothing more than an overhauled F 13 with a 310 hp Junkers L.5 engine. The production models started coming out in 1927, and the production line remained open until 1934, when the 199th plane was constructed. Immediately following the W 33, the prototype of the W 34 took to the air. This aircraft, equipped with pontoons, went through a series

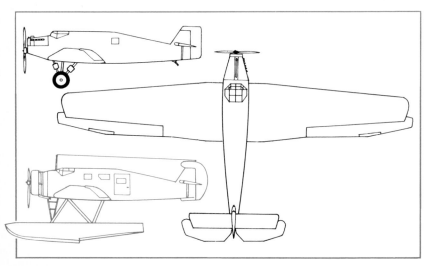

of tests together with the W 33, and some one hundred W 34s were manufactured before production ended.

The W 33s and 34s were successfully used by airlines in Canada, South America, and Africa. And with the secret redevelopment of the Luftwaffe, the military air force, a great number of Junkers were used for communication, patrol, and training services. The Bremen's trans-Atlantic flight highlighted the continuing success of the W 33. The flight was planned in 1927. Originally, two aircraft were to make the crossing together, the Bremen and another W 33, the Europa. The two planes were modified to accommodate a more powerful L.5 engine. Four extra fuel tanks provided a total fuel capacity of 650 gallons (3,000 l). The first flight was attempted on August 14, 1927. The two aircraft took off from Dessau, but bad weather drove them back. The Bremen alone made another attempt eight months later, and this time it was a success.

Aircraft: **Junkers W 33 (landplane)**
Manufacturer: **Junkers Flugzeuge und Motorenwerke A.G.**
Type: **Civil transport**
Year: **1927**
Engine: **Junkers L.5, 6-cylinder in-line, liquid-cooled, 310 hp**
Wingspan: **58 ft 3 in (17.75 m)**
Length: **34 ft 6 in (10.50 m)**
Height: **11 ft 8 in (3.56 m)**
Weight: **5,500 lb (2,500 kg)**
Cruising speed: **93 mph (150 km/h)**
Ceiling: **14,100 ft (4,300 m)**
Range: **620 mile (1,000 km)**
Crew: **2–3**
Passengers: **6**

Aircraft: **Junkers W 34 (landplane)**
Manufacturer: **Junkers Flugzeuge und Motorenwerke A.G.**
Type: **Civil transport**
Year: **1927**
Engine: **Gnome-Rhône Jupiter VI, 9-cylinder radial, air-cooled, 420 hp**
Wingspan: **58 ft 3 in (17.75 m)**
Length: **33 ft 8 in (11.00 m)**
Height: **—**
Weight: **5,900 lb (2,700 kg)**
Cruising speed: **108 mph (175 km/h)**
Ceiling: **20,600 ft (6,300 m)**
Range: **530 mile (850 km)**
Crew: **2–3**
Passengers: **6**

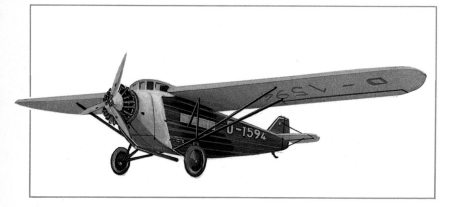

Arado V 1

In 1928 Deutsche Lufthansa ordered a long-distance plane for its postal services from the Arado–Handelsgesellschaft company. This new manufacturer had only recently begun producing planes, a variety of trainers most of which were monoplanes. The company was originally founded in 1917 as a subsidiary of the Flugzeugbau Friedrichshafen GmbH, but it suspended all activity in the years after the end of World War I. The company was briefly involved in building ship hulls and was reorganized in 1924 as an aircraft manufacturer. The Arado company was to become famous throughout the world during World War II, because of the Ar 234s, the first jet bombers ever built.

The V 1 was the company's first attempt at developing a commercial plane. Arado answered Lufthansa's request with a high-wing monoplane. Structured in metal and wood and

Aircraft: **Arado V 1**
Manufacturer: **Arado-Handelsgesellschaft GmbH**
Type: **Civil transport**
Year: **1928**
Engine: **B.M.W. Hornet, 9-cylinder radial, air-cooled, 500 hp**
Wingspan: **59 ft (18.00 m)**
Length: **39 ft 4 in (12.00 m)**
Height: **—**
Weight: **5,180 lb (2,350 kg)**
Maximum speed: **124 mph (200 km/h)**
Ceiling: **—**
Crew: **2**
Passengers: **4**

covered with fabric and plywood, the aircraft was powered by a 500 hp B.M.W. Hornet radial engine. After test flights, the V 1 was put on display at the Berlin air show in October 1928. Then Lufthansa put it into service as an experimental postal transport plane. But the aircraft had a very short career: it crashed on December 19, 1929. Nevertheless, in barely a year it had effected several long-distance flights, including Berlin–Seville, a distance of 1,610 miles (2,591 km), in fifteen hours, and Berlin–Istanbul in eleven hours.

Roland II

Adolf Rohrbach, the man who designed the ill-fated four-engine
Zeppelin–Staaken E.4/20, founded his
own aircraft manufacturing company
in 1922. The first design to go into
production was a three-engine transport plane that took over construction
technique and general structure from
the E.4/20. This plane was called the
Rohrbach Ro VIII Roland, and the
final version of the aircraft was known
as the Roland II.

Nine Roland IIs in all were built for
Deutsche Lufthansa. At first they were
used on the same routes as the Ro
VIII, to England, Switzerland, Austria, and Italy; but in 1936 they were
centred on two other runs: Hamburg–
Copenhagen–Malmö and Berlin–
Munich. Five planes were transferred
from Lufthansa to the Spanish airline
Iberia and saw service between Mad-
rid and Barcelona.

Adolf Rohrbach also built commercial transport seaplanes. The first

Aircraft: **Roland II**
Manufacturer: **Rohrbach-Metall-
Flugzeugbau GmbH**
Type: **Civil transport**
Year: **1929**
Engine: **Three Junkers L.5, 6-cylinder in-
line, liquid-cooled, 280 hp each**
Wingspan: **86 ft 3 in (26.28 m)**
Length: **53 ft 9 in (16.40 m)**
Weight: **16.300 lb (7.400 kg)**
Cruising speed: **110 mph (177 km/h)**
Ceiling: **17,550 ft (5,350 m)**
Range: **800 mile (1,300 km)**
Crew: **2**
Cargo: **5,500 lb (2,500 kg) (10 passengers)**

was the Ro V Rocco, a twin-engine
plane that could carry ten passengers.
This aircraft was powered by two
650 hp Rolls-Royce Condor III engines. Rohrbach's second seaplane
was a more ambitious enterprise, the
Romar, a three-engine plane that
could carry twelve passengers across
the Atlantic. But the plans for these
planes did not seem very promising.
Only one Ro V Rocco was built in
1927 and saw service for a few months
on the Lubeck–Oslo route. Three
Romars were built for Lufthansa.
They were not considered satisfactory
for Atlantic service and flew Baltic
runs from 1929 till 1933.

Dornier Do X

The Dornier Do X was powered by twelve engines producing a total of 7,200 hp; it weighed 52 tons at take-off; and it could carry 150 passengers. The largest aeroplane in the world at the time, the Do X was an unfortunate giant. This 1930s Jumbo disappointed the expectations of its designer, Claude Dornier. What he had hoped for was a gigantic luxury aeroplane that could make regular trans-Atlantic flights. Harassed by continual structural problems, difficulties with the engines, and poor efficiency, the single German Do X and the two aircraft built for Italy were soon forgotten.

Design was begun in 1926, and in a little less than three years the prototype was ready for its maiden flight. After a long series of tests, it looked as if all the problems had been ironed out on October 21, 1929. That was the day the Do X took to the air for an hour with 169 people aboard: a ten-man crew, one hundred and fifty 'official' passengers, and nine stowaways. Although the flight provided good publicity for the aircraft, it exaggerated the seaplane's possibilities, for the cabin could only properly accommodate seventy-two passengers.

It was an all-metal plane in structure, the hull was metal-skinned and the wings were covered in a mixture of materials. The twelve engines were originally 525 hp Siemens Jupiter radials, installed in pairs on the upper wing. The hull had three decks. The

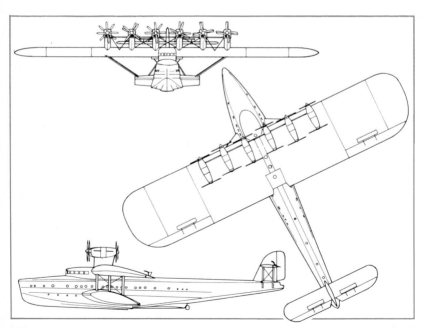

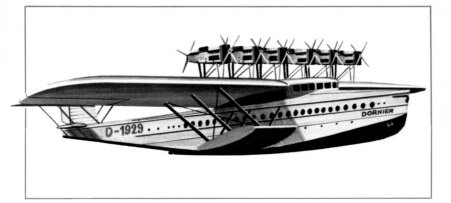

main deck housed the passengers, the lower deck held fuel tanks (about 3,500 gallons; 1,600 l) and baggage, while the upper deck accommodated crew quarters, the radio cabin, the engine cabin, and the cockpit.

After the first test flights difficulty was encountered with the engines. The rear engines had a poor cooling system and power fell, so the plane could barely manage to reach an altitude of 1,300 feet (420 m). The engines were replaced with 600 hp Curtiss engines, 12-cylinder Vs, liquid-cooled. Although the over-heating problem was solved, the plane still had difficulty reaching altitudes above 1,600 feet (500 m). Another publicity flight was undertaken in 1930, when the Do X set off on an around-the-world demonstration flight that lasted ten months. After flying to Brazil, the plane reached New York on August 27, 1931. The flight was not a great success, because of a host of problems that again demonstrated its poor efficiency. Nevertheless, Italy ordered

Aircraft: **Dornier Do X**
Manufacturer: **Dornier Werke GmbH**
Type: **Civil transport**
Year: **1929**
Engines: **Twelve Curtiss Conquerors, 12-cylinder V, liquid-cooled, 600 hp each**
Wingspan: **157 ft 6 in (48.00 m)**
Length: **131 ft 4 in (40.03 m)**
Height: **33 ft 2 in (10.10 m)**
Weight: **114,600 lb (52,000 kg)**
Cruising speed: **118 mph (190 km/h)**
Ceiling: **1,600 ft (500 m)**
Range: **1,050 mile (1,700 km)**
Crew: **10**
Passengers: **72**

two Do Xs in 1931. These aircraft were powered by twelve 550 hp Fiat A.22R engines mounted in six aerodynamic housings. These two planes, the Umberto Maddalena and the Alessandro Guidoni, were earmarked for service with the SANA company on the Trieste–Venice–Genoa–Marseilles–Barcelona–Gibraltar–Cadiz route, but they were never put in service. Instead they were assigned to the Italian Royal Air Force for experimental flights. They were in service for only a short time before they were dismantled.

Junkers G 38ce

Hugo Junkers began his attempts to create a 'flying wing' in 1907 and came rather close to achieving just that with the design of the G 38, which he began in 1928. This aircraft had an enormous wing (Span- 144 ft 4 in; 44 m. Width: 32 ft 9 in; 10 m. Thickness: 5 ft 7 in; 1.7 m). Not only did the wing house engines and fuel tanks, but it could accommodate four passengers, two on each side. The other thirty passengers were housed in a conventional fuselage that was all but invisible when compared to the wings. Only two of these aircraft were ever built. They saw service on several international routes of Deutsche Lufthansa until 1936. One of the planes survived until the first year of the Second World War. It was destroyed in Athens during a bombing raid.

The G 38 made its maiden flight on November 6, 1929, and was delivered to Lufthansa in June of the following year. This enormous aircraft had the general structural characteristics that had become typical of Junkers aircraft: all metal structure and corrugated duralumin covering. The aircraft was powered by four engines: two 400 hp 6-cylinder in-line Junkers L.8s and two 800 hp 12-cylinder V Junkers L.88s. The engines were entirely enclosed within the wings but could be reached during flight. The oil and water radiators were housed in a

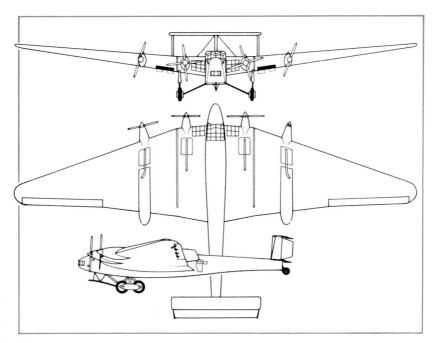

retractable unit on the lower surface of the wing. The massive undercarriage, with aerodynamic fairing, consisted of two pairs of wheels for each strut.

The second G 38 was delivered on September 1, 1931, and was somewhat different from the prototype. In particular, the fuselage was enlarged to make room for two decks, and there were ailerons the full length of the wing, a feature that was to reappear in almost all later Junkers. The spacious passenger cabin was luxuriously decorated. Behind the pilot's cabin on the upper deck was an eleven-passenger cabin. On the lower deck two smaller cabins could accommodate another eleven passengers, and six passengers could also be seated inside the wings. There was a splendid view from the wings because of the large windows in the leading edges. There was also a smokers' cabin for four at the rear of the plane and two seats in the nose.

Aircraft: **Junkers G 38ce**
Manufacturer: **Junkers Flugzeuge und Motorenwerke A.G.**
Type: **Civil transport**
Year: **1930**
Engine: **Four Junkers L.88a, 12-cylinder V, liquid-cooled, 800 hp each**
Wingspan: **144 ft 4 in (44.00 m)**
Length: **76 ft 1 in (23.20 m)**
Height: **23 ft 7 in (7.20 m)**
Weight: **52,900 lb (24,000 kg)**
Cruising speed: **112 mph (180 km/h)**
Ceiling: **8,200 ft (2,500 m)**
Range: **2,100 mile (3,500 km)**
Crew: **7**
Passengers: **34**

Among the prestige routes flown by the two Lufthansa G 38s was Berlin–Munich–Venice–Rome and Berlin–Copenhagen–Stockholm. The G 38 manufacturing licence was sold to Japan, where six military bomber versions were constructed. These aircraft were known as Ki-20 or Type 92.

135

Junkers Ju 52/3m

The Junkers Ju 52/3m made an important name for itself in civil aviation during the 1930s and then became one of the leading aircraft of World War II. In the period between the two world wars this slow, reliable, and extremely tough three-engine plane made a decisive contribution to the development of air transport. Its role was comparable to that of two rather similar aircraft, the Fokker F.VIIb-3m and the Ford Trimotor. Between 1932 and 1939 some two hundred Ju 52/3ms were built and sold to about thirty airlines around the world.

The Ju 52 prototype made its maiden flight on October 13, 1930, and like the major transport planes Junkers had built before (F 13 and W 33), it was powered by a single engine. However the general line, structure and dimensions were the same. The seventh aircraft off the production line became the real prototype of the three-engine plane with the installation of three 575 hp B.M.W. Hornet radials. This aircraft took to the air for the first time in April 1932. Its performance and general characteristics were so fine that it was decided that future Ju 52s would all be three-engine planes.

A low-wing monoplane, all-metal in structure, and covered in corrugated sheet duralumin, the Ju 52/3m could

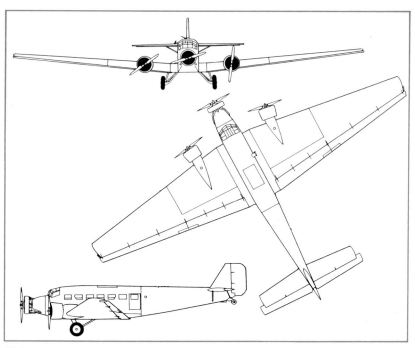

accommodate 17 passengers and a crew of two or three. It was an extremely adaptable plane, and in World War II it became a sort of 'plane-of-all-work': cargo transport, troop transport, paratroop transport, glider towing, air ambulance, mine detection, and even bombing. A great number of variant models were produced in peace and war. The differences in numbering were necessary to distinguish the various engines employed. Almost all the engines on the market were applied to Ju 52s, from German B.M.W.s to the American Pratt and Whitney Wasp and the British Bristol Pegasus, among radial engines, not to mention in-line and V engines such as the Hispano–Suiza and the Junkers Jumo diesel.

Most of the pre-World War II Ju 52/3ms saw service with Deutsche Lufthansa; 78 were still on duty on December 31, 1940. They were used on routes around the world, in Europe and in the Far East. Twenty-eight European, South American, and Af-

Aircraft: **Junkers Ju 52/3m**
Manufacturer: **Junkers Flugzeuge und Motorenwerke A.G.**
Type: **Civil transport**
Year: **1932**
Engine: **Three B.M.W. Hornet, 9-cylinder radial, air-cooled, 525 hp each**
Wingspan: **95 ft 11 in (29.25 m)**
Length: **62 ft (18.90 m)**
Height: **18 ft 2 in (5.54 m)**
Weight: **20,200 lb (9,200 kg)**
Cruising speed: **152 mph (245 km/h)**
Ceiling: **17,000 ft (5,200 m)**
Range: **568 mile (914 km)**
Crew: **2**
Passengers: **15–17**

rican airlines used this versatile three-engine plane. Total production of the Ju 52/3m, in peace and war, reached 4,835 aircraft. And the plane continued in use after the War in several countries, including Spain and France. For a number of years there were no less than 85 Ju 52s in service in France.

Heinkel He 70 G

In the spring of 1933 the Heinkel He 70 was named the fastest passenger transport in Europe. It earned this title by flying at a speed of 221 mph (357 km/h). And it was precisely for this kind of performance that this elegant monoplane was originally designed. It set eight world speed records.

The Heinkel He 70 was a slender, low-wing monoplane, with attractively aerodynamic lines and a four-passenger cabin. The elliptical-plan wing and the retractable undercarriage increased its high aerodynamic coefficients. The 630 hp B.M.W. VI engine was housed in an aerodynamic fairing, and drove a two-blade metal propeller. There was a military as well as a commercial version of the aircraft. Two hundred and ninety-six were built for the burgeoning Luftwaffe, and the 28 commercial aircraft saw service on various European runs of the Deutsche Lufthansa.

Aircraft: **Heinkel He 70 G**
Manufacturer: **Ernst Heinkel A.G.**
Type: **Civil transport**
Year: **1933**
Engine: **B.M.W. VI, 12-cylinder V, liquid-cooled, 630 hp**
Wingspan: **48 ft 7 in (14.80 m)**
Length: **39 ft 4 in (12.00 m)**
Height: **10 ft 2 in (3.10 m)**
Weight: **7,630 lb (3,460 kg)**
Cruising speed: **190 mph (305 km/h)**
Ceiling: **18,300 ft (5,600 m)**
Range: **620 mile (1,000 km)**
Crew: **1**
Passengers: **4**

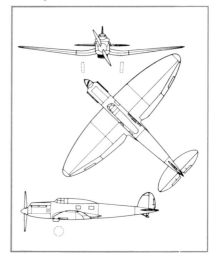

Heinkel He 51

One of the first combat biplanes of the new German air force was the Heinkel He 51, and with this plane the new-born Luftwaffe was to test its potential in the Spanish Civil War. This single-seat fighter was fairly agile and fast, and was armed with two machine guns.

Delivery of the aircraft began in the middle of 1934, and a total of seven hundred biplanes were manufactured. Each new manufacturing run made structural improvements in the aircraft. When Germany intervened on the side of Nationalist forces in the Spanish Civil War, six He 51s were sent to Spain in July 1936. As the war went on, the number of He 51s in Spain increased to one hundred and thirty-five, in service in the Nationalist air force and in the German Condor Legion. In combat, however, the He 51 turned out too inferior to the Russian Polikarpov I-15 fighter. In 1938 the He 51 became a trainer.

Aircraft: **Heinkel He 51**
Manufacturer: **Ernst Heinkel A.G.**
Type: **Fighter**
Year: **1934**
Engine: **B.M.W. VI, 12-cylinder V, liquid-cooled, 750 hp**
Wingspan: **36 ft 1 in (10.99 m)**
Length: **27 ft 6 in (8.38 m)**
Height: **10 ft 6 in (3.20 m)**
Weight: **4,200 lb (1,900 kg)**
Maximum speed: **205 mph (330 km/h)**
Ceiling: **25,200 ft (7,700 m)**
Range: **350 mile (570 km)**
Armament: **2 machine guns**
Crew: **1**

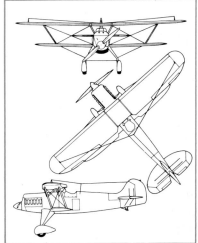

Junkers Ju 86

The Junkers Ju 86 was designed for duty as a commercial transport and as a military bomber. Although the plane was more famous in its military role, it had an important European commercial career in the 1930s. Some fifty planes were used by eight airlines around the world, including South African Airways, which had a fleet of eighteen Ju 86s.

The project was started in 1934, and two prototypes were ready within a few months. The first made its maiden flight on November 4, 1934. There was an unusual technical innovation in the construction of these planes: they were powered by a pair of Diesel engines, 600 hp Junkers Jumo 205C engines. There were many difficulties at first in adapting these engines, but finally production began, and the first airlines began ordering planes. The Junkers Ju 86 was very modern in style, an all-metal aircraft with oval-section fuselage and a retractable undercarriage. The passenger version could carry ten people, while the transport version provided 12.2 cubic

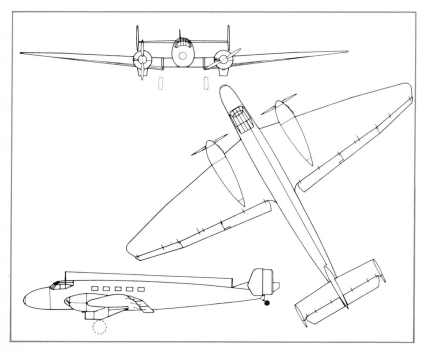

metres (430 cubic feet) of cargo space.

Swissair was the first company to take delivery of the Ju 86, and one of its planes was assigned to the night postal run between Zurich and Frankfurt. Deutsche Lufthansa soon built up a fleet of sixteen Ju 86s. South African Airways took eighteen, but their version was powered by Pratt and Whitney Hornet radial engines generating 800 hp. Actually, there had been general reluctance to use diesel engines in aircraft, and the unreliability of the first engines installed in the Ju 86 discouraged some customers. The Junkers company resolved the problem at once. It developed various types of Ju 86 equipped with different engines, including 770 hp B.M.W. radials, 745 hp Rolls-Royce Kestrels (12-cylinder V, liquid-cooled), and American Pratt and Whitney Hornet radials.

The military Ju 86 began its career in 1936, when the first bombers were delivered to the Luftwaffe. The Swed-

Aircraft: **Junkers Ju 86**
Manufacturer: **Junkers Flugzeuge und Motorenwerke A.G.**
Type: **Civil transport**
Year: **1934**
Engine: **Two Rolls-Royce Kestrel XVI, 12-cylinder V, liquid-cooled, 745 hp each**
Wingspan: **73 ft 10 in (22.50 m)**
Length: **57 ft 2 in (17.52 m)**
Height: **15 ft 9 in (4.80 m)**
Weight: **16,900 lb (7,700 kg)**
Cruising speed: **177 mph (284 km/h)**
Ceiling: **20,000 ft (6,100 m)**
Range: **680 mile (1,100 km)**
Crew: **2**
Passengers: **10**

ish air force also acquired forty Ju 86E bombers and built sixteen more under licence. Although the exact production figures are not available, serial numbers make it certain that almost a thousand were manufactured, mostly in the bomber version.

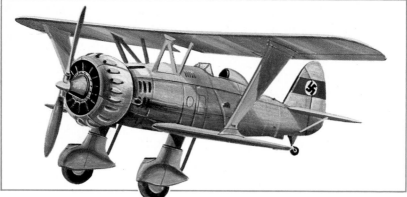

Henschel Hs 123

The last biplane to see service with the Luftwaffe was the Henschel Hs 123, which proved to be an effective ground attack plane during the first years of World War II. It began its career in 1935, when it was selected as an attack fighter by the German air force. The prototype took to the air on May 8, 1935, and then a small number of production models were manufactured to try out the plane under normal operating conditions. In 1936 five were sent to Spain for service in the German Condor Legion. Although it was an efficient aircraft, it was considered obsolete in comparison with the newer monoplane fighters that were starting to make their appearance. (The Luftwaffe itself was already using monoplane fighters.) The outbreak of World War II found the Hs 123 in service with ground attack units, and it saw duty during the invasion of Poland and France.

Aircraft: **Henschel Hs 123**
Manufacturer: **Henschel Flugzeugwerke A.G.**
Type: **Attack fighter**
Year: **1935**
Engine: **B.M.W. 132 Dc, 9-cylinder radial, air-cooled, 880 hp**
Wingspan: **34 ft 5 in (10.50 m)**
Length: **27 ft 4 in (8.33 m)**
Height: **10 ft 6 in (3.21 m)**
Weight: **4,890 lb (2,220 kg)**
Maximum speed: **212 mph at 3,900 ft (341 km/h at 1,200 m)**
Ceiling: **29,500 ft (9,000 m)**
Range: **530 mile (860 km)**
Armament: **2 machine guns; 4 bombs 110 lb (50 kg) each**
Crew: **1**

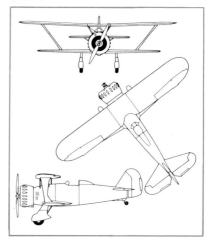

D

1929 Dornier Do R4 Super Wal II. Wingspan: 93 ft 6 in (28.50 m). Length: 77 ft 5 in (23.60 m). Cruising speed: 111 mph (178 km/h). Engines: Four 510 hp Gnome–Rhône Jupiter radials. After the great commercial success of the Do J Wal model, Dornier built a larger and more powerful version of the plane. This was the Super Wal. The sixteen aircraft built in Germany were all employed by Deutsche Lufthansa on its Scandinavian routes. The plane was also manufactured in Italy and Spain. The SANA line in Italy used six planes.

1929 Opel-Sander Rak 1. The Rak 1 was a glider powered by small rockets, built by Fritz von Opel. It was first tested in Rebstock on September 30, 1929. The flight was just under two miles (three kilometres). A year earlier another German, Fritz Stamer, had built what is considered the first rocket aircraft in history. A Canard-type glider, christened Ente, it was powered by two Sander rockets. Tests carried out in Wasserkuppe on June 11, 1928, were not very successful.

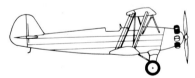

1932 Focke Wulf Fw 44. Wingspan: 29 ft 6 in (9.00 m). Length: 23 ft 11 in (7.28 m). Maximum speed: 118 mph (190 km/h). Engine: 150 hp Siemens Sh 14a radial. This was the first plane designed for Focke Wulf by Kurt Tank, who was to become famous for his World War II aircraft. This biplane was one of the most popular light aircraft and training planes of its time.

1934 Bücker Bu 131 Jungmann. Wingspan: 24 ft 3 in (7.40 m). Length: 21 ft 10 in (6.66 m). Maximum speed: 109 mph (175 km/h). Engine: 80 hp Hirth HM 60R. The first of a famous series of light aerobatic planes, the Bücker Bu 131 Jungmann was built by Carl Bücker, a former test pilot who founded his own company in 1933. This agile biplane with its classic lines was a great success on the export market. In Germany it was used as a trainer for the new air force.

1934 Dornier Do 23. Wingspan: 84 ft (25.60 m). Length: 61 ft 7 in (8.77 m). Maximum speed: 162 mph (260 km/h). Engines: Two 750 hp B.M.W. VI U. A transition model in the semi-clandestine Luftwaffe, the Dornier Do 23 was introduced in 1934 as a civil transport plane. But it had really been designed as a bomber. Subsequently it equipped German bomber squadrons. In 1937 it was replaced by its more illustrious successor, the Do 17.

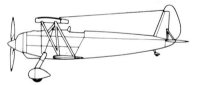

1934 Arado Ar 68. Wingspan: 36 ft 1 in (11.00 m). Length: 31 ft 2 in (9.50 m). Maximum speed: 205 mph (330 km/h). Engine 675 hp B.M.W. VI. After the Heinkel He 51, the Arado Ar 68 was the second fighter biplane developed for the Luftwaffe. But it had a short career. Delays in assembly and in engine manufacture slowed deliveries, and in 1936 the plane was virtually superseded by the revolutionary new Messerschmitt Bf 109.

Italy

Italy was late in entering the field of civil aviation. Although the first companies were founded in 1923 (Aero Espresso Italiana, the AEI, and the Società Italiana Servizi Aerei, SISA) and 1925 (The S.A. Navigazione Aerea, SANA, and the Transadriatica), regular commercial flights were not inaugurated until 1926. This delay was due to the economic and political crisis that followed World War I. Nevertheless Italy was the first country officially to recognize air postal services. Single flights had been made as early as the spring of 1918, when an airmail flight was set up between Civitavecchia, near Rome, and the island of Sardinia. Military aircraft flew the route to test the possibility of establishing a regular air mail service. On November 25, 1918, a mail service was set up in the northern Adriatic, serving Venice, Trieste, Pola, and Fiume. Another mail service was begun on March 2, 1919 Padua and Vienna). Caproni planes carried the mail every three days.

Notwithstanding these achievements, the popularisation of the aeroplane as a commercial vehicle was delayed by public indifference and by economic problems. By May 1919 there were regular postal flights between Rome and Naples, Rome and Pisa, and Milan and Venice (by dirigible). By January 1920, little had changed, except that aeroplanes replaced the dirigibles. There were still only three routes: Rome–Pisa–Milan, Turin–Milan–Venice, and Genoa–Pisa. By this time France, Great Britain, and Germany had already accumulated a great deal of experience, and the groundwork had already been laid for the further development of civil aviation.

Italian civil aviation dates from 1926. On April 1, the Transadriatica line opened its Rome–Venice route, and SISA inaugurated its Turin–Venice–Trieste line on the same day. SANA began service between Genoa, Rome, and Naples on April 7, and on August 1, Aero Espresso made its first flight from Brindisi to Istanbul. Two new companies were founded, the Società Aerea Mediterranea (SAM) in February 1927, and the Avio Linee Italiane (ALI) in October 1928. By the early 1930s these six companies were operating over a large area with flights to Rhodes, Tripoli, and Berlin. Although Germany and France were far ahead, Italy had made considerable progress since 1926. In terms of total passengers carried, Italy, with 40,000 passengers in 1930, was in third place, behind Germany and France and ahead of Great Britain.

The second half of the 1930s was certainly the golden age of Italian civil aviation. Record flights and racing titles as well as the famous trans-Atlantic flights gave Italy worldwide prestige in aviation. The aviation industry was growing to meet military demands, and Italian aircraft manufacturers were producing high-performance planes that could compete with those of the most technologically advanced countries in the world. Civil aviation continued to expand until the outbreak of World War II.

On August 28, 1934, a national airline was founded. Like France, Germany, and Great Britain, Italy felt the need to concentrate available resources and improve its commercial facilities. Thus a new company was established, the Società Ala Littoria, which absorbed SISA, Aero Espresso, SANA, and SAM. (SAM had absorbed Transadriatica in 1931.) The only remaining independent company, Avio Linee Italiane, continued its own expansion independently of Ala Littoria.

Ala Littoria's expansion was aided by the government. The company increased its colonial flights and extended its European routes. On April 1, 1935, the Budapest route was opened. On July 29, the flight to Paris by way of Marseilles was inaugurated. On December 7, 1936, Cadiz and Spanish Morocco were added. In 1937 routes were extended to Central Europe, to

Prague in May and to Bucharest in October. And routes to Spain were increased in 1938.

Avio Linee Italiane also continued to expand. Services on existing routes were amplified (including flights to Munich and Berlin), and internal routes were extended. One of these, the line serving Venice, Milan, and Turin, was extended to Paris and London.

In the years just before World War II, Italy developed several intercontinental routes. After Ala Littoria established routes to Italy's African colonies (Eritrea, Somalia, Abyssinia), trans-Atlantic flights to South America were begun. A new company was founded for this purpose, the Linee Aeree Transcontinentali Italiane (LATI), which inaugurated regular flights between Rome and Rio de Janeiro in December 1939. The route was serviced by SIAI-Marchetti SM.83s. The route, which had to avoid French and British territories, was kept in service until the end of 1941. These weekly flights represented the first regular passenger service across the South Atlantic following the withdrawal from service of the German Zeppelin dirigibles. After surmounting a host of bureaucratic and political obstacles, LATI succeeded in getting authorization in 1941 to extend its routes to Argentina. The first Buenos Aires flight was made in September of that year. However this success, was shortlived as LATI had to suspend all its services on December 22, because of the United States fuel blockade. Other fuel sources could not be diverted from military uses.

Savoia S.17

Aircraft: **Savoia S.17**
Manufacturer: **Idrovolanti Savoia**
Type: **Competition**
Year: **1919**
Engine: **Isotta-Fraschini V6, 6-cylinder in-line, liquid-cooled, 250 hp**
Wingspan: **26 ft 6 in (8.07 m)**
Length: **27 ft 2 in (8.28 m)**
Height: **10 ft (3.05 m)**
Weight (empty): **1,610 lb (730 kg)**
Weight (loaded): **2,075 lb (940 kg)**
Maximum speed: **152 mph (245 km/h)**
Ceiling: **20,300 ft (6,200 m)**
Crew: **1–2**

It was the fog that dominated the third competition in the Schneider Trophy Series, which was held at Bournemouth, England, on September 10, 1919. This was the first Schneider Trophy race after the end of World War I. The fog plus a host of organizational difficulties were responsible for misunderstandings and confusion. Finally the race was suspended and the excellent performance of the Savoia S.17 and its pilot, Guido Janello, never got into the record books. Indeed, the Italian plane was the only one to complete the race, maintaining an average speed of 125 mph (201 km/h), but an involuntary infraction of the rules led to its disqualification. Flying through heavy fog along what he considered the correct course, Janello made his turns around a non-regulation marker. The Italian group at the race protested to the F.A.I. and com-

plained of the poor organization of the competition, but to no avail. The race was cancelled and put off until the following year in Venice.

The plane that Janello flew was a modified version of the Savoia S.13 seaplane, an aircraft designed just after the end of World War I as a reconnaissance and fighter plane. The Savoia S.17 had the general characteristics of a central-hull biplane, but the aerodynamic lines were improved and a 250 hp Isotta–Fraschini engine was installed. Like its predecessor the Savoia S.17 was extremely manoeuvreable and tough.

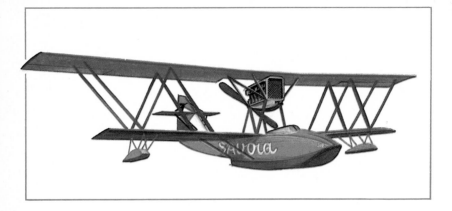

Savoia S.12

After the unfortunate cancellation of the race in Bournemouth, the fourth Schneider Trophy race was held in Venice, September 18–21, 1920. It was not an especially exciting event, because the only planes ready to fly were Italian. Although the French and the English intended to compete, they were unable to get their planes ready in time. There were four Italian planes entered in the race, two Macchis and two Savoias. The Savoias were the S.12 and the S.19 the Macchis were the M.12 and the M.19. The Savoia S.19 was designed expressly for Schneider Trophy racing but, like the two Macchis, it had difficulties during the preliminary races because of hasty preparation of the aircraft and had to withdraw. The only aircraft to remain in the race was the Savoia S.12, a biplane constructed for military service at the end of World War I. Thanks to its intrinsic resilience, it was

Aircraft: **Savoia S.12**
Manufacturer: **Idrovolanti Savoia**
Type: **Competition**
Year: **1920**
Engine: **Ansaldo V-12, liquid-cooled, 500 hp**
Wingspan: **43 ft 2 in (13.16 m)**
Length: **32 ft 8 in (9.95 m)**
Height: **12 ft 6 in (3.81 m)**
Weight (empty): **2,625 lb (1,191 kg)**
Weight (loaded): **3,835 lb (1,740 kg)**
Maximum speed: **105 mph (169 km/h)**
Crew: **1–2**

the only plane that managed to take to the air in the bad weather that dogged the preliminary flights.

Luigi Bologna piloted the S.12 through the qualifying tests on September 18. The next day it was decided to run the course. But bad weather forced Bologna to come down after five laps. He tried again on September 21, and this time he completed the circuit. The ten laps were flown in two hours, ten minutes, and thirty-five seconds, at an average speed of 107.18 mph (172.48 km/h). It was the first official win for Italy. The next race, in Venice again the following year, was also won by Italy.

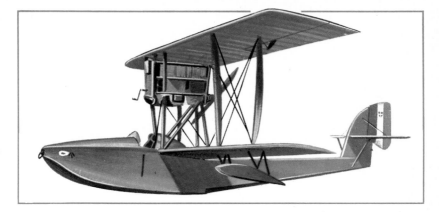

Macchi M.7bis

Italy won the Schneider Trophy for the second time in Venice in August 1921. The winning plane was the Macchi M.7 piloted by Giovanni De Briganti: Like the 1920 version it was an all-Italian race. The English did not enter, and the only French competitor, Sadi Lecointe, had to withdraw his Nieuport when it was damaged during trials. After tough preliminaries, three planes entered the finals, two Macchi M.7s, De Briganti's and another piloted by Piero Corgniolino, and Arturo Zanetti's Macchi M.19. Zanetti led during the first laps, but an engine shaft broke and a fire started, and Zanetti made a forced landing. Corgniolino had to withdraw from the race too, while De Briganti finished the circuit at an average speed of more than 110 mph (180 km/h).

The Macchi M.7 was designed toward the end of World War I as a seaplane fighter by Tonini.

Aircraft: **Macchi M.7bis**
Manufacturer: **Società Aeronautica Nieu-port Macchi**
Type: **Competition**
Year: **1921**
Engine: **Isotta-Fraschini V6bis, 6-cylinder in-line, liquid-cooled, 260 hp**
Wingspan: **32 ft 8 in (9.95 m)**
Length: **26 ft 7 in (8.10 m)**
Height: **9 ft 10 in (2.99 m)**
Weight (empty): **1,710 lb (775 kg)**
Weight (loaded): **2,380 lb (1,080 kg)**
Maximum speed: **160 mph (257 km/h)**
Crew: **1**

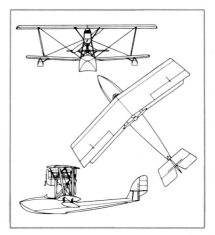

Caproni Ca 60 Transaereo

The design of the Caproni Ca 60 was an extremely ambitious programme, especially considering that it was undertaken just after the end of World War I. Eight engines generated a total of 3,200 hp. Nine wings, in sets of three, were installed on an enormous fuselage measuring 77 feet (23.45 m) in length. In theory it should have been able to transport one hundred passengers. Alas, this enormous plane proved a complete failure. During its second and last test flight, over Lake Maggiore, it barely managed to rise sixty feet before nosing down and crashing in the lake. Nevertheless it is of historic interest. When it was built, it was the largest plane in the world, the first triple triplane in history, and the first aircraft designed to carry 100 passengers across the Atlantic.

Caproni had a great deal of success during World War I in the construction of multi-engine bombers, and the Ca 60 design was based on this experience. Most of the structure was wood with metal reinforcing. The three sets of three wings were installed in the middle and at the ends of the huge fuselage, which looked rather like the hull of a ship. The plane was powered by American Liberty engines, which were installed in unusual fashion: four on the middle front wing and four on the middle back. Of each set of four engines, the two middle

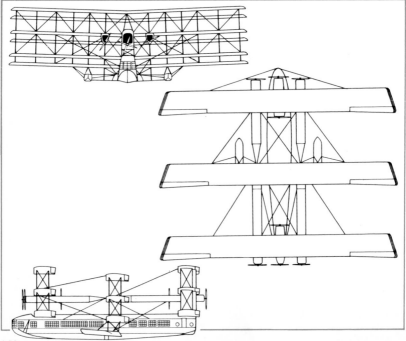

engines were installed in tandem and drove four-blade propellers. The two outer engines on the sides drove two-blade propellers. A firm structure connected the forward and rear engines thereby reinforcing the wings and making it possible for crewmembers to reach the engines during flight. The fuselage had two enormous pontoons to make it easier to take off from water, and inside there was spacious accommodation for one hundred passengers. Pairs of seats ran down the length of the plane, which had large and unusual windows.

The unfortunate test flight took place on March 4, 1921, at Sesto Calende. The chief test pilot of the Caproni company, Semprini, was at the controls. After a few floating trials, the plane was loaded with a weight equal to that of sixty passengers to give the aircraft the necessary equilibrium in the water. Then Semprini decided to try taking off. After a long approach run, with all eight engines at maximum power, the plane

Aircraft: **Caproni Ca 60 Transaereo**
Manufacturer: **Società Aviazione Ing. Caproni**
Type: **Civil transport**
Year: **1921**
Engine: **Eight Liberty, 12-cylinder V, liquid-cooled, 400 hp each**
Wingspan: **98 ft 5 in (30.00 m)**
Length: **77 ft (23.45 m)**
Height: **30 ft (9.15 m)**
Weight: **55,100 lb (26,000 kg)**
Maximum speed: **80 mph (130 km/h)**
Range: **410 mile (660 km)**
Crew: **8**
Cargo: **12,000 lb (5,445 kg) (100 passengers)**

lifted off from the waters of Lake Maggiore and rose several feet in the air. But at about 60 ft (20 m) the plane nosed over and headed down. All the pilot's attempts to right the plane came to nothing. The Caproni nosed down into the water and crashed. Semprini got out in time, and the wreck was subsequently hauled to the surface. While Caproni was considering whether or not to repair the aircraft and resume testing, a fire broke out and destroyed the remains of the plane.

Dornier Do J Wal

More than half of the three hundred or so Dornier Do J Wals constructed in various models were built in Italy. In 1922 the Dornier company completed the prototype of what was to be one of the most popular seaplanes in the world for more than fifteen years. But the peace treaty at the end of World War I forbade Germany from building aircraft of that class. Thus a new company was founded in Italy, in Marina di Pisa, for the manufacture of this plane, the Costruzioni Meccaniche Aeronautiche S.A. (CMASA). Through this new company the commercial success of the Wal was assured. In 1927 and 1928 the aircraft was also built in Spain and Holland, though there it was produced mainly in a military version. In 1932 the Dornier company itself began production of two larger and more powerful models of this aircraft, and continued turning out Wals until 1936.

The Wal was a central-hull monoplane flying boat driven by two engines installed in tandem over the middle of the wing. Over a period of fourteen years no less than twenty variant models of the plane were produced. They differed in size, weight, engine, and use. The first variant model, built by CMASA in 1923, was equipped with a pair of

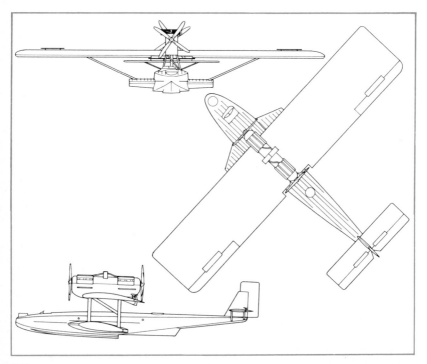

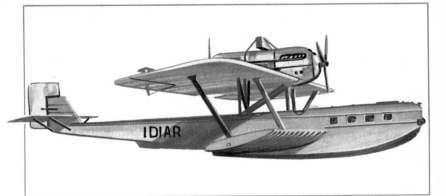

360 hp Rolls-Royce Eagle IX engines or two 300 hp Hispano–Suizas and could accommodate eight-to-ten passengers plus two crew members, the latter in an open cockpit. The first orders came from Spain, and soon after Brazil, Colombia, and Germany bought the aircraft. The German Aero-Lloyd company used four Wals on the Danzig–Stockholm run. Confirmation of the plane's exceptional qualities came first from Spain, where in 1926 a Wal, baptized Plus Ultra, flew some 6,259 miles (10,072 km) from Seville to Buenos Aires in 59 hours and 35 minutes. A year earlier Roald Amundsen had used a Wal in his unsuccessful attempt to fly over the North Pole.

Italy was a major consumer of Wals. Some thirty passenger versions were put in service on Italian lines. The SANA company inaugurated its Genoa–Rome–Naples–Palermo route in 1926; in 1928 a Rome–Barcelona–Tripoli service was introduced; and the next year there was a line between Genoa and Alexandria. The Aero

Aircraft: **Dornier Do J Wal**
Manufacturer: **C.M.A.S.A.**
Type: **Civil transport**
Year: **1923**
Engine: **Two Rolls-Royce Eagle IX, 12-cylinder V, liquid-cooled, 360 hp each**
Wingspan: **73 ft 10 in (22.50 m)**
Length: **56 ft 7 in (17.25 m)**
Height: **17 ft (5.20 m)**
Weight: **12,500 lb (5,700 kg)**
Cruising speed: **87 mph (140 km/h)**
Ceiling: **11,400 ft (3,500 m)**
Range: **1,350 mile (2,200 km)**
Crew: **2**
Passengers: **8–10**

Espresso company used the Wal on flights to Athens and Istanbul. The first improved German versions that appeared in 1933 were used in the Wal's more impressive flights, the trans-Atlantic postal flights to South America. The first experimental flight took place in May 1933, and seven months later the regular route was opened. By August 1935 (a year and a half after the service began) the Lufthansa Wals had made a hundred Atlantic crossings. When the aircraft were finally withdrawn from service, they had made a total of 328 successful crossings.

Savoia Marchetti S 16ter

On April 20, 1925, the small S.16ter, a single-engine biplane flying boat took off on the longest flight yet to have been undertaken. With Francesco De Pinedo as pilot and Ernesto Campanelli as flight engineer, the plane touched down on three continents. It flew from Sesto Calende, on Lake Maggiore, to Rome, Melbourne, Tokyo, and back to Rome. After 67 landings the plane returned on November 7, 1925. The plane flew some 33,000 miles (53,000 km) in 360 hours in the air. This was two years before Charles Lindbergh's solo crossing of the Atlantic and one year before Richard Byrd's flight over the North Pole.

The Savoia Marchetti S.16ter was adapted from a civil transport plane, the S.16, which was designed and built in 1919 and shown at the Paris air show the same year. A flying boat, this central-hull biplane was powered by an engine with a pusher propeller, by then a well-established formula with both the Savoia and Macchi companies. Its purchase price at the time was 16,000 French francs, relatively inexpensive for a high-performance plane that could carry five or six passengers. Yet the plane was not a commercial success. In 1921 the SIAI–Marchetti company, which was still known as the Idrovolanti Savoia company, built a bomber version of the aircraft. This was the S.16bis. It was the first seaplane bomber adopted by the Italian military air force, which had been organized as a separate branch of the

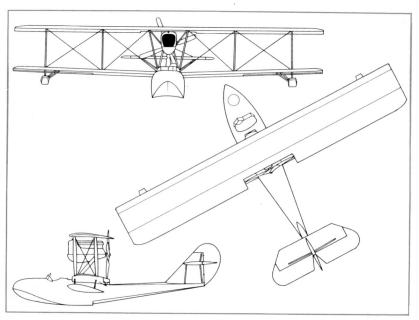

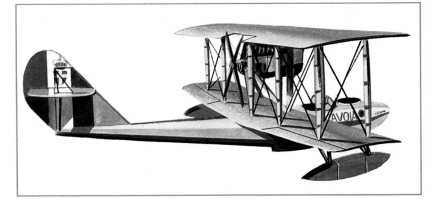

military on March 23, 1923. The S.16ter made its appearance in the same year. In effect it was a longer and more powerful version of its predecessor. It was powered by a 400 hp Lorraine–Dietrich engine in place of the 300 hp Fiat A.12bis used by its two predecessors. The structure and general configuration were relatively unchanged: a central hull, wings of equal length joined by struts and metal cables.

Despite its excellent performance the S.16ter was not an immediate success. (3 minutes and 30 seconds to reach 3,000 feet; 1,000 m. 55 minutes to reach 15,000 feet; 5,000 m.) In September 1920 an S.16 established a record for the longest non-stop flight by a seaplane, flying from Sesto Calende to Helsinki with Umberto Maddalena at the controls. In 1924 the S.16ter established a seaplane record for altitude, carrying half a ton of cargo to 15,081 feet (4,597 m). De Pinedo's flight the following year confirmed the plane's toughness and reliability. The S.16ter that Francesco

Aircraft: **Savoia Marchetti S.16ter**
Manufacturer: **Società Idrovolanti Alta Italia**
Type: **Passenger transport**
Year: **1923**
Engine: **Lorraine-Dietrich (Isotta-Fraschini), 12-cylinder V, liquid-cooled, 400 hp**
Wingspan: **50 ft 10 in (15.50 m)**
Length: **32 ft 6 in (9.91 m)**
Height: **12 ft (3.66 m)**
Weight: **5,800 lb (2,600 kg)**
Cruising speed: **93 mph (150 km/h)**
Ceiling: **9,800 ft (3,000 m)**
Range: **620 mile (1,000 km)**
Crew: **1**
Passengers: **4**

De Pinedo flew was called Gennariello, and it outdistanced by 3,700 miles (6,000 km) the American record established in 1924 with the Douglas World Cruiser.

In 1926, after its record flights, the S.16 began to appear on the commercial market, especially the bis and ter models. At the end of 1926 the Aero Espresso company took two S.16ters, and in 1929 the SISA bought four as training planes. The Società Incremento Turismo Aereo (SITA) used two S.16bis, three S.16ter, and one S.16, with a 300 hp Fiat engine, on the San-Remo–Genoa route.

Fiat CR.1

The Fiat CR.1 was the first of the fighters to be designed by Celestino Rosatelli, the Fiat designer who was to become world-famous. This aircraft was also the first all-Italian fighter to enter service after the end of World War I. The design was begun in 1923, and the production model appeared the following year. The production model differed from the prototype in the adoption of a 320 hp Isotta–Fraschini engine in place of the 300 hp Hispano–Suiza. Aside from the change of engine, there were no significant differences. It was a single-seat biplane, unusual because the lower wing was noticeably larger than the upper wing. It was a fine-performance aircraft and extremely manoeuvreable. Heavy production of CR.1s was undertaken to equip fighter units of the Italian air force. In total, about one hundred planes were built, beginning in 1924. The plane was also used by military aerobatic squadrons.

Aircraft: **Fiat CR.1**
Manufacturer: **Fiat S.A.**
Type: **Fighter**
Year: **1924**
Engine: **Isotta-Fraschini Asso, 8-cylinder V, liquid-cooled, 320 hp**
Wingspan: **29 ft 4 in (8.95 m)**
Length: **20 ft 6 in (6.24 m)**
Height: **7 ft 10 in (2.40 m)**
Weight: **2,546 lb (1,155 kg)**
Maximum speed: **168 mph (270 km/h)**
Ceiling: **24,440 ft (7,450 m)**
Range: **405 mile (650 km)**
Armament: **2 machine guns**

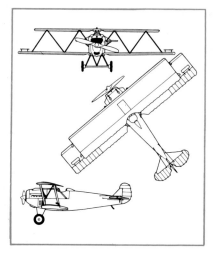

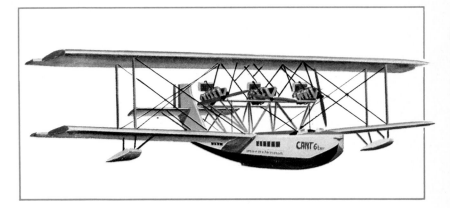

Cant 6ter

The Cantieri Navali Triestino built only two Cant 6ter aircraft, so this aircraft cannot be said to have had a truly commercial career. Yet it did represent one of the shipbuilding company's early approaches to aviation. In later years, up to the outbreak of World War II, the name Cant was to become synonymous with excellence in the manufacture of transport seaplanes. The company reached the peak of its renown during the war.

The prototype of the Cant appeared in January 1926 as a demonstration plane. A central-hull biplane, it was originally powered by three 400 hp Isotta–Fraschini engines and could accommodate eleven passengers in addition to the two members of the crew. The skeleton of the aircraft was of wood, while the skin was fabric. The three engines were lined up between the wings and supported by a complicated system of struts attached to the fuselage. The radiators were

Aircraft: **Cant 6ter**
Manufacturer: **Cantieri Navali Triestino**
Type: **Civil transport**
Year: **1926**
Engine: **Three Isotta-Fraschini, 12-cylinder V, liquid-cooled, 400 hp each**
Wingspan: **76 ft 1 in (23.20 m)**
Length: **49 ft (14.94 m)**
Height: **—**
Weight: **15,400 lb (7.000 kg)**
Maximum speed: **121 mph (195 km/h)**
Ceiling: **—**
Range: **—**
Crew: **2**
Passengers: **11**

mounted above the rear of each engine, and the wooden propellers were two-blade.

The prototype, registered as I-ONIO, was derived from a flying boat bomber Cant had built in 1925. The second 6ter was purchased by the Società Italiana Servizi Aerei (SISA), which used the aircraft as a training plane. This plane was powered by three 200 hp S.P.A. engines.

SIAI–Marchetti SM.55C
SIAI–Marchetti SM.55X

Aircraft: **SIAI-Marchetti SM.55C**
Manufacturer: **SIAI-Marchetti**
Type: **Civil transport**
Year: **1926**
Engine: **Two Isotta-Fraschini (Lorraine-Dietrich), 12-cylinder V, liquid-cooled, 400 hp each**
Wingspan: **78 ft 9 in (24.00 m)**
Length: **54 ft 1 in (16.50 m)**
Height: **16 ft 5 in (5.00 m)**
Weight: **15,900 lb (7,200 kg)**
Cruising speed: **106 mph (170 km/h)**
Ceiling: **12,400 ft (3,800 m)**
Range: **680 mile (1,100 km)**
Crew: **3**
Passengers: **9–11**

The SM.55 prototype established fourteen records. Francesco De Pinedo flew it around the world for a total distance of 27,230 miles (43,820 km). The plane set a series of endurance and distance records. And it made two Atlantic crossings in formation, in 1930 and 1933, with Italo Balbo at the controls. The SM.55 was world-famous from the middle 1920s until the middle of the 1930s. Alessandro Marchetti's plane was a remarkable aircraft.

The SM.55 appeared in 1924. The air force was looking for a torpedo-launching seaplane, and the designer found several original solutions for the technical problems that had to be met. It was a twin-hull flying boat, and the tail was supported by two booms extending from the hulls. The two engines were installed above the central section of the wing on a trellis-like

structure. The cockpit was in the wing between the two hulls, while fuel tanks, radio, gun and sighting turret were housed in the hulls. Torpedoes or bombs were suspended from the lower side of the wing between the two hulls. Not only did the plane perform well on water and in the air, but it was designed in such a way that one could easily reach any part of the craft and, if necessary, replace the installations.

Nevertheless, the air force commission found the plane too unorthodox for its tastes, and two years went by before the aircraft's merits were fully

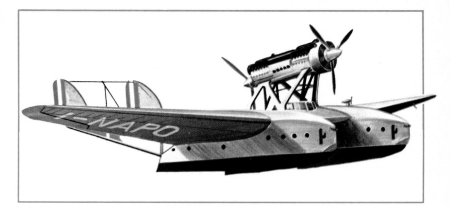

appreciated. The Italian air force ordered the SM.55 in 1925 and was so satisfied with its performance that 170 models were manufactured beginning in 1926. There were several variant models, with different structural details and varying performance, weight, and size. In some cases more powerful engines were installed. There were three military versions, the A, M, and X models and two civilian versions, the C and P models. In place of armament and military equipment, the civilian models had room for nine to twelve passengers. These planes saw service, beginning in 1926, with the Aero Espresso company, the Società Area Mediterranea (SAM), and the Ala Littoria. Until 1937 they flew Mediterranean routes.

The first of the SM.55s long-range flights took place in 1927. Francesco De Pinedo and Carlo Del Prete flew one of the first military SM.55s, the Santa Maria; the armament was removed and structural reinforcements were applied. At 7.35 on the

Aircraft: **SIAI-Marchetti SM.55X**
Manufacturer: **SIAI-Marchetti**
Type: **Long-range flying boat**
Year: **1933**
Engine: **Two Isotta-Fraschini Asso, 12-cylinder V, liquid-cooled, 800 hp each**
Wingspan: **78 ft 9 in (24.00 m)**
Length: **54 ft 1 in (16.50 m)**
Height: **16 ft 5 in (5.00 m)**
Weight: **22,000 lb (10,000 kg)**
Cruising speed: **149 mph (240 km/h)**
Ceiling: **16,400 ft (5,000 m)**
Range: **2,400 mile (4,000 km)**
Crew: **4**
Cargo: **11,000 lb (5,000 kg)**

morning of February 13 they took off from the seaplane port of Elmas, Sardinia, and flew to Africa, South America, and North America. Because of the negligence of one of the spectators in New Orleans, the Santa Maria caught fire and burned. The return flight was made aboard another SM.55, which touched down in Rome on June 16. A total of 28,000 miles (43,820 km) had been flown across four continents. In 1928 another flight across the South Atlantic was made with the Brazilian fliers Braga and De Barros aboard. In June of the same year Umberto Maddalena and Stefano Cagna took part in the search for the wreck of Umberto Nobile's dirigible in the polar region. In May and June Italo Balbo and Francesco De Pinedo undertook the first mass air cruise in history: sixty-one planes flew more than 1,700 miles (2,800 km) across the Mediterranean. A second group flight in the eastern Mediterranean was made the following year, logging 2,900 miles (4,667 km).

But the SM.55 is probably most famous for the two trans-Atlantic flights of 1930 and 1933. On December 17, 1930, four squadrons of three aeroplanes – with two in reserve – set off from Orbetello under the command of Italo Balbo. The fourteen planes, all SM.55As, reached Rio de Janeiro on January 15, 1931, after flying 6,400 miles (10,400 km) at an average speed of 115 mph (185 km/h). The 1933 flight was in commemoration of the tenth anniversary of the founding of the Italian air force. Twenty-five SM.55Xs, again under the command of Italo Balbo, flew from Orbetello to New York and back to Rome. They flew 12,300 miles (19,800 km) in this double crossing of the North Atlantic.

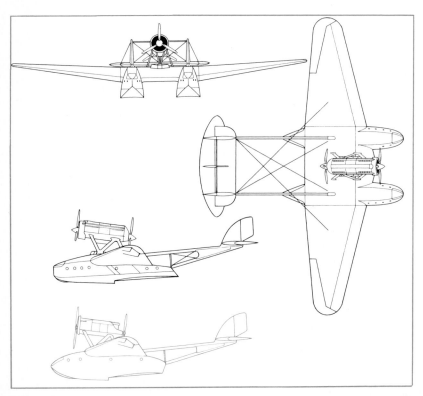

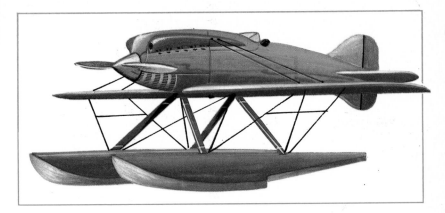

Macchi M.39

The ninth competition in the Schneider Trophy series, held in 1926, was won by a Macchi M.39, piloted by Mario De Bernardi. The trophy had been won by England in 1922, and by America in 1923 and 1925. The race was held in Norfolk, Virginia, on November 11–13, 1926. The English did not enter in 1926 and dedicated their efforts to preparing their planes for the 1927 race. So it was a race between American and Italian planes. There were three Macchi M.39s in the race, piloted by De Bernardi, Arturo Ferrarin, and Adriano Bacula. The design was a masterpiece of aerodynamics and purity of line. And the M.39 became the model for a series of seaplane racers, English as well as Italian. First impressions were not misleading. De Bernardi won the trophy with an average speed of about 246 mph (295 km/h) while Bacula came in third with an average speed of more than 210 mph (335 km/h).

Aircraft: **Macchi M.39**
Manufacturer: **Aeronautica Macchi**
Type: **Competition**
Year: **1926**
Engine: **Fiat A.S.2, 12-cylinder V, liquid-cooled, 880 hp**
Wingspan: **30 ft 5 in (9.26 m)**
Length: **22 ft 1 in (6.73 m)**
Height: **—**
Weight (empty): **2,781 lb (1,261 kg)**
Weight (loaded): **3,472 lb (1,575 kg)**
Maximum speed: **259 mph (416 km/h)**
Ceiling: **—**
Range: **—**
Crew: **1**

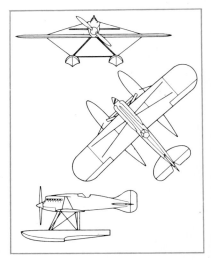

Fiat CR.20

Continuing the series begun in 1923 with the CR.1, Celestino Rosatelli designed the CR.20 in 1926. This fighter remained a 'classic' until the middle of the 1930s and was outstanding for its aerobatic ability. The prototype took to the air in the summer of 1926, and production was soon under way. A total of approximately 450 aircraft were built in various models. The CR.20 was an all-metal, single-seat biplane, powered by a 400 hp Fiat A.20 engine and armed with two machine guns. The plane saw service in the Italian air force until the eve of World War II. The CR.20 saw its first military action during the Italian campaign in Libya and continued in service even after tougher, more modern fighter aircraft appeared on the scene. Among variant models the CR.20B was a trainer, the CR.20-I was a seaplane, and the CR.20AQ was a high-altitude fighter.

Aircraft: **Fiat CR. 20**
Manufacturer: **Fiat S.A.**
Type: **Fighter**
Year: **1926**
Engine: **Fiat A.20, 12-cylinder V, liquid-cooled, 400 hp**
Wingspan: **32 ft 2 in (9.80 m)**
Length: **22 ft (6.71 m)**
Height: **9 ft 2 in (2.79 m)**
Weight: **3,080 lb (1,395 kg)**
Maximum speed: **168 mph (270 km/h)**
Ceiling: **23,000 ft (7,000 m)**
Range: **460 mile (750 km)**
Armament: **2 machine guns**
Crew: **1**

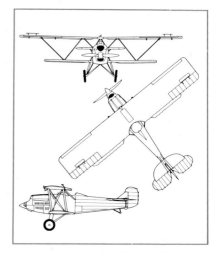

Cant 10ter

Aircraft: **Cant 10ter**
Manufacturer: **Cantieri Navali Triestino**
Type: **Civil transport**
Year: **1926**
Engine: **Lorraine-Dietrich (Isotta-Fraschini), 12-cylinder V, liquid-cooled, 400 hp**
Wingspan: **50 ft 2 in (15.30 m)**
Length: **36 ft 7 in (11.50 m)**
Height: **13 ft 4 in (4.06 m)**
Weight: **6,600 lb (3,000 kg)**
Cruising speed: **93 mph (150 km/h)**
Ceiling: **13,700 ft (4,200 m)**
Range: **370 mile (595 km)**
Crew: **1**
Passengers: **4**

After the commercial failure of the 6ter model, the Cantieri Navali Triestino built a smaller flying boat that was chosen for the first regular commercial route in Italy. This plane was the Cant 10ter, a central-hull flying boat that was very similar in structure to the 6ter. The new aircraft was powered by a 400 hp Lorraine–Dietrich engine and could carry four passengers. It entered commercial service in 1926, when the seven aircraft built that year were delivered to the Società Italiana Servizi Aerei (SISA), which planned to use them on the Trieste–Venice–Pavia–Turin route. This line was inaugurated in 1926, and further expanded with the opening of a second route connecting Trieste to Zara, Ancona, and Venice. A later model of the Cant 10ter appeared in 1930. Four aircraft were manufactured and equipped with 500 hp Isotta–Fraschini engines.

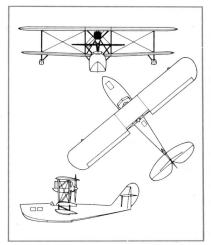

SIAI–Marchetti SM.64

Between May 31 and July 5, 1928, a number of records were established by an Italian aeroplane expressly designed and constructed for endurance flying. A world endurance record was established with 58 hours and 53 minutes in the air. A world closed-circuit distance record of 4,764 miles (7,666 km) was established. A world speed record over 3,000 miles (5,000 km) at an average of 86 mph (139 km/h) was set. And a world straight-line distance record was set on a flight of 4,466 miles (7,188 km) from Montecelio to Natal. The plane that set these records was the SIAI–Marchetti SM.64, a masterpiece of aerodynamic technology. Such exceptional attention was paid to detail that a landing strip was specially designed to exploit the aircraft's particular qualities. This landing strip at Montecelio, near Guidonia, Italy, was built on a slanting gradient that broadened toward the end. It was from here that the SM.64 took off on its record-making flights.

This aircraft was the result of a meeting between two passionate enthusiasts – Alessandro Marchetti and Arturo Ferrarin. Both men singly had dreamt of a specially designed aircraft that could undertake endurance flights. The project got under way with the support of the Italian air ministry. The SIAI company built the aircraft, the Fiat company built a special version of its A.22 engine, and the air force built a specially designed runway for the plane's take-offs. Alessandro Marchetti has his SM.64 ready in March 1928, and its first flight took place on April 10 at the Cameri airfield. The aircraft was altogether original. A single-engine monoplane, it had twin tail booms and a fixed undercarriage, and a streamlined cockpit was installed in the middle of the wing just underneath the engine, which (like the SM.55 flying boat engine) had a nacelle located above the fuselage. The engine housing was made of duralumin and smoothly cowled to reduce air resistance. The wing housed the fuel tanks, 27 in all holding a total of 1,500 gallons

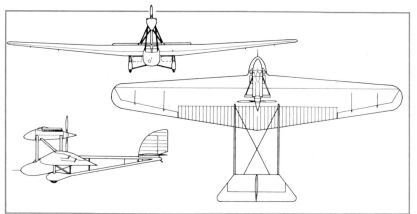

(7,000 L), and the cooling system. The aircraft was divided into waterproof compartments in case of a forced landing on water. The wing also had a sleeping compartment.

After test flights at Cameri, Arturo Ferrarin, Carlo Del Prete, and Flight Engineer Cappannini took the SM.64 to Montecelio. There were more tests and trial flights, and then, on the night of May 31, the first great run. The closed circuit was flown fifty-one times and, at 3.30 on the afternoon of June 2, the aeroplane landed, having established a record: 58 hours, 53 minutes, and 15 seconds in the air covering a distance of 4,764 miles 63 yards (7,666.617 km). The next run followed a month later. On July 3, Ferrarin and Del Prete took off with a full cargo for Brazil. They sighted the coast of South America on July 5. An emergency landing that damaged the plane brought the men down near Natal. On board another aircraft, Ferrarin and Del Prete were involved in an accident, and Del Prete lost his life.

Aircraft: **SIAI-Marchetti SM.64**
Manufacturer: **SIAI-Marchetti**
Type: **Competition**
Year: **1928**
Engine: **Fiat A 22T, 12-cylinder V, liquid-cooled, 590 hp**
Wingspan: **70 ft 6 in (21.49 m)**
Length: **29 ft 6 in (8.99 m)**
Height: **12 ft 1 in (3.68 m)**
Weight (empty): **5,300 lb (2,400 kg)**
Weight (loaded): **15,400 lb (7,000 kg)**
Maximum speed: **146 mph (235 km/h)**
Ceiling: **—**
Range: **7,150 mile (11,505 km) (theoretical maximum)**
Crew: **2–3**

The aircraft was brought back to Italy, overhauled, and equipped with a variable-pitch propeller. This reconstructed plane was called the SM.64bis. Piloted by Fausto Cecconi and Umberto Maddalena, the plane set a new closed-circuit endurance record on May 31, 1930: 67 hours and 13 minutes in the air covering a distance of 5,088 miles 916 yards (8,188.8 km). This was the last record set by the SM.64. On March 19, 1931, during a routine flight, the plane crashed at sea and went down with its crew, Maddalena, Cecconi, and the flight engineer, Giuseppe Damonte.

Caproni Ca 90

The Caproni Ca 90 was the largest land plane in the world at the time it was built. Only the German Dornier Do X had been larger, with a wingspan just over 4 feet (1 m) greater and some twenty tons heavier when fully loaded. Although it never went on the production line, the Ca 90 was duly famous. A year after its first flight it had set a number of altitude, endurance, and maximum load records.

It was built in 1929, when the air force seemed to be interested in large multi-engine planes. The Caproni Ca 90 was designed as a heavy bomber. The aircraft was exceptional for its size and power at the time. The lower wing of this giant biplane was considerably larger than the upper wing, and the aircraft was powered by six 1,000 hp, 18-cylinder V, Isotta–Fraschini Asso engines. The structure was of welded steel tubes. The nose was covered in duralumin, and the rest of the aircraft was covered in fabric. The giant undercarriage consisted of four wheels mounted in two pairs and a smaller moveable rear wheel. The spacious, square-section fuselage could accommodate the eight-man crew, armament, and military equipment. Its cargo capacity was 33,000

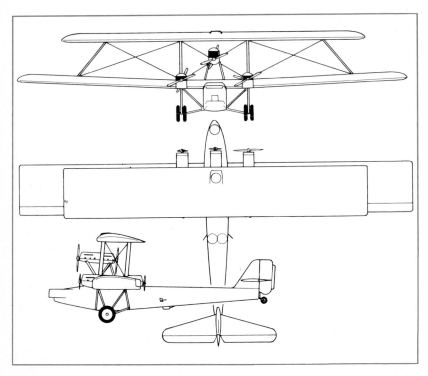

pounds (15,000 kg) including 17,600 pounds (8,000 kg) of bombs. The six engines were installed in three pairs, the two lateral pairs on the lower wing and the central pair over the fuselage between upper and lower wing. The forward propellers were two-blade, while the rear ones were four-blade. Defensive armament consisted of seven machine guns distributed around the aircraft, including one in the middle of the upper wing.

The plane's performance confirmed the designer's calculations, which had already been substantiated by a series of tests performed on the various components of the aircraft at the Milan Polytechnic. The plane's top speed was 127 mph (204 km/h), while landing speed was just about 56 mph (90 km/h). The operational ceiling was about 15,000 feet, and its endurance was seven hours, equivalent to a range of about 800 miles (1,300 km). The aircraft's capability was firmly established in 1930, when it set a new world record for maximum load. With

Aircraft: **Caproni Ca 90**
Manufacturer: **Società Italiana Caproni**
Type: **Heavy bomber**
Year: **1929**
Engine: **Six Isotta-Fraschini Asso, 18-cylinder V, liquid-cooled, 1,000 hp each**
Wingspan: **152 ft 10 in (46.58 m)**
Length: **88 ft 4 in (26.92 m)**
Height: **35 ft 5 in (10.79 m)**
Weight: **66,000 lb (30,000 kg)**
Maximum speed: **127 mph (204 km/h)**
Ceiling: **14,700 ft (4,500 m)**
Range: **800 mile (1,290 km)**
Armament: **7 machine guns: 17,600 lb (8,000 kg) of bombs**
Crew: **8**

22,000 pounds (10,000 kg) of cargo aboard, the Ca 90 reached an altitude of 10,682 feet (3,256 m) and remained in the air for three hours and thirty-one minutes. But the plane's superb capabilities were never proven in regular service, either by the air force or commercially. Had the Caproni Ca90 been transformed into a commercial aircraft (as other countries adapted bombers), it would have been an exceptional passenger plane.

SIAI–Marchetti SM.66

The great sporting and commercial success of the SIAI–Marchetti SM.55 gave the factory in Sesto Calende the impetus to develop a bigger and better three-engine flying boat. This new aircraft, which made its appearance in 1932, was the SM.66. Some twenty of these planes remained in service until the outbreak of World War II.

The SM.66 was very similar in concept to its illustrious predecessor. It, too, was a double central-hulled craft with booms supporting the tail unit. But the wings were much longer, and the power was increased. There were three engines instead of two, and they were housed in three separate units. The pusher propellers were four-blade. Because of the SM.66s greater power and size, it could carry more passengers and cargo than its predecessor. Between fourteen and eighteen passengers could be housed in the two cabins. The cockpit was installed in the middle of the wing, and the crew consisted of two pilots and a navigator. A tunnel through the wing made it possible for the crew to reach the two passenger compartments.

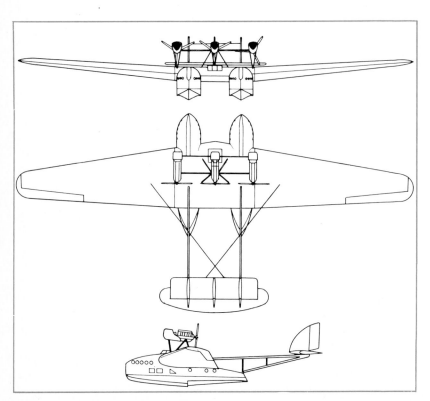

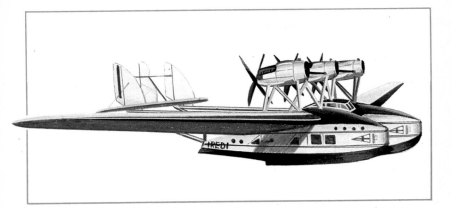

The prototype was equipped with three 550 hp Fiat A.22 R engines, but after tests these engines were replaced by 750 hp Fiat A.24 R engines, the standard power-plant provided in the production models. The plane's performance was outstanding: maximum speed of 164 mph (264 km/h); cruising speed of 146 mph (234 km/h); landing speed of 69 mph (111 km/h). It took the plane 7 minutes and 50 seconds to reach 2,000 metres altitude; $13\frac{1}{2}$ minutes to reach 3,000 metres; 21 minutes and 25 seconds to reach 4,000 metres; and 35 minutes and 2 seconds to reach 5,000 metres (over 16,000 ft).

The first airlines to buy SM.66s were the Aero Espresso (three planes), SANA (four planes), and SAM (seven planes). But the company that acquired the largest number was Ala Littoria, with no less than twenty-three planes, most of which were still in service on the eve of World War II. In April 1934 the SM.66 replaced the SM.55 on the Rome–Tripoli–Tunis route, and three years later they

Aircraft: **SIAI-Marchetti SM.66**
Manufacturer: **SIAI-Marchetti**
Type: **Civil transport**
Year: **1932**
Engine: **Three Fiat A 24.R, 12-cylinder V, liquid-cooled, 750 hp each**
Wingspan: **108 ft 3 in (33.00 m)**
Length: **54 ft 6 in (16.63 m)**
Height: **16 ft 1 in (4.89 m)**
Weight: **24,090 lb (10,930 kg)**
Cruising speed: **146 mph (234 km/h)**
Ceiling: **18,530 ft (5,650 m)**
Range: **800 mile (1,290 km)**
Crew: **3**
Passengers: **14–18**

entered service on the run from Brindisi to Athens, Rhodes, and Alexandria. These planes had a long operational career, thanks to their toughness and resilience. After serving commercial routes in the Mediterranean, the SM.66 also served during the early stages of World War II. Having doffed their commercial colours for camouflage grey, they saw duty as naval rescue planes.

SIAI–Marchetti SM.71

After the success of its seaplanes, especially the SM.55 and the SM.66, the SIAI–Marchetti company turned to the production of land transport planes. The SM.71, which made its appearance in 1932, was an elegant aircraft that saw service for five years, first with SAM and then with Ala Littoria, on short-and medium-range flights.

The SM.71 project got under way in 1930, and the SIAI–Marchetti company followed one of the most popular formulas of the period, a formula that

had already been applied to several outstanding aircraft: the three-engine, high-wing monoplane. SM71 was a high-performance transport that could carry from eight to ten passengers plus a three-man crew a distance of about 620 miles (1,000 km). The fuselage was built of steel tubes, while the wings were built of wood. The fuselage and tail were fabric-covered, the front of the cabin was covered in duralumin, and the wings were covered with plywood and a layer of fabric. The passengers were comfortably lodged in a cabin with sliding windows. The engine installation was simple and 'clean'. Completely cowled,

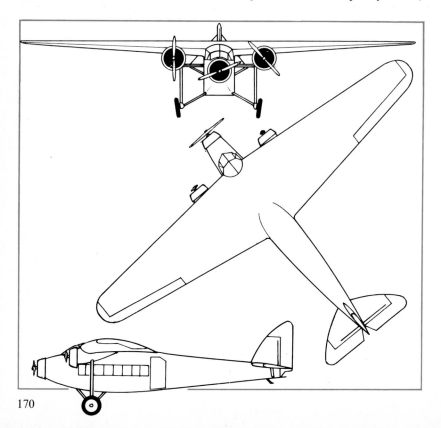

the engines were installed one at the nose of the aircraft and the other two in pods attached to the wings. The engines were of two kinds, the 240 hp Walter Castor or the 370 hp Piaggio Stella VII, both air-cooled radials. The propellers were two-bladed and made of metal.

The test flights of the prototype were very successful: maximum speed of 165 mph (270 km/h); cruising speed of 142 mph (229 km/h); and landing speed of about 60 mph (100 km/h). The plane could reach over 3,000 feet (1,000 m) altitude in two minutes and fifty-four seconds; 6,000 feet (2,000 m) in six minutes and thirty-eight seconds; 3,000 metres in eleven minutes and fifty-one seconds; 4,000 metres in nineteen-and-one-half minutes; and 5,500 metres in forty-two minutes and eleven seconds.

The first six aircraft were consigned to SAM, four with Walter Castor engines and two with Piaggios. The six planes were assigned to the Rome–Brindisi route at the beginning, and

Aircraft: **SIAI-Marchetti SM.71**
Manufacturer: **SIAI-Marchetti**
Type: **Civil transport**
Year: **1932**
Engine: **Three Piaggio Stella VII, 7-cylinder radial, air-cooled, 370 hp each**
Wingspan: **69 ft 6 in (21.20 m)**
Length: **45 ft 11 in (14.00 m)**
Height: **—**
Weight: **11,342 lb (5,149 kg)**
Cruising speed: **142 mph (229 km/h)**
Ceiling: **19,300 ft (5,900 m)**
Range: **750 mile (1,200 km)**
Crew: **3**
Passengers: **8–10**

from February 4, 1934, they also saw service on the Tirana–Salonika route. In the end they flew the entire run from Rome to Salonika. Subsequently Ala Littoria took over five of SAM's six SM.71s. One of these was lost in an accident in 1935, but the others remained operational until 1937. over the years some SM.71s were slightly modified; the most significant improvement being the fairing of the two wheels of the undercarriage and the addition of a steerable, faired tail wheel.

Macchi MC.72

The Macchi MC.72 was designed and built for Schneider Trophy racing but lost the last competition in the series by a hair's breadth. The last seaplane racer ever built, the Macchi MC.72 won immortality on October 23, 1934, over Lake Garda, with Francesco Agello at the controls. The plane set an all-time seaplane speed record, 440.698 mph (709.202 km/h). Forty years on, that record still stands for the category, notwithstanding the enormous progress that has been made in aviation in the past decades.

The Macchi MC.72 was the last racing seaplane that Mario Castoldi designed. It had been hoped that the aircraft would be ready for the 1931 Schneider Trophy had it not been for difficulties and delays in applying the final touches to the aircraft, it seems likely that the Englishman John H. Boothman's Supermarine S.6B would have had a harder time winning the race at Lee on Solent that year. Mario Castoldi applied all the experience he had gained with the M.39, the M.52, and the M.67 to his design for the MC.72. What was new about the MC.72 and what made it outstanding was its engine. The Fiat company had created a new engine by joining two units, A.S.5 12-cylinder V engines, in a single element of more than 12,500-gallon cylindering. This engine generated more than 3,000 hp at 3,300 rotations per minute. Each engine had its own shaft and reduction gear, and a special transmission passed on the power to two coaxial propeller shafts that drove counter-rotating two-blade metal propellers.

In effect the aircraft was built for its

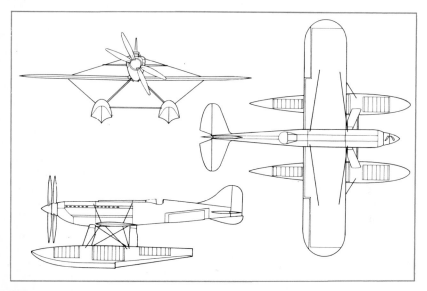

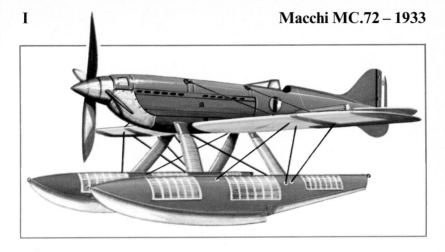

engine. The front part of the plane was in steel-tube construction, and the rear part of the fuselage and the tail were built of wood. The cooling pipes ran along the edge of the wing, down the struts, along the front of the pontoons and under the fuselage, just behind the cockpit. The fuel tanks and two radiators each for oil-cooling were housed in the pontoons.

The first flights took place at the Scuola di Alta Velocità (the high-speed flying school) in Desenzano, on Lake Garda, in June 1931. The pilot lost his life during the difficult tests when the engine transmission system broke down. Tests continued for a long time, and this delay prevented the plane from racing for the Schneider Trophy. The first positive results were obtained in the spring of 1933. The five MC.72s that Macchi built passed through the final delicate stages of preparation and were now fully air-worthy. On April 10, over Lake Garda, Francesco Agello set his first world speed record, flying at

Aircraft: **Macchi MC.72**
Manufacturer: **Aeronautica Macchi S.p.A.**
Type: **Competition**
Year: **1933**
Engine: **Fiat AS.66, 24-cylinder V, liquid-cooled, 3,000 hp**
Wingspan: **31 ft 1 in (9.48 m)**
Length: **27 ft 4 in (8.33 m)**
Height: **10 ft 10 in (3.30 m)**
Weight (empty): **5,500 lb (2,500 kg)**
Weight (loaded): **6,409 lb (2,907 kg)**
Maximum speed: **442.102 mph (711.462 km/h)**
Ceiling: —
Range: —
Crew: **1**

423.843 mph (682.078 km/h). In Ancona on October 8, 1933, Lt. Col. Cassinelli established a 100-km (about 60 miles) speed record with 391.09 mph (629.370 km/h). And on October 23, 1934, flying the last MC.72 to be built (registered 181). Francesco Agello again established a world speed record. During four runs the aircraft reached a maximum speed of 442.102 mph (711.462 km/h) and maintained an average speed of 440.69 mph (709.202 km/h).

SIAI–Marchetti SM.73

The SIAI–Marchetti company was famous, especially during World War II, for a series of engine aircraft they started building in the 1930s. The first of these planes to make its appearance was a civil transport plane, the 73, which made its debut in 1934. This aircraft laid the foundation of a construction formula that proved sound for many years and resulted in some exceptionally fine planes. Some of the 73s were requisitioned by the Italian air force and served all through the war as troop transports. They were remarkably long-lived and tough aircraft.

The prototype took to the air for the first time on June 4, 1934. A triple-engine low-wing monoplane, this aircraft had a wood-and-metal skeleton and fabric-and-plywood skin. This first plane had a row of windows down both sides of the fuselage. The propellers were wood, four-blade for the central engine and two-blade for the side engines. The production model had a different arrangement of windows, and all the engines had three-blade metal propellers. The tail and rudder were also modified. The first engines were 600 hp Gnome Rhône Mistral 9K radials, and they were also installed in the first five production models, whose delivery to Sabena, the Belgian airline, began in 1935. Later a

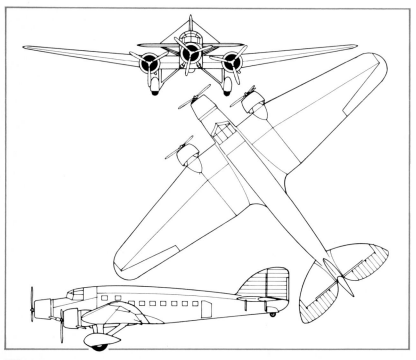

variety of engines were installed in the SM.73, including the 700 hp Piaggio Stella X.RC, the 770 hp Wright Cyclone GR-1820, the 750 hp Alfa Romeo 126 RC, and the 615 hp Walter Pegasus II M2. All the variant models were outstanding in performance and cargo capacity. Some planes carried up to eighteen passengers and a five-man crew.

The SM.73 was a great commercial success. The first five planes, consigned to Sabena, flew the London–Paris–Brussels–Hamburg–Copenhagen–Malmö route, the line that connected Brussels with Lille and Ostend, and the London–Ostend run. The Italian Ala Littoria company bought about twenty SM.73s in various models, equipped with Piaggio, Alfa Romeo, and Wright Cyclone engines. Ala Littoria flew the planes along the main routes of Europe, North Africa, and East Africa. The Avio Linee Italiane took six SM.73s. Three aircraft were sold to ČSA, the Czechoslovakian airline, in 1937, and two

Aircraft: **SIAI-Marchetti SM.73**
Manufacturer: **SIAI-Marchetti**
Type: **Civil transport**
Year: **1934**
Engine: **Three Alfa Romeo 126 RC 34, 9-cylinder R radial, air-cooled, 750 hp each**
Wingspan: **78 ft 9 in (24.00 m)**
Length: **57 ft 3 in (17.44 m)**
Height: **15 ft 1 in (4.59 m)**
Weight: **23,800 lb (10,800 kg)**
Cruising speed: **174 mph (280 km/h)**
Ceiling: **23,000 ft (7,000 m)**
Range: **620 mile (1,000 km)**
Crew: **4–5**
Passengers: **18**

more soon afterward. These were the only planes equipped with Walter Pegasus II M2 engines. In 1937 seven SM.73s were built under licence in Belgium for Sabena, which used these aircraft on its toughest runs, on the route from Brussels to Elisabethville in what was then the Belgian Congo. These were modified SM.73s: they carried only eight passengers instead of the standard eighteen. This flight took almost two days: 44 hours flying time.

Fiat CR.32

The Fiat CR.32 occupies a special place among the immortals in aviation history. It was one of the last biplane fighters ever built, a typical example of the generation of combat planes that preceded World War II. When it appeared in 1933, the plane Celestino Rosatelli designed was an immediate success because of its high performance. The plane saw combat duty during the Spanish Civil War. Nevertheless, the plane's success was not all to the good. For it inspired technicians and military men to concentrate on developing biplanes when the rest of the world was following the logical evolution to monoplanes. Thus Italy continued to produce combat biplanes for several more years. Among such planes was the CR.32, an excellent aircraft in itself but subject to the limitations of the biplane formula,

especially where armament and speed were concerned. When World War II started, the Italian air force had a combat nucleus of CR.42s and CR.32s with a few of the new monoplanes, the Fiat G.50 and the Macchi MC.200; while the English and the Germans had much more advanced fighters, such as the Hawker Hurricane, the Supermarine Spitfire, and the Messerschmitt Bf 109. Italy was at least three years behind the others.

The CR.32 design was started by Clestino Rosatelli in 1931. It was the logical development of another plane just off the production line, the C.30. The new plane was to be faster and more manoeuvreable. The new fighter was smaller with a decreased wingspan and various improvements. But the configuration and general structure of the two planes were the same. The skeleton was all metal, and the skin was fabric, except for the metal nose. The wings were simple and

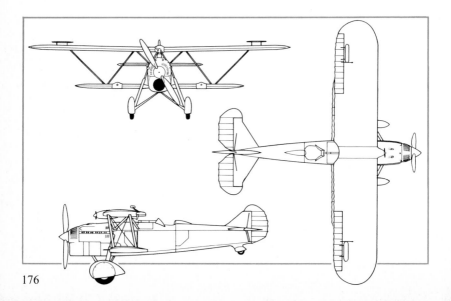

robust, and the lower wing was typically much smaller than the upper one. The CR.32 had the same engine as the CR.30, a 600 hp Fiat, 12-cylinder V, liquid-cooled, driving a two-blade metal propeller.

The prototype took to the air for the first time on April 28, 1933, and proved itself airworthy at once. The next year production began, and by the spring of 1935 the first aircraft were delivered to air force units. The 1st fighter wing, stationed at Campoformido, was the first to be fully equipped with the new fighter. Soon the 2nd, 4th and 3rd wings also received their CR.32s. Meanwhile production went ahead on a vast scale. A total of 383 CR.32s were produced in the original version. Three other versions were also manufactured. Of the CR.32bis, the second model, 328 planes were manufactured. Of the third model, the CR.32ter, designed in 1937, 100 planes were produced. The fourth model, the CR.32quater, brought the grand total of CR.32s to

Aircraft: **Fiat CR.32**
Manufacturer: **Fiat S.A.**
Type: **Fighter**
Year: **1935**
Engine: **Fiat A.30 RA, 12-cylinder V, liquid-cooled, 600 hp**
Wingspan: **31 ft 2 in (9.50 m)**
Length: **24 ft 5 in (7.45 m)**
Height: **8 ft 8 in (2.63 m)**
Weight: **4,080 lb (1,850 kg)**
Maximum speed: **233 mph at 9,800 ft (375 km/h at 3,000 m)**
Ceiling: **28,900 ft (8,800 m)**
Range: **460 mile (760 km)**
Armament: **2 machine guns**
Crew: **1**

1,212. The four versions differed in armament and in minor structural details. The last CR.32 off the production line appeared in the spring of 1939, when the manufacture of its successor, the CR.42 got under way.

In 1936 the first of a total of 380 CR.32s were delivered to the Nationalist Aviacion del Tercio in Spain. The plane also saw combat on the Greco-Albanian front and in the Mediterranean and East Africa during the first year of World War II. The 177 serviceable CR.32s on charge at the outbreak of the war remained in front line duty until April 1941.

Caproni Ca 133
Caproni Ca 101

The Caproni Ca 133 underwent many years service as a civil transport plane, especially on African routes, before seeing war service in East Africa and Russia. Of about 275 Ca 133s manufactured, most were earmarked for military service as transport, logistical support, and paratroop planes. But more than a dozen were delivered to Ala Littoria, which kept them in service until just before World War II.

The Caproni Ca 133 was a direct development of the 1930 Caproni Ca 101, an all-metal fabric-covered high-wing monoplane. There were several models of the Ca 101, differing in number (one or two) and power of engines installed, e.g. the 200 hp Alfa

Romeo, the 370 hp Piaggio Stella, and the 240 hp Walter Castor. Most of the Ca 101s were also military aircraft, but a few were used by the Società Nord-Africa Aviazione, Ala Littoria, and SAM, which flew eight passengers at a time on East African flights. The military version, powered by three 270 hp Alfa Romeo engines, were assigned to some night bombing units of the Italian air force. This aircraft had two or three machine guns, mounted on the back and sides, and could carry a payload of one-half ton of bombs. The Ca 101 saw combat first in the Ethiopian campaign and, despite its obsolescence, was in service during the first years of World War II.

In 1935 an improved version of the Ca 101 was developed, the Ca 133. The two aircraft were conceptually

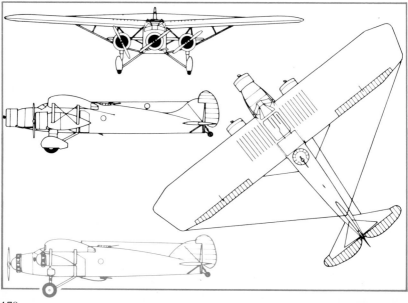

Caproni Ca 133 – 1935

identical, including the same structure and configuration, and even the same wing. But the Ca 133 was a significantly superior plane, both in aerodynamic form and in power. The Ca 133 was powered by three 460 hp Piaggio P.VII C.16 engines, smoothly housed in pods suspended from the fuselage. It was a high-performance plane and could carry a larger payload than its predecessor. The passenger version of this aircraft, which was used on routes connecting Rome with Italian colonies in Africa, could carry eighteen passengers plus a two-man crew. The military version carried eighteen fully equipped servicemen. The Ca 133 saw service throughout World War II on all fronts: in Africa, Albania, Greece, and Russia. Twelve Ca 133s took part in Italy's foray over the English Channel, the Italian air corps' Belgian operations in October 1940. Ca 133s also provided logistical support for a short time for the fighter squadrons that flew alongside the German Luftwaffe.

Aircraft: **Caproni Ca 133**
Manufacturer: **Società Italiana Caproni**
Type: **Civil transport**
Year: **1935**
Engine: **Three Piaggio P.VII C.16, 7-cylinder radial, air-cooled, 460 hp each**
Wingspan: **69 ft 8 in (21.23 m)**
Length: **50 ft 4 in (15.34 m)**
Height: **13 ft 2 in (4.00 m)**
Weight: **14,800 lb (6,700 kg)**
Cruising speed: **143 mph (230 km/h)**
Ceiling: **18,000 ft (5,500 m)**
Range: **840 mile (1,350 km)**
Crew: **2**
Passengers: **16**

Aircraft: **Caproni Ca 101**
Manufacturer: **Società Italiana Caproni**
Type: **Bomber**
Year: **1930**
Engine: **Three Alfa Romeo D.2, 9-cylinder radial, air-cooled, 270 hp each**
Wingspan: **64 ft 6 in (19.68 m)**
Length: **47 ft 1 in (14.35 m)**
Height: **12 ft 9 in (4.00 m)**
Weight: **11,317 lb (5,133 kg)**
Maximum speed: **124 mph (200 km/h)**
Ceiling: **20,000 ft (6,100 m)**
Range: **620 mile (1,000 km)**
Armament: **2–3 machine guns: 1,100 lb (500 kg) of bombs**
Crew: **3**

SIAI-Marchetti SM.74

The SM.74 was the first four-engine plane that the SIAI-Marchetti company ever manufactured. Only three aircraft were constructed, but they saw long years of service in peace and war. The SM.74 was flown by Ala Littoria first on the Rome–Marseilles–Lyons–Paris route and then on the Rome–Brindisi line. When World War II broke out, the three planes were transferred to the military. They saw service in Africa as troop and cargo carriers, and then were used to evacuate civilians and wounded. All three were destroyed in military action. The last one was damaged during a bombing raid over the Rome–Urbe airport on July 19, 1943.

The prototype first took to the air on November 16, 1943, and during its test flights established a world record. It flew some 620 miles (1,000 km) at 200 mph (322 km/h) with a load of ten tons. The SM.74 was a high-wing monoplane. The wing was constructed of wood, while the fuselage was built of metal with wood and fabric covering. Two of the aircraft were powered by four 700 hp Piaggio Stella X.RC engines; the third was powered by 845 hp Alfa Romeo Pegasus III engines. Lodged in NACA cowls, the engines drove two-position three-blade metal propellers. The passenger cabin was about 26 feet (8 m) long and

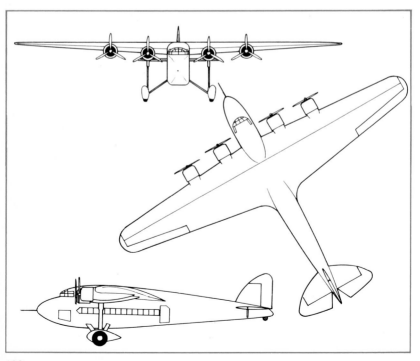

had a bar as well as sanitary facilities. Passenger capacity varied from a maximum of 27, for distances up to 620 miles (1,000 km), to a minimum of 16, for distances up to 1,200 miles (2,000 km). Since the plane had to climb to high altitudes in order to cross the Alps, the passengers were equipped with individual oxygen masks. The SM.74's test flight performances were excellent. The aircraft could reach about 3,000 feet (1,000 m) in two minutes and forty-eight seconds; 9,000 feet (3,000 m) in eight minutes and fifty-five seconds; and 15,000 feet (5,000 m) in nineteen minutes and forty-three seconds.

The first SM.74 was delivered to the Rome Urbe airport on March 27, 1935, and inaugurated the Rome–Marseilles–Lyons–Paris route on July 18. The other two aircraft were delivered later in the year. Beginning in the summer of 1936, the three SM.74s flew the Rome–Brindisi line and later made flights to Libya. On the eve of the war the planes were transferred to

Aircraft: **SIAI-Marchetti SM.74**
Manufacturer: **SIAI-Marchetti**
Type: **Civil transport**
Year: **1935**
Engine: **Four Piaggio Stella X.RC, 9-cylinder radial, air-cooled, 700 hp each**
Wingspan: **97 ft 4 in (29.68 m)**
Length: **70 ft 1 in (21.36 m)**
Height: **18 ft 1 in (5.50 m)**
Weight: **30,800 lb (14,000 kg)**
Cruising speed: **186 mph (300 km/h)**
Ceiling: **23,000 ft (7,000 m)**
Range: **620 mile (1,000 km)**
Crew: **4**
Passengers: **27**

the Reyia Aeronautica.

Soon the planes were sent to the vicinity of Benghazi, which was their base during the war. The first SM.74 to be destroyed (the second that was built) crashed into a mountain on October 23, 1921. The second to go was the prototype, which was destroyed on the ground during an air raid on November 2, 1941. The last SM.74 had more than one accident, but survived until July 1943.

1920 Macchi M.18. Wingspan: 51 ft 9 in (15.77 m). Length: 31 ft 7 in (9.62 m). Maximum speed: 106 mph (170 km/h). Engine: 250 hp Isotta-Fraschini. After its success in building fighter and reconnaissance seaplanes during World War I, the Macchi company incorporated all its past experience in the design of this maritime reconnaissance plane. Most of the M.18s saw service as naval reconnaissance aircraft, but a few were used for civil transport.

1922 Ansaldo A.300/4. Wingspan: 36 ft 6 in (11.12 m). Length: 28 ft 5 in (8.66 m). Maximum speed: 120 mph (193 km/h). Engine: 300 hp Fiat A.12bis. Seven hundred A.300s saw reconnaissance service for several years in Italy's air force. Derived from the famous World War I S.V.A., the A.300 was built in seven different models, the most popular of which was the A.300/4.

1924 Fiat BR.1. Wingspan: 56 ft 3 in (17.14 m). Length: 34 ft (10.36 m). Maximum speed: 144 mph (232 km/h). Engine: 700 hp Fiat A-14. This was the first bomber designed by Celestino Rosatelli. It made its appearance in 1924 as an improved model of the 1919 B.R. On December 23, 1924, a Fiat BR.1 set an altitude record of 16,915 ft (5,516 m) with a cargo of 3,300 lb (1,500 kg). There were some structural difficulties with the plane that made it unsteady in flight.

1924 Breda A.4. Wingspan: 35 ft 9 in (10.89 m). Length: 27 ft 1 in (8.20 m). Maximum speed: 87 mph (140 km/h). Engine: 130 hp Colombo 110 D. One of the earliest and most popular air force training planes, the Breda A.4 saw many years of service in flying schools and in the air force academy. This simple tough plane appeared in 1924 and was produced in various models, including single-seater and seaplane versions powered by a 180-hp Hispano–Suiza engine.

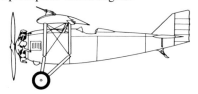

1925 Ansaldo A.C.3. Wingspan: 41 ft 7 in (12.67 m). Length: 23 ft 9 in (7.24 m). Maximum speed: 141 mph (226 km/h). Engine: 450 hp Gnome–Rhône Jupiter radial. This plane was derived from the French Dewoitine fighters, which the Ansaldo company built under licence. The A.C.3 was designed as an attack plane and carried four machine guns, two on the fuselage and two mounted on the wings. On November 21, 1926, an A.C.3 established a world altitude record with Donati at the controls: 38,913 ft (11,861 m).

1927 Romeo Ro.1. Wingspan: 49 ft 9 in (15.16 m). Length: 30 ft 9 in (9.37 m). Maximum speed: 153 mph (246 km/h). Engine: 420 hp Bristol Jupiter radial. This reconnaissance plane had a long operational life, and many Ro.1s were still in service on the eve of World War II. The Romeo Ro.1 was the licence version of the Dutch Fokker C V.

I

1927 C.R.D.A. Cant 25. Wingspan: 39 ft 4 in (12,00 m). Length: 28 ft 8 in (8.75 m). Maximum speed: 151 mph (243 km/h). Engine: 410 hp Fiat A.20. The Cant 25 was one of the finest seaplane fighters of the 1920s and 1930s and was kept in service for more than twelve years. The M model, which appeared in 1931, was the chief production model. An improved version, the AR model, appeared later. The Cant 25M carried two machine guns, and its wings could be folded back for housing on aircraft carriers.

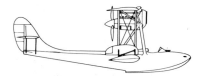

1929 Macchi M.41bis. Wingspan: 36 ft 6 in (11.12 m). Length: 28 ft 5 in (8.66 m). Maximum speed: 163 mph (262 km/h). Engine: 440 hp Fiat A.20. This fighter flying boat, a contemporary of the Cant 24, was designed by Castoldi (the designer of Agello's MC. 72). It was in service for about ten years with naval fighter units. The plane had two machine guns mounted on the nose and could also carry a small load of bombs.

1930 Breda 19. Wingspan: 29 ft 6 in (9.00 m). Length: 21 ft 8 in (6.60 m). Maximum speed: 130 mph (210 km/h). Engine: 220 hp Alfa Romeo Lynx radial. This was one of the most famous training and aerobatic planes of the 1930s. It was used by some of the air force's aerobatic units. The famous 'Pattuglia Folle' (the 'Mad Patrol') took full advantage of the plane's outstanding characteristics in its memorable aerial stunts.

1930 Breda 25. Wingspan: 32 ft 6 in (9.90 m). Length: 26 ft (7.92 m). Maximum speed: 123 mph (197 km/h). Engine: 240 hp Alfa Romeo D2 radial. The most popular of all of Breda's training planes was the 25, which made its debut in about 1930. It equipped many Italian air force units for almost fifteen years, and was still in service at the end of World War II. One of the variant models was a seaplane trainer.

1935 Cant Z.501. Wingspan: 73 ft 2 in (22.30 m). Length: 48 ft 7 in (14.80 m). Maximum speed: 165 mph (265 km/h). Engine: 900 hp Isotta–Fraschini Asso XI RC 15. Built in 1934, this large monoplane flying boat (with central hull construction) saw many years of service as a naval reconnaissance aircraft. It also saw duty as a convoy escort and as a coastal and rescue plane during the war. More than two hundred Z.501s were constructed.

1935 Meridionali Ro 37. Wingspan: 36 ft 4 in (11.08 m). Length: 28 ft 3 in (8.62 m). Maximum speed: 199 mph (320 km/h). Engine: 550 hp Fiat A.30 RAbis. This reconnaissance plane first saw combat during the Spanish Civil War and was used by most of the air force's reconnaissance squadrons during World War II. In addition to two or three machine guns, the plane carried some small bombs.

Japan

Japan was not one of the pioneering countries in the history of aviation. It entered the field many years after Europe and America, but after catching up with other countries, Japan produced planes that could compete in quality and quantity with those of the rest of the world.

Japan became interested in aviation during the golden age of pioneer aviation, when the whole world was developing a certain enthusiasm for flying machines. In 1910 two Japanese officers were sent to Europe to learn to fly. At that time, the most interesting developments in aviation were taking place in France. Late in the same year, the two officers returned to Japan with two aircraft, one of them a Farman biplane. These two flying machines represented the beginning of Japanese aviation. Soon an improved version of the Henri Farman was built in an army plant, after a design developed by one of the two army officers. With this first Japanese-built plane, the era of the heavier-than-air craft was launched in the Far East.

The problem now was to develop technical expertise and make up for lost time. At the outset Japan had to rely on the experience of others. A variety of European-built aircraft were purchased, and technicians and industrialists set to work to study and improve these planes. The Japanese government invited foreign experts and engineers, chiefly French, English, and German, to make their contribution to the new industry. Japan relied on foreigners in the development of its own air industry throughout the 1920s. It was in this period that the three chief Japanese manufacturers (Mitsubishi, Nakajima, and Kawasaki) came to the forefront and began to leave their mark on international aviation. At the same time many students and technicians went to the United States for university studies and for on-the-job training in the aviation industry.

Nakajima Hikoki K.K. was the oldest aeroplane factory in Japan. It was founded on December 6, 1917, by Chikuhei Nakajima and Seibei Kawanishi. In 1931 the company produced the first all-Japanese fighter plane. The company became an enormous industrial complex that not only constructed planes, but also manufactured the components necessary for assembling planes and engines. Kawasaki Kokuki Kogyo K.K. was founded in 1918 as a subsidiary of Kawasaki Jukogyo, the heavy industry complex, but soon became independent with two major plants and four minor ones of its own. Two of the minor plants produced aeroplanes and the other two built engines. Mitsubishi Jukogyo K.K. first took an interest in aviation in 1918. In 1920 it separated its aviation activities from its various engineering and shipbuilding enterprises. By World War II Mitsubishi had become the most important Japanese company in the production of heavy aircraft and engines.

These three giant manufacturers bore the brunt of supplying the Japanese armed-forces, during World War II. Between the three of them, Nakajima, Kawasaki, and Mitsubishi produced three-quarters of all the combat planes and four-fifths of all the aeroplane engines manufactured in Japan between 1941 and 1945. This was an impressive achievement when one thinks that, in those five years, Japan built a total of 68,888 aeroplanes and 116,577 engines.

Other aeroplane manufacturers emerged in the 1920s and 1930s. Aichi Kokuki K.K., the fourth most important company, began building aeroplanes in 1920 and engines in 1927. Kawanishi Kokuki K.K. began building seaplanes in 1928 and went on to specialize in the construction of large hydroplanes. Tachikawa Hikoki K.K. was founded in 1928. It was smaller than the others but nevertheless became one of the leading builders of transport and training planes. And several other factories were built in the 1930s.

Although the Japanese air industry caught up with the rest of the world and produced a great number of planes, relatively few were designed for the civil sector. While Europe and the United States had seen enormous development of the aeroplane for transport, communication, and sport, Japan concentrated primarily on military aircraft. The Imperial Army and Imperial Navy competed in building better military aircraft. The rest of the world had little idea of what was happening in Japan, and hence underestimated the country's potential.

Indeed, Japan had two well-developed air forces when World War II began. The Japanese naval air force was larger and better-equipped than the army air force. As early as 1912 the navy had sent officers to France and America to learn to fly and had bought Farman and Curtiss seaplanes. When the first officers returned to Japan, the first air training school was established for pilots. In 1913 a seaplane support ship, the *Wakamiya Maru*, was built. Japanese pilots had a chance to test their mettle during World War I, when the naval air force sank a German mine-layer. The navy increased its flying capacities and developed a large programme of aircraft-carrier production. The *Hosho*, laid down in 1919, was the second ship ever to be built as an aircraft carrier. Earlier carriers had been converted passenger liners or military ships.

Mitsubishi 1MF1

The first Japanese carrier-borne fighter plane was designed by an Englishman, Herbert Smith, who designed some of the best-known combat aircraft manufactured by Sopwith during World War I. Smith went to Japan in 1921 to study the needs of the Imperial Navy, which was looking for a fighter plane to be carried aboard its first aircraft carrier, the *Hosho*. The design of the plane was finished toward the end of the year. The test flights were successful, and the navy ordered production from the Mitsubishi company. The Mitsubishi 1MF1, known as Type 10, made its first carrier take-offs and landings in February 1923, and delivery to naval aviation units began soon after. Production continued until late 1928. A total of 128 aircraft were manufactured and saw service until 1929. The Mitsubishi company manufactured seven models of the 1MF, which differed in structural details.

Aircraft: **Mitsubishi 1MF1**
Manufacturer: **Mitsubishi Jukogyo K.K.**
Type: **Fighter**
Year: **1923**
Engine: **Hispano-Mitsubishi, 8-cylinder V, liquid-cooled, 300 hp**
Wingspan: **30 ft 6 in (9.30 m)**
Length: **22 ft (6.71 m)**
Height: **9 ft 8 in (2.95 m)**
Weight: **2,510 lb (1,140 kg)**
Maximum speed: **147 mph at 6,500 ft (237 km/h at 2,000 m)**
Ceiling: **23,000 ft (7,000 m)**
Endurance: **2 hr 30 min**
Armament: **2 machine guns**
Crew: **1**

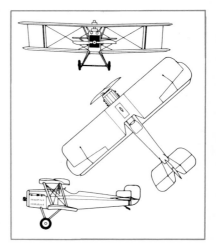

Kawasaki Type 88 (KDA-2)

In its concern to close the gap between its own aviation industry and that of Europe and America, Japan invited foreign engineers and designers to work in its aeroplane factories. In 1923, the German Richard Vogt, for example, became chief designer for Kawasaki Kokuki Kogyo, a company that had hitherto built French planes and engines under licence. Among Vogt's first projects was a reconnaissance biplane built for the army and known as Type 88. The first prototype appeared early in 1927 and six months later was officially approved and put into production. Type 88 was very impressive for speed, both in horizontal flight and in reaching higher altitudes. Some seven hundred 88s were built and remained in service for about ten years. The plane saw combat duty against China in 1932, where it also doubled as a light bomber.

Aircraft: **Kawasaki Type 88 (KDA-2)**
Manufacturer: **Kawasaki Kokuki Kogyo K.K.**
Type: **Reconnaissance**
Year: **1928**
Engine: **BMW-Kawasaki, 12-cylinder V, liquid-cooled, 500 hp**
Wingspan: **49 ft 10 in (15.20 m)**
Length: **40 ft 3 in (12.28 m)**
Height: **11 ft 2 in (3.40 m)**
Weight: **6,800 lb (3,100 kg)**
Maximum speed: **130 mph (210 km/h)**
Ceiling: **17,000 ft (5,200 m)**
Endurance: **5 hr**
Armament: **2–3 machine guns; 440 lb (200 kg) of bombs**
Crew: **2**

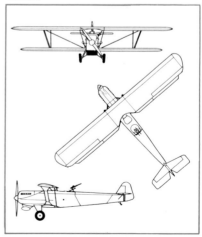

Nakajima Army Type 91

The first fighter plane that was all-Japanese in design appeared in 1931 and became first-line equipment with the army's air force. The requirement was issued in 1927, and both Nakajima and Mitsubishi submitted projects. The Mitsubishi prototype had an accident, and the Nakajima remained the only competitor, even though its fighter did not get off to a brilliant start. The army technical authorities were not impressed with the high-wing monoplane structure of the aircraft, and turned it down. The authorities then considered ordering an American plane, the Curtiss P-1C. A few months later they changed their mind and agreed to consider a modified version of the Nakajima prototype. This plane, the 91, performed very well in tests, and in December 1931, Army Type 91 planes were delivered to fighter squadrons. A total of 320 Type 91s were built.

Aircraft: **Nakajima Army Type 91**
Manufacture: **Nakajima Hikoki K.K.**
Type: **Fighter**
Year: **1931**
Engine: **Bristol Jupiter-Nakajima, 9-cylinder radial, air-cooled, 500 hp**
Wingspan: **36 ft 1 in (10.99 m)**
Length: **23 ft 10 in (7.26 m)**
Height: **9 ft 2 in (2.79 m)**
Weight: **3,370 lb (1,530 kg)**
Maximum speed: **186 mph at 6,500 ft (299 km/h at 2,000 m)**
Ceiling: **29,500 ft (9,000 m)**
Range: **370 mile (600 km)**
Armament: **2 machine guns**
Crew: **1**

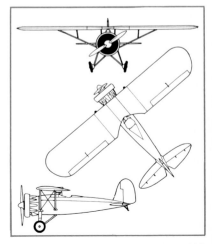

Mitsubishi B2M

This plane, built expressly as a torpedo-launching aircraft, was also designed abroad for Japan. The British Blackburn company (along with two other English companies, Sopwith and Handley–Page) submitted designs to the Japanese navy for a plane to replace the B1M, which was also a British design. The first B2M prototype was built in England in 1929 and delivered to the Japanese authorities in February 1930. Three more prototypes were built in Japan, and a long series of tests were made. The plane went into production in 1932. By 1935 a total of one hundred and eight planes (including the four prototypes) had been built. The Mitsubishi B2M remained in service for some years. The two most popular versions were the B2M1 and the B2M2. The latter appeared in 1934 and incorporated several modifications of the original plane.

190

Aircraft: **Mitsubishi B2M**
Manufacturer: **Mitsubishi Jukogyo K.K.**
Type: **Torpedo bomber**
Year: **1932**
Engine: **Hispano-Mitsubishi, 12-cylinder V, liquid-cooled, 600 hp**
Wingspan: **49 ft 11 in (15.22 m)**
Length: **33 ft 8 in (10.27 m)**
Height: **12 ft 2 in (3.71 m)**
Weight: **7,900 lb (3,600 kg)**
Maximum speed: **132 mph (213 km/h)**
Ceiling: **14,700 ft (4,500 m)**
Range: **600 mile (960 km)**
Armament: **2 machine guns; 1,700 lb (800 kg) of bombs**
Crew: **2**

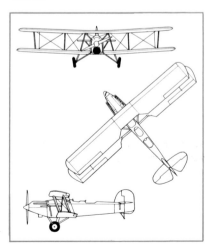

Mitsubishi Ki-2

After considering the German Junkers K 37, the Japanese army decided to look for a Japanese design for a three-seat twin-engine bomber that could carry a half-ton payload. The Mitsubishi Jukogyo company was approached because of its experience in bomber construction. The prototype of the new aircraft was ready in the spring of 1933. The plane performed well in test flights but some modifications were made to the forward part of the fuselage. By the end of the year the authorities accepted the plane. By 1936 a total of one hundred and thirteen planes had been built. In 1936 a new model, the Ki-2-2, went into production. The new model was equipped with more powerful engines, a retractable undercarriage, and a closed cockpit. The Ki-2 had a long operational career. It saw service in the war with China, and some of them were still being used as training planes at the outbreak of World War II.

Aircraft: **Mitsubishi Ki-2**
Manufacturer: **Mitsubishi Jukogyo K.K.**
Type: **Bomber**
Year: **1933**
Engine: **Two Nakajima Kotobuki, 9-cylinder radial, air-cooled, 570 hp**
Wingspan: **65 ft 6 in (19.96 m)**
Length: **41 ft 4 in (12.60 m)**
Height: **15 ft 2 in (4.64 m)**
Weight: **10,040 lb (4,550 kg)**
Maximum speed: **158 mph at 9,800 ft (255 km/h at 3,000 m)**
Ceiling: **23,000 ft (7,000 m)**
Range: **560 mile (900 km)**
Armament: **2 machine guns; 660 lb (300 kg) of bombs**
Crew: **3**

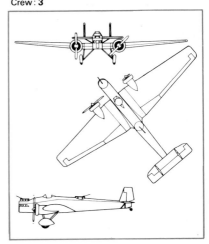

Kawasaki Ki-10

The last biplane fighter built for the Japanese army was a small and highly manoeuvreable aircraft. Although it marked the end of an era, it influenced combat plane construction for years to come. Indeed, all the Japanese fighters that saw service in World War II were distinguished by extreme manoeuvrability and high performance. These results were generally achieved at the expense of defence and armament. The Ki-10 prototype made its appearance in March 1935, in direct competition with a Nakajima monoplane design. The designers of the Ki-10 were Takeo Doi, Imachi, and Tojo, who produced a fast, highly manoeuvrable plane with extremely pure lines. After a few modifications to increase its speed, the Ki-10 was accepted and put into production. Three hundred aircraft were built between 1935 and 1937, and Ki-10s saw duty against China.

Aircraft: **Kawasaki Ki-10**
Manufacturer: **Kawasaki Kokuki Kogyo K.K.**
Type: **Fighter**
Year: **1935**
Engine: **Kawasaki Ha.9.IIa, 12-cylinder V, liquid-cooled, 850 hp**
Wingspan: **31 ft 4 in (9.55 m)**
Length: **23 ft 7 in (7.20 m)**
Height: **9 ft 10 in (3.00 m)**
Weight: **3,640 lb (1,650 kg)**
Maximum speed: **250 mph at 9,800 ft (400 km/h at 3,000 m)**
Ceiling: **32,800 ft (10,000 m)**
Range: **680 mile (1,100 m)**
Armament: **2 machine guns**

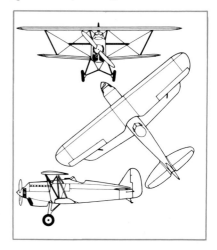

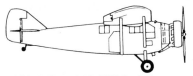

1930 Mitsubishi K3M. Wingspan: 51 ft 3 in (15.62 m). Length: 31 ft 4 in (9.54 m). Maximum speed: 146 mph (234 km/h). Engine: 340 hp Hitachi Amakaze radial. One of the most popular aircrew trainers, the K3M was built in a variety of versions to a total of 624 aircraft. The navy commissioned the plane which went into service in 1930. An army version was developed soon after. This simple robust plane could carry an instructor plus three or four trainees.

1933 Yokosuka K5Y. Wingspan: 36 ft 1 in (11.00 m). Length: 26 ft 5 in (8.05 m). Maximum speed: 132 mph (212 km/h). Engine: 340 hp Hitachi Amakaze radial. This aircraft went into production in 1933, and more K5Y biplanes were built than any other training plane. The production line was in continuous operation until 1945, notwithstanding the appearance of far more modern planes. The Yokosuka K5Y was the most popular all-round plane in the naval air force, and a total of 5,770 aircraft were built.

1934 Kawanishi E7K. Wingspan: 45 ft 11 in (14.00 m). Length: 34 ft 2 in (10.41 m). Maximum speed: 148 mph (238 km/h). Engine: 500 hp Hiro type 91, 12-cylinder W. The Kawanishi E7K, which entered service in 1934, was one of the most popular pre-war naval reconnaissance planes. A total of 530 aircraft were built in several models. They saw duty with combat and support vessels and were also used as land-based coastal patrol planes.

1934 Aichi D1A. Wingspan: 37 ft 4 in (11.37 m). Length: 30 ft 10 in (9.40 m). Maximum speed: 174 mph (280 km/h). Engine: 580 hp Nakajima Kotobuki 2 Kai radial. A two-seat biplane, the Aichi D1A was designed as a carrier-borne dive bomber. This extremely tough and manoeuvreable plane was modelled after the Heinkel He 66, one of which had been imported directly from the German factory. A total of 590 planes were built and saw service with such aircraft carriers as the *Akagi*, the *Kaga*, and the *Ryujo*.

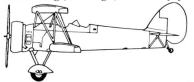

1935 Tachikawa Ki-9. Wingspan: 33 ft 10 in (10.32 m). Length: 24 ft 8 in (7.58 m). Maximum speed: 149 mph (240 km/h). Engine: 350 hp Hitachi Ha-13a radial. Like the navy's Yokosuka K5Y, this biplane trainer was in production until the end of World War II. A total of 2,618 aircraft were built, of which 2,395 were built between 1935 and 1942. The Ki-9 was a trainer in the army's air force.

1935 Nakajima E8N. Wingspan: 36 ft (10.98 m). Length: 28 ft 11 in (8.81 m). Maximum speed: 186 mph (300 km/h). Engine: 580 hp Nakajima Kotobuki 2 Kai radial. The plane was designed as a naval reconnaissance aircraft, but in the years just preceding World War II it also saw intensive service as a catapult plane aboard cruisers, battleships, and support vessels. It was still in service during the first year of the war, when it was replaced by more advanced aircraft. A total of 755 E8Ns were built.

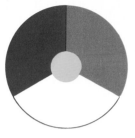

Holland

The history of aviation in Holland is synonymous with the name of Fokker. When Anthony Fokker, the great Dutch aircraft designer, managed to escape from Germany and return to Holland, he was already world-famous for his combat planes. When he decided to build an aeroplane construction plant in Holland, conditions were almost ideal. There was practically no competition, and the market was wide-open, for Dutch civil aviation was still in its infancy.

In the first phase of his career Fokker had produced a number of combat planes, but after the war his first major success was a commercial plane, the F.II. This was the grandfather of a series of transports that he was to design during the next fifteen years. The F.II can also be considered as the ancestor of modern Dutch transport aircraft. The appearance of the F.II coincided with the inauguration of one of the world's major airlines, KLM (Royal Dutch Airlines), which used the F.II to commence its flights from Holland to England. The collaboration of Fokker and KLM was one of the most successful in aviation history. Most of Fokker's designs were developed specifically for KLM, and it was because of Fokker that KLM was able to take its place in the vanguard of civil aviation. The collaboration came to an abrupt end in 1934, when KLM's founder, Albert Plesman, turned down Fokker's most ambitious project, the F.XXXVI, in favour of the American Douglas DC-2, which had already appeared on the market.

By this time, however, Fokker was as famous for civil aircraft as he was for combat planes. Several of Fokker's planes have become immortal in the history of aviation. For example, the F.VIIs, perhaps the most famous of all the Fokkers, alone indicate the importance of the Dutch contribution to commercial aviation.

Anthony Fokker was not satisfied to be in the vanguard of European aeroplane manufacture. He set up a business in America as well, where he had been selling export models. The American factory also developed original designs of its own.

Fokker F.II

Aircraft: **Fokker F.II**
Manufacturer: **Fokker**
Type: **Civil transport**
Year: **1920**
Engine: **B.M.W., 6-cylinder in-line, liquid-cooled, 185 hp**
Wingspan: **52 ft 10 in (16.10 m)**
Length: **38 ft 3 in (11.65 m)**
Height: **10 ft 5 in (3.17 m)**
Weight: **4,176 lb (1,894 kg)**
Maximum speed: **93 mph (150 km/h)**
Ceiling: **—**
Range: **750 mile (1,200 km)**
Crew: **2**
Passengers: **4**

KLM's first flight to England with its own plane took place on September 30, 1920. The aeroplane, a Fokker F.II, flew from Amsterdam to Croydon in over three hours following the route of Louis Blériot. The Dutch airline had only recently bought two F.IIs. This aircraft is considered to be the grandfather of all the transport planes Fokker built. The prototype of this high-wing monoplane was actually built in the Schwerin factory in Germany and made its maiden flight in October 1919. The plane's flight to Holland was a rather adventurous enterprise, because of German export restrictions. A total of about thirty Fokker F.IIs were built and sold to various new airlines. The plane, which was also sold in Germany, was very successful.

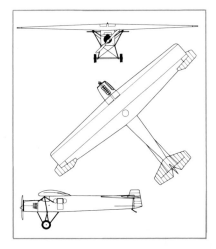

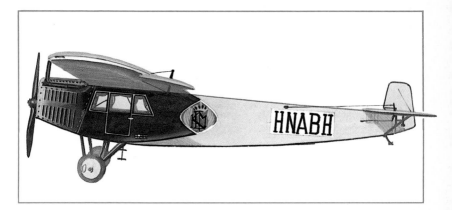

Fokker F.III

Aircraft: **Fokker F.III**
Manufacturer: **Fokker**
Type: **Civil transport**
Year: **1921**
Engine: **Siddeley Puma, 6-cylinder in-line, liquid-cooled, 240 hp**
Wingspan: **57 ft 10 in (17.62 m)**
Length: **36 ft 4 in (11.07 m)**
Height: **12 ft (3.65 m)**
Weight: **4,200 lb (1,900 kg)**
Cruising speed: **84 mph (135 km/h)**
Ceiling: **—**
Range: **420 mile (675 km)**
Crew: **1**
Passengers: **5**

In 1920 Fokker began building a larger and more powerful version of its successful F.II. The new aircraft, the F.III, had the same welded-steel tube structure of its predecessor and was also a high-wing monoplane. The increase in size and power improved the plane's performance and made it possible to increase passenger capacity to five. A characteristic of the plane was that the cockpit was not aligned with the engine. The original engine was a 240 hp Siddeley Puma, but this was later replaced by a 350 hp B.M.W. and then by a 360 hp Rolls-Royce Eagle. The F.III was as successful as the F.II and was sold to KLM and other European airlines. About thirty aircraft were manufactured in Holland, and others were built under licence in Germany.

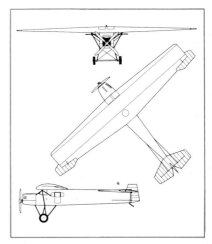

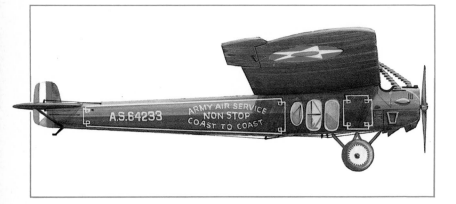

Fokker T-2 (F.IV)

Aircraft: **Fokker T-2**
Manufacturer: **Fokker**
Type: **Transport**
Year: **1921**
Engine: **Liberty 12-A, 12-cylinder V, liquid-cooled, 400 hp**
Wingspan: **81 ft 4 in (24.79 m)**
Length: **49 ft 1 in (14.79 m)**
Height: **11 ft 10 in (3.60 m)**
Weight: **10,760 lb (4,880 kg)**
Maximum speed: **96 mph (155 km/h)**
Ceiling: —
Range: —
Crew: **2**
Passengers: **10**

The Fokker F.IV did not enjoy the same success as its two predecessors, the F.II and the F.III. Bigger and more powerful, with a passenger capacity of ten, the F.IV was built in 1921. Unfortunately, the airlines were not interested in such a large aircraft. The only two F.IVs built were finally sold to the United States Army, which used them as transport planes and renamed them T-2 (transport) and A-2 (ambulance). One of them (T-2) broke several world records by flying non-stop from coast to coast in May 1923, with MacReady and Kelly at the controls. The other plane was turned into an ambulance plane and renamed A-2. It could carry two stretcher patients and medical personnel.

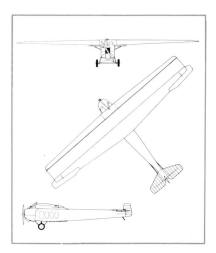

Fokker C VD

The C V did more than any other plane to establish the name of Fokker in military aviation in the period between the two World Wars. The plane saw service for fifteen years in a dozen countries. The C V prototype first took to the air in May 1924 and proved itself a fine performer. Its great success was due chiefly to its great versatility and easy maintenance. To meet various military requirements, the plane was designed with wings that could be easily interchanged. A variety of different engines could be installed, depending on the role assigned to a particular model. The plane could accommodate radial and vee engines of varying power. The C VD model had a sesquiplane wing and simplified struts. The C V plane saw service in the Dutch air force. It was sold abroad and manufactured under licence in many European countries.

Aircraft: **Fokker C VD**
Manufacturer: **Fokker**
Type: **Reconnaissance**
Year: **1926**
Engine: **Bristol Jupiter, 9-cylinder V, air-cooled, 450 hp**
Wingspan: **41 ft (12.50 m)**
Length: **31 ft 4 in (9.55 m)**
Height: **11 ft 6 in (3.50 m)**
Weight: **4,222 lb (1,915 kg)**
Maximum speed: **200 mph (320 km/h)**
Ceiling: **19,600 ft (6,000 m)**
Range: **740 mile (1,200 km)**
Armament: **2 machine guns**
Crew: **2**

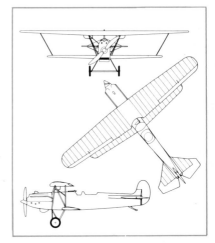

Fokker F.VIIa-3m
Fokker F.VIIa

The Fokker F.VIIs, which started to appear in 1924, were one of the most famous series of aircraft ever built. The F.VIIs made an important contribution to civil aviation in the 1920s and 1930s, as well as taking part in some of the most important sporting events of the period. It was in the first F.VIIa-3m, the Josephine Ford, that Richard E. Byrd and Floyd Bennett flew over the North Pole on May 9, 1926.

The first F.VII was built in 1924. It was a high wing monoplane, with the typical Fokker structure and configuration, designed as a long-range transport plane. Its endurance was demonstrated by the prototype's flight from Amsterdam to Jakarta with a cargo of mail. The five F.VIIs built were sold to KLM, and Fokker had a much-improved model, the F.VIIa, ready in 1925. The new model was structurally identical to its predecessor, but it had smoother aerodynamic lines and a redesigned undercarriage. It could also accommodate a variety of engines, generating between 350 and 525 hp. The F.VIIa was a success, and forty-two aircraft were sold throughout Europe. The plane was purchased in Switzerland, Denmark, France, Poland, Hungary, and Czechoslovakia, as well as Holland.

Anthony Fokker then went to the United States in May 1925 to study the market there and visit his American subsidiary, the Netherlands Air-

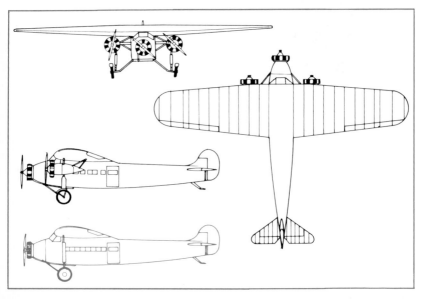

craft Manufacturing Company. It was here that he learned of Henry Ford's new interest in aviation. The American automobile manufacturer had set up a race, the Ford Reliability Tour, which started in Detroit and covered about 2,000 miles (3,200 km). Anthony Fokker decided to enter the race. He had his chief designer, Platz, add two engines to the F.VIIa to make it faster and safer. The aircraft was overhauled in three months, and it was this plane, the F.VIIa-3m, that took part in the race. Ford bought the plane and then turned it over to Richard E. Byrd for use in his Arctic explorations.

This modified version resulted in a better aircraft. It was so much better that the single-engine planes were now provided with supports under the wing-system so that they could be transformed into three-engine planes on request. The F.VIIa-3m was sold to a great many European airlines and, with its successor, the F.VIIb-3m, became one of the outstanding transport planes of the period.

Aircraft: **Fokker F.VIIa**
Manufacturer: **Fokker**
Type: **Civil transport**
Year: **1925**
Engine: **Bristol Jupiter, 9-cylinder radial, air-cooled, 480 hp**
Wingspan: **63 ft 4 in (19.30 m)**
Length: **47 ft 1 in (14.35 m)**
Height: **12 ft 10 in (3.91 m)**
Weight: **8,050 lb (3,650 kg)**
Cruising speed: **96 mph (155 km/h)**
Ceiling: **8,500 ft (2,600 m)**
Range: **700 mile (1,130 km)**
Crew: **2**
Passengers: **8**

Aircraft: **Fokker F.VIIa-3m**
Manufacturer: **Fokker**
Type: **Civil transport**
Year: **1926**
Engine: **Three Wright Whirlwind, 9-cylinder radial, air-cooled, 240 hp each**
Wingspan: **63 ft 4 in (19.30 m)**
Length: **47 ft 10 in (14.57 m)**
Height: **12 ft 10 in (3.91 m)**
Weight: **8,787 lb (3,986 kg)**
Maximum speed: **118 mph (190 km/h)**
Ceiling: **—**
Range: **1,600 mile (2,600 km)**
Crew: **2**
Passengers: **8**

Fokker F.VIIb-3m

The Fokker F.VIIb-3m Southern Cross flew across the Pacific Ocean, from San Francisco to Brisbane, Australia, in 83 hours and 38 minutes in 1928, distance of about 7,300 miles (11,900 km). The Southern Cross set out on May 31, 1928, and for two years continued to make record-breaking trans-oceanic flights. In the summer of 1930, Charles Kingsford Smith with a three-man crew completed an around-the-world flight of 50,000 miles (80,450 km). Amongst the records established during these flights was the first flight to New

Zealand, on September 10, 1928; a flight from Sydney, Australia, to Croydon, England, in 12 days, 14 hours, and 18 minutes; and an east-west Atlantic crossing of 2,000 miles (3,220 km) on June 24–25, 1930.

This plane, which was to become the most popular and most successful Fokker transport, was developed almost by accident. The famous English explorer George Hubert Wilkins, who owned a three-engine F.VIIa-3m, asked for a larger aircraft of the same type but with greater range for exploitation flights. The new plane was also

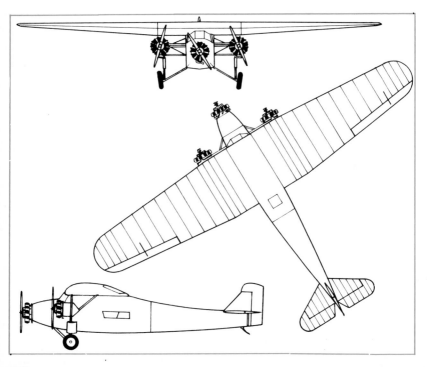

a high-wing monoplane with three engines. It was of steel-tube construction, the fuselage was covered, and the wings were covered with wood. The plane could accommodate any radial engine then manufactured, including the 300 hp Wright Whirlwind, the 365 hp Gnome–Rhône Titan, and the 215 hp Armstrong-Siddeley Lynx. The plane could carry eight–ten passengers plus a two-man crew.

The Fokker F.VIIb-3m led the vanguard in commercial aviation at once. Seventy aircraft were built by the Fokker company, and another seventy or so were constructed under licence elsewhere, in Belgium, Czechoslovakia, Poland, France, Italy, and England. The planes built in England by the Avro company were known as Avron Tens, while the F.VIIb-3ms in America were called F.10 and F.10A. The American subsidiary sold its planes directly to US operators. The F VIIb-3m flew everywhere in the world. Air France,

Aircraft: **Fokker F. VIIb-3m**
Manufacturer: **Fokker**
Type: **Civil transport**
Year: **1928**
Engine: **Three Wright Whirlwind, 9-cylinder radial, air-cooled, 300 hp each**
Wingspan: **71 ft 3 in (21.71 m)**
Length: **47 ft 7 in (14.50 m)**
Height: **12 ft 10 in (3.90 m)**
Weight: **11,700 lb (5,300 kg)**
Cruising speed: **111 mph (178 km/h)**
Ceiling: **14,400 ft (4,400 m)**
Range: **740 mile (1,200 km)**
Crew: **2**
Passengers: **8–10**

Swissair, Ala Littoria, and KLM flew the plane, and it was also sold in Australia, Canada, Spain, and Japan.

Variant models were also built, including the F.VIIb-3m/M bomber and the F.VIIb-3m/W seaplane. Amelia Earhart's Friendship, the plane she flew across the Atlantic in 1928, was a F.VIIb-3m/W seaplane.

Fokker F.XXXVI

The revolution in transport flying caused by the appearance of the Douglas DC-2 left a number of victims. One of these was the F.XXXVI, one of the last commercial designs that Fokker developed in the period between the two World Wars. This giant four-engine plane, which could carry thirty-two passengers, had been designed and developed especially for KLM to expand and improve its Far Eastern service. The appearance of the DC-2 and, more important, KLM's victory in the London–Melbourne race in October 1934 with its own DC-2, convinced the company that they should abandon the Fokker project and buy the Douglas.

In fact, there was no comparison between the two aircraft. The Fokker F.XXXVI was part of the past, with its metal skeleton and wood-and-fabric skin. Although it represented the best in European technology, it could not compete with the DC-2, the plane of the future.

The F.XXXVI was designed in 1932. And it was Albert Plesman, the founder of KLM, who approached Anthony Fokker. The two men discussed the project on June 6, 1932, and

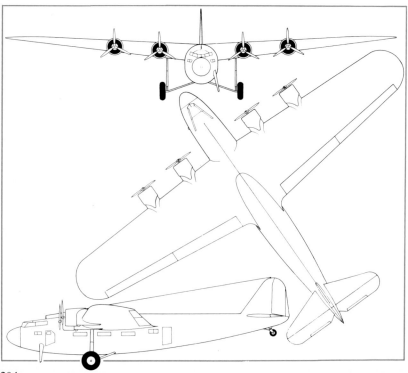

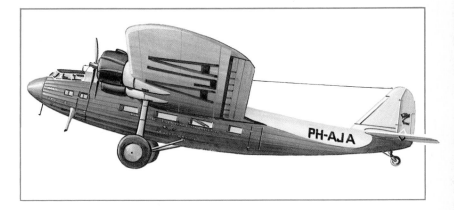

decided to try something new, a four-engine transport plane. KLM wanted to buy six aircraft capable of carrying thirty-two passengers on European routes and sixteen with berths on flights to the East. The maximum speed was to be about 155 mph (250 km/h).

Five months later Fokker had built a dummy of the fuselage and in 1933 began work on the prototype. The F.XXXVI was the largest transport plane built in Europe. It was a high-wing monoplane, with fixed under-carriage, powered by four 750 hp Wright Cyclone radial engines. Its cruising speed was 150 mph (240 km/h) and its range was 840 miles (1,350 km). The first flight took place on June 22, 1934, and tests were conducted for several months. All the results were more than satisfactory, but the Douglas appeared at almost the same time.

KLM cancelled its order, and production was suspended. The prototype, christened Arend (Eagle) re-

Aircraft: **Fokker F.XXXVI**
Manufacturer: **Fokker**
Type: **Civil transport**
Year: **1934**
Engine: **Four Wright Cyclone, 9-cylinder radial, air-cooled, 750 hp each**
Wingspan: **108 ft 3 in (33.00 m)**
Length: **77 ft 5 in (23.60 m)**
Height: **19 ft 8 in (5.99 m)**
Weight: **36,300 lb (16,500 kg)**
Cruising speed: **149 mph (240 km/h)**
Ceiling: **14,400 ft (4,400 m)**
Range: **840 mile (1,350 km)**
Crew: **4**
Passengers: **32**

mained a prototype. After much controversy, KLM bought the plane and used it on its London Amsterdam–Berlin route. The plane was sold to the Scottish Aviation Society in 1939 and was used for navigation training during the war. Meanwhile Anthony Fokker bought the Dutch rights for building the Douglas DC-2 and sold these planes to KLM.

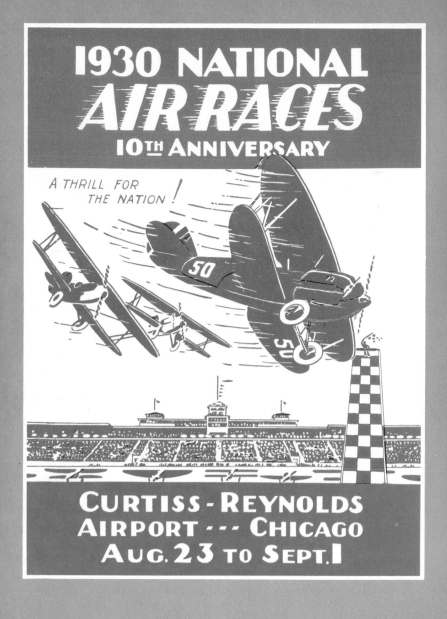

United States of America

Despite the Wright brothers' pioneering achievement, the development of the aeroplane and the growth of commercial aviation in the United States were slow processes. While Europe was discovering air transport and acquiring valuable experience, the United States dedicated most of its energies to developing military aviation. When the United States entered World War I, it was totally dependent on France and Britain for aviation material. It was clear that America had fallen behind foreign industries. Thus, the country decided to catch up with its foreign competitors, and military aviation became a top priority. At the same time military aircraft took part in one area of civil aviation competition flying. The United States won the Schneider Trophy in 1923 and 1925. The Curtiss NC-4 trans-Atlantic flight in 1919 and the round-the-world flight of the Douglas World Cruisers were also made in military aircraft. Military and civil aircraft also flew side by side in the races that were so popular in America in the 1920s. Indeed, most of the civilian racing planes were hand-built aircraft created by aficionados. Although these planes were highly sophisticated, they were precious toys more than they were vehicles.

There was no great impetus to develop commercial aviation, much less passenger aircraft. In the first place, rail service throughout the United States was highly developed. And long-distance trains were actually faster than the slow and uncomfortable biplanes of the period. Ground service and suitable airfields did not exist. Furthermore, the American aircraft industry's situation was different from that of the industries of its wartime allies. France, Great Britain, and Italy found themselves with an enormous surplus of aircraft after the war. And although Germany was strictly limited by the terms of the peace treaty, the German manufacturers had extensive resources. But American production at this time was at a relatively modest level. Commercial aircraft still needed research and design. And this took time.

Thus American civil aviation started in a relatively limited sector, airmail transport. As early as 1917 the US Post Office had initiated plans for an airmail service. After a number of problems, most of them connected with the problem of acquiring suitable aircraft, the first route was inaugurated on May 15, 1918, between New York and Washington, D.C. The planes were slow biplanes, the Curtiss JN-4H Jennys, which had seen service as military trainers. On August 12 these planes were replaced by biplanes specially built by Standard Aircraft Co. By early 1919 the postal fleet numbered some 120 aircraft, including about 100 war surplus de Havilland D.H.4s. The airmail network gradually expanded. Airmail service reached Chicago on May 15, and by September 8, 1920, when the Omaha–Sacramento route was opened, airmail service reached San Francisco. The east–west flight took 34 hours and 20 minutes, while the west–east flight lasted 29 hours and 15 minutes. Aircraft were changed six times during the trans-continental flight, in Cleveland, Chicago, Omaha, Cheyenne, Salt Lake City, and Reno. The service was a success, and in 1927 the postal authorities turned over the administration of airmail flights to private companies. Boeing Air Transport took over the route between Chicago and San Francisco, and National Air Transport handled the Chicago–New York route. By September 1, 1927, when the last Post Office-administered flight was made, the airmail planes had flown over ten million miles (sixteen million kilometres) and carried more than six million pounds (3 million kilogrammes) of mail. The year 1923 saw the highest quantity of mail transport, with 67,875,000 letters carried.

It was in 1927, the same year Lindbergh made his historic trans-Atlantic flight, that the aeroplane entered the field of passenger transport in the United States. The airmail service had fostered the growth of several small companies that served subsidiary routes, such companies as Colonial Air Transport, the Robertson Aircraft Corporation, National Air Transport, Western Air Express, Varney Speed Lines, and the Ford Motor Company's airline. Western Air Express was the first to initiate regular passenger service. Its first flight took off on May 23, 1926, and Western was soon followed by other companies. But the first large-scale undertakings were only begun after Lindbergh's flight, which aroused enormous interest in flying throughout America. American industry was finally convinced that the aeroplane was a safe and reliable means of transport, and that it had a commercial future. Trans-continental Air Transport (TAT) was the first major air company to be founded in this new climate of enthusiasm. The company was established on March 16, 1928, and its stockholders included the Wright and Curtiss companies as well as the Pennsylvania Railroad. The technical director was the man-of-the-hour, Charles Lindbergh.

From this point on, the history of American aviation is a continuing story of new companies, reorganizations, consolidations, and developments that culminated in the 1930s with the creation of the Big Four, the leading companies in American civil aviation: American Air

Lines, the result of the successive consolidation of fifteen airlines; United Air Lines, created by six companies; Eastern Air Lines, the combination of two companies; and Transcontinental and Western Air (TWA), the consolidation of two groups. A fifth giant made its appearance on the scene, Pan American Airways. Pan Am became the largest international line in the world. Alongside these colossal companies, a host of smaller companies were also established. By 1930 there were more than forty companies, with a total of about 500 aircraft and an overall total of about 30,000 route miles. This enormously rapid expansion of civil aviation put America in the forefront of world aviation. In 1929 about 160,000 passengers were carried, about 10,000 more passengers than in 1928, and almost 50,000 more passengers than were carried by Germany, which was in second place.

At the same time the manufacture of aircraft in the United States increased enormously. A second-rank producer just after World War I, America led the world by the 1930s. Aircraft manufactured by Boeing, Douglas, Lockheed, and Sikorsky – to mention only the most important companies – were known throughout the world. But perhaps the most important new plane to make its appearance in this period was the Boeing 247. This plane, which appeared in 1933, was the first truly modern commercial aircraft. It marked the beginning of a new era in aviation.

The appearance of the Boeing 247 had other consequences as well. It demonstrated how much the survival of a major air line depends on the efficiency of the aircraft it uses. United Air Lines managed to obtain a monopoly of the 247s, which caused a crisis in its direct competitor, TWA. The Boeing was faster, more comfortable, and more efficient than any other commercial plane in the air. TWA commissioned the Douglas company to develop what was to become the father of a whole line of famous transport planes, the DC-1. The Douglas was so successful that by the end of the 1930s it served eight per cent of American air lines. A total of 268 aircraft were in service on domestic routes.

The development of Pan American Airways followed a different course. It was the only trans-continental service in the United States. The company was founded on March 14, 1927, and inaugurated its first route on October 19, between Key West, Florida, and Havana, Cuba. The aircraft was a Fairchild seaplane lent to the company. With the backing of bankers and industrialists, the company expanded rapidly. In 1929 it developed several Caribbean routes. By the next year it had reached the southernmost end of South America. In 1935 it inaugurated its trans-Pacific routes. In 1938 it reached Alaska, and in 1939 it flew across the Atlantic. By 1940 it was flying to New Zealand. On the eve of World War II, Pan Am operated the most extensive routes in the world. In less than twenty years America had established itself as the world leader in aviation.

Navy/Curtiss NC-4

Barely a month before the historic non-stop Atlantic crossing made by Alcock and Brown in their Vickers Vimy, three large seaplanes set out on an Atlantic crossing of their own. This was not a non-stop crossing and only one of the aircraft completed the flight, a Navy/Curtiss NC-4. This aircraft became the first plane in the world to fly all the way across the Atlantic, from Rockaway, Long Island, to Lisbon, Portugal. (The longest lap was that from the coast of New-foundland to the Azores.)

The NC-4 was the fourth in a series of seaplanes built in the last year of World War I to protect Allied convoys from German submarines. It was a joint effort of the U.S. Navy and the Curtiss company that produced the large central-hull, three-engine bi-plane. The first NC was powered by three 400 hp Liberty engines. The Navy/Curtiss NC-1 made its maiden flight on October 4, 1918, and one-and-a-half months later it established

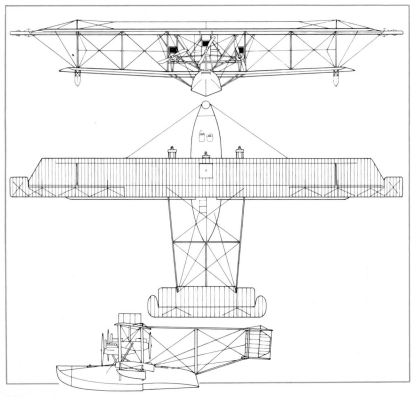

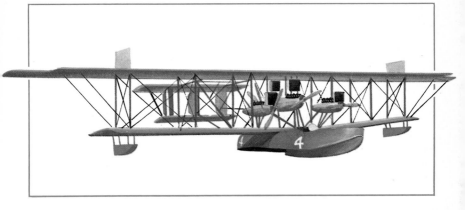

a world passenger transport record by carrying 51 people. Although the test flights were successful, it was decided that three engines could not provide sufficient power for long ocean flights, and a fourth engine was added. The second plane, the NC-2, took to the air on April 12, 1919, with its four Liberty engines installed in two tandem pairs. The third plane, the NC-3, established the perfected formula of the aircraft, which was that of the NC-4 as well: three tractor engines plus a fourth, pusher engine in the middle nacelle.

With the end of the war, there was no need for convoy defence, so it was decided to test the planes' capabilities in a trans-Atlantic crossing. On May 16, 1919, three aircraft, the NC-1, NC-3, and NC-4, set out on the longest leg of the flight, from Trepassey Bay, Newfoundland, to Horta in the Azores, a distance of about 1,400 miles (2,250 km). The NC-1 and the NC-3 made forced sea landings and did not continue the flight. The third plane, the NC-4, with Albert C. Read

Aircraft: **Navy/Curtiss NC-4**
Manufacturer: **Curtiss Aeroplane and Motor Co.**
Type: **Reconnaissance**
Year: **1919**
Engine: **Four Liberty 12, 12-cylinder V, liquid-cooled, 400 hp each**
Wingspan: **126 ft (38.40 m)**
Length: **68 ft 3 in (20.80 m)**
Height: **24 ft 6 in (7.46 m)**
Weight: **27,386 lb (12,422 kg)**
Maximum speed: **85 mph (137 km/h)**
Ceiling: **4,500 ft (1,370 m)**
Range: **1,470 mile (2,360 km)**
Armament: **2 machine guns**
Crew: **6**

at the controls, reached the Azores and took off again for Portugal on May 20. On April 31 the plane flew to Plymouth, England, where it was given a triumphal welcome.

After the Atlantic crossing, the NC-4 was shown around the United States and then turned over to the Smithsonian Institution in Washington, D.C., where it is still on display to mark man's first flight across the Atlantic Ocean.

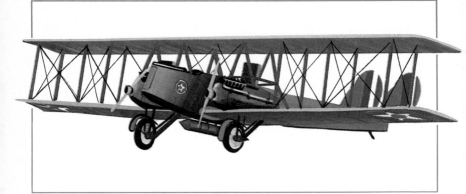

Martin MB-2

Aircraft: **Martin MB-2**
Manufacturer: **Glenn L. Martin Co.**
Type: **Bomber**
Year: **1919**
Engine: **Two Liberty 12, 12-cylinder V, liquid-cooled, 420 hp each**
Wingspan: **74 ft 2 in (22.60 m)**
Length: **42 ft 8 in (13.00 m)**
Height: **14 ft 8 in (4.47 m)**
Weight: **12,064 lb (5,472 kg)**
Maximum speed: **100 mph (160 km/h)**
Ceiling: **8,500 ft (2,600 m)**
Range: **560 mile (900 km)**
Armament: **5 machine guns; 3,000 lb (1,360 kg) of bombs**
Crew: **4**

During World War I the United States relied on European aircraft manufacturers, but after the war a great effort was made not to be outdistanced, especially by British and French aircraft manufacturers. It was in this context that the Glenn L. Martin Company was commissioned to design a new bomber to succeed the British heavy bomber Handley Page 0/400, which had been built in the United States under licence from the owner. It was in 1917 that the American company set out to produce a better aircraft than the 0/400. This new aircraft, the MB-1, took to the air in August 1918. One year later an improved version, designed for night bombing, was introduced, the MB-2. This was a twin-engine biplane powered by two 420 hp Liberty engines. One hundred and thirty planes were built and remained in service with the Army Air Force until 1927.

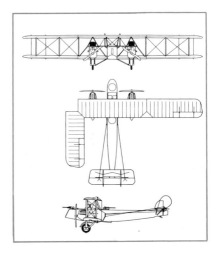

Dayton–Wright RB Racer

Perhaps the most advanced and original airplane designed in 1920 was the Dayton–Wright RB Racer, but it never had a chance to achieve its full potential. The plane was designed with the help of Orville Wright and built especially for the 1920 competition for the Gordon Bennett Cup. (This was the oldest aeroplane racing trophy, the first race being held in Rheims in 1909.) This fast, compact monoplane had to withdraw from the race after the first lap because of a broken control cable. Sabotage was suspected at the time. The RB Racer was undoubtedly the most interesting aircraft in the race. It was the only monoplane in the race and was built of balsa and plywood. It had a manually retractable undercarriage, and the cockpit was closed. Aside from its smooth aerodynamic lines, the wing angle could be adjusted. The 250 hp engine was a 6-cylinder in-line.

Aircraft: **Dayton-Wright RB Racer**
Manufacturer: **Dayton-Wright Airplane Co.**
Type: **Competition**
Year: **1920**
Engine: **Hall-Scott, 6-cylinder in-line, liquid-cooled, 250 hp**
Wingspan: **21 ft 2 in (6.45 m)**
Length: **22 ft 8 in (6.91 m)**
Height: **8 ft (2.44 m)**
Weight (empty): **1,400 lb (630 kg)**
Weight (loaded): **1,850 lb (840 kg)**
Maximum speed: **200 mph (320 km/h)**
Ceiling: **15,000 ft (4,600 m)**
Endurance: **1 hr 30 min**
Crew: **1**

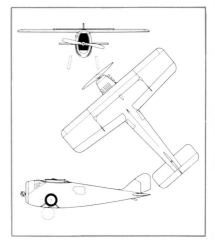

Verville R-1 (VCP-1/VCP-R)

The last competition in the Gordon Bennett Cup race series took place in 1920, the year France retained the cup permanently. But American enthusiasm for aeroplane racing was so keen that only a couple of months later a new race was inaugurated, the Pulitzer Trophy, offered by the famous publishing brothers, Ralph, Herbert, and Joseph Pulitzer Jr. It was a simple speed race. Any plane from any country could compete. The only restriction was the ability to fly faster than 100 mph (160 km/h). A limit of 75 mph (120 km/h) landing speed was later introduced in 1922 for reasons of safety. The first race was held on November 27, 1920, at Mitchell Field, Long Island, over a course 116 miles 100 yards (186.77 km) long. Forty-five thousand people turned out for the race. After rigorous preliminaries, a total of thirty-seven planes qualified

Aircraft: **Verville R-1 (VCP-1/VCP-R)**
Manufacturer: **Verville**
Type: **Competition**
Year: **1920**
Engine: **Packard 1A-2025, 12-cylinder V, liquid-cooled, 638 hp**
Wingspan: **28 ft 2 in (8.58 m)**
Length: **24 ft 2 in (7.37 m)**
Height: **8 ft 8 in (2.64 m)**
Weight (empty): **2,450 lb (1,110 kg)**
Weight (loaded): **3,200 lb (1,450 kg)**
Maximum speed: **186 mph (299 km/h)**
Ceiling: **—**
Endurance: **1 hr 15 min**
Crew: **1**

for the race. The winner was a plane that had taken part in the final competition for the Gordon Bennett Cup on September 28. It was the Verville R-1, the first competition racing plane built for the US Army Air Force. Piloted by Corliss Mosely, the plane maintained an average speed of 156.50 mph (251.85 km/h). Sometime later, during a test flight, the Verville R-1 touched 186 mph (300 km/h). As a result of this, the criticisms of those who believed the plane to be of little value because of its weight (empty 2,450 lb; 1,110 kg) were completely refuted.

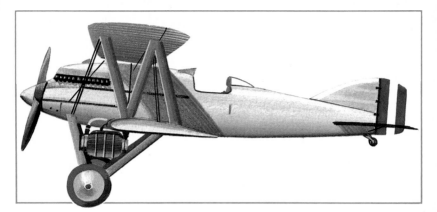

Curtiss CR-1

The CR-1 was a biplane designed exclusively for speed. The US Navy ordered the plane from the Curtiss company early in 1921 so that it could compete in the annual Pulitzer Trophy race. The first of two aircraft was finished on August 1, the second a week later. The CR-1 was an extremely elegant plane, and aerodynamics had provided the primary criterion in its construction. A special version of the Curtiss CD-12 engine was installed. The 405 hp engine was cooled by two ring radiators installed on the undercarriage. Only one CR-1 took part in the race, which was held on November 3 in Omaha, Nebraska. The navy decided at the last minute not to take part, so the CR-1 was entered by the Curtiss company. Piloted by Bert Acosta, this elegant biplane outdistanced all its competitors and won the trophy with an average speed of 176.71 mph (284.36 km/h).

Aircraft: **Curtiss CR-1**
Manufacturer: **Curtiss Aeroplane and Motor Co.**
Type: **Competition**
Year: **1921**
Engine: **Curtiss CD-12, 12-cylinder V, liquid-cooled, 405 hp**
Wingspan: **22 ft 8 in (6.91 m)**
Length: **21 ft (6.40 m)**
Height: **8 ft 4 in (2.53 m)**
Weight (empty): **1,728 lb (783 kg)**
Weight (loaded): **2,158 lb (978 kg)**
Maximum speed: **185 mph (298 km/h)**
Ceiling: —
Endurance: **1 hr 30 min**
Crew: **1**

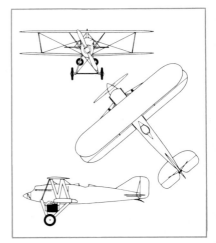

Curtiss–Cox Cactus Kitten

The Cactus Kitten was the only triplane ever to take part in competition flying. It was the third racing plane that Curtiss built for the oil magnate S. E. J. Cox. The first plane, also called the Cactus Kitten, was a monoplane designed in 1920. The second, the Texas Wildcat, built at the same time as the first Kitten, was a biplane. Both these aircraft were built for the Gordon Bennett Cup race in 1920. Despite their technical details and aerodynamic lines, they never achieved their full potential. The third plane was built for the 1921 Pulitzer Trophy race. It was substantially similar to the other two planes, except that it was a triplane. The extra wing was installed so that the aircraft could land at a speed within the limits prescribed by the regulations. Tested in October by Bert Acosta, the plane proved to be an excellent racer, but it came in second, behind the outstanding Curtiss CR-1.

Aircraft: **Curtiss-Cox Cactus Kitten**
Manufacturer: **Curtiss Aeroplane and Motor Co.**
Type: **Competition**
Year: **1921**
Engine: **Curtiss C-12, 12-cylinder V, liquid-cooled, 435 hp**
Wingspan: **20 ft (6.10 m)**
Length: **19 ft 3 in (5.87 m)**
Height: **8 ft 6 in (2.59 m)**
Weight (empty): **1.936 lb (878 kg)**
Weight (loaded): **2,406 lb (1,091 kg)**
Maximum speed: **196 mph (315 km/h)**
Ceiling: **25,000 ft (7,600 m)**
Endurance: **1 hr 10 min**
Crew: **1**

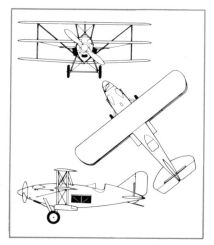

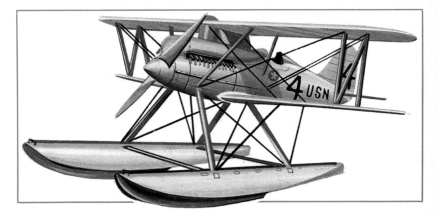

Curtiss CR-3

The seventh competition in the Schneider Cup series, in 1923, was the first to be won by an American plane. The race was held on September 27–28 at Cowes, on the Isle of Wight. The race demonstrated that America had caught up with the rest of the world in aviation and was now able to produce the fastest and highest-performing planes in the world. The winner of the race was a Curtiss CR-3, an improved seaplane version of the CR-1. Aside from the floats, the rudder surface was larger, and cooling radiators were installed on the wings. The two CR-3s that entered the race took first and second places. The winning plane was piloted by David Rittenhouse at an average speed of 177.37 mph (285.45 km/h). The second-place plane, with Rutledge Irvine at the controls, flew at an average speed only about 2 mph (3 km/h) slower.

Aircraft: **Curtiss CR-3**
Manufacturer: **Curtiss Aeroplane and Motor Co.**
Type: **Competition**
Year: **1923**
Engine: **Curtiss D-12, 12-cylinder V, liquid-cooled, 450 hp**
Wingspan: **22 ft 8 in (6.91 m)**
Length: **25 ft (7.63 m)**
Height: **10 ft (3.05 m)**
Weight (empty): **2,119 lb (961 kg)**
Weight (loaded): **2,746 lb (1,246 kg)**
Maximum speed: **188 mph (302 km/h)**
Ceiling: **22,000 ft (6,700 m)**
Range: **520 mile (840 km)**
Crew: **1**

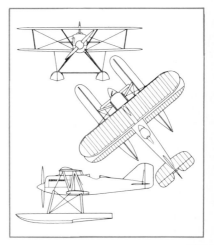

Douglas DWC/0-5 World Cruiser

Around the world in 175 days! On April 6, 1924, four Douglas World Cruisers took off from Seattle, Washington, on a round-the-world flight that covered 27,553 miles (44,341 km). These four planes – the Seattle, the Chicago, the Boston, and the New Orleans – were adapted from a torpedo bomber that the Douglas company had built for the US Navy. All the military equipment was removed, the controls and the fuel tanks were modified and a radio direction-finder was installed. Only two of the aircraft completed the flight, arriving home on September 28, 1924. The Seattle was lost in Alaska on April 30, and the Boston went down over the Atlantic on August 3.

The progenitor of the DWC was the Douglas DT-1, the first military aircraft the Douglas company built (1921). It was a single-seat biplane, driven by a 400 hp Liberty engine. The plane had an undercarriage and two pontoons for coming down on water. After test flights, the navy asked for some modifications, and only one of the three prototypes ordered was

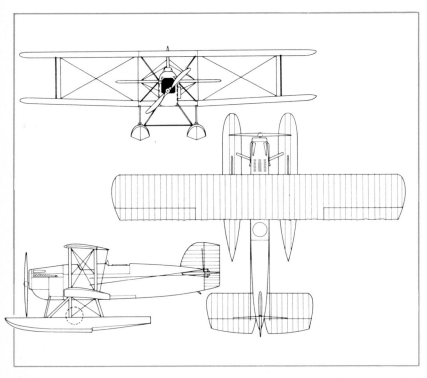

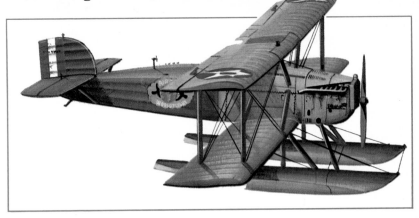

actually completed. This was the DT-1. The other two aircraft were finished as two-seaters and had a single radiator installed in front of the engine, instead of the double radiator that was installed on the fuselage of the prototype. The production model was called the DT-2, and a total of 132 were manufactured. Delivery to the US navy began in 1922. The plane could carry a torpedo weighing 1,830 pounds (830 kg). The wings of the plane could be folded up for easier carriage aboard ship. Because the plane could come down on land or sea, it became very popular in a variety of models. With the new radial engines that replaced the liquid-cooled Liberty, the plane was more reliable and easier to service.

In 1923 the US Army became interested in the plane. The army was looking for a plane to compete with five other countries in an around-the-world flight. The prototype of this plane, the Douglas DWC, was prepared in July and August, 1923, and

Aircraft: **Douglas DWC/0-5 World Cruiser**
Manufacturer: **Douglas Aircraft Co.**
Type: **Reconnaissance seaplane**
Year: **1924**
Engine: **Liberty 12 A, 12-cylinder V, liquid-cooled, 420 hp**
Wingspan: **50 ft (15.24 m)**
Length: **35 ft 2 in (10.72 m)**
Height: **15 ft 1 in (4.60 m)**
Weight (empty): **4,268 lb (1,936 kg)**
Weight (loaded): **8,800 lb (4,000 kg)**
Maximum speed: **100 mph (160 km/h)**
Ceiling: **7,000 ft (2,100 m)**
Range: **2,100 mile (3,500 km)**
Crew: **2**

four more planes were delivered in March 1924. After the flight, the army ordered five more DWCs in a reconnaissance model. These planes, the Douglas 0-5, were substantially like the DWC, except that their fuel capacity was lower and they carried military equipment and armament. These planes were manufactured as seaplanes for overseas duty.

Army/Curtiss R3C-2
Army/Curtiss R3C-1

The Schneider Trophy contest skipped a year in 1924. The seventh competition, in 1923, had been won by America. The eighth race was scheduled for October 25, 1924, but most of the contestants found it impossible to get their aircraft ready in time. In a spirit of good sportsmanship the Americans agreed to postpone the eighth competition in the series until the following year. The race was held on October 26, 1925, in Baltimore. It was hard-fought, with British, Italian, and American planes competing for the cup. Again the Americans won. This time the winning pilot was Jimmy Doolittle, an army pilot who was to become world-famous during World War II. The plane he flew was a seaplane racer, the Curtiss R3C-2. The average speed was 232.57 mph (374.27 km/h), and the maximum speed 245.67 mph (395.35 km/h), a new world record.

Only a few days earlier the land counterpart of the R3C-2 had won the Pulitzer Trophy race, which was held at Mitchell Field on October 10. This plane, the R3C-1, a Curtiss biplane piloted by Cyrus Bettis, had outdistanced all its rivals by touching a speed of 248 mph (400 km/h).

R3Cs were direct descendants of the CR-1 racer that appeared in 1921 and the CR-3 seaplane that had made America's first Schneider Trophy win in 1923. An intermediate plane in this series was the R2C, which the navy developed for the 1923 race in the Pulitzer Trophy series. Two R2Cs were built, and they won first and second place in the Pulitzer race. The

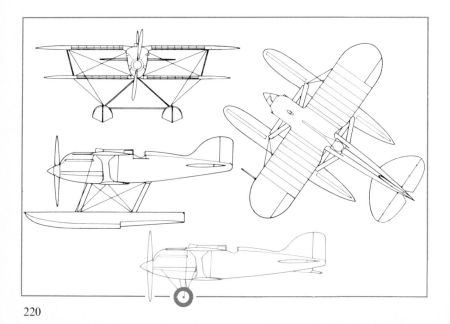

pilot of the winning plane, Alford J. Williams, flew at an average speed of 243.64 mph (392.08 km/h). The two R2Cs were transformed into seaplanes and prepared for the 1924 edition of the Schneider Trophy race.

The cancellation and postponement of that race led the army and the navy to order a new version of the plane from the Curtiss company. The R3C, in both land and seaplane versions, was fundamentally similar to its direct predecessor. However, it incorporated several technical and structural improvements, including a new engine capable of generating 610 horsepower and a new wing profile for greater speed. The plane's success in both the Schneider and Pulitzer races in 1925 removed any doubts that might have existed about the aircraft's high quality. The navy ordered another model of the seaplane, this one with a 700 hp engine, for the 1926 Schneider race. A bit of bad luck and some superb flying by the Italian Macchi M.39 dashed the plane's hopes of victory in 1926.

Aircraft: **Army/Curtiss R3C-1**
Manufacturer: **Curtiss Aeroplane and Motor Co.**
Type: **Competition**
Year: **1925**
Engine: **Curtiss V-1400, 12-cylinder V, liquid-cooled, 610 hp**
Wingspan: **22 ft (6.71 m)**
Length: **20 ft 1 in (6.12 m)**
Height: **6 ft 9 in (2.05 m)**
Weight (empty): **1,792 lb (813 kg)**
Weight (loaded): **2,182 lb (990 kg)**
Maximum speed: **285 mph (458 km/h)**
Ceiling: **26,400 ft (8,000 m)**
Range: **—**
Crew: **1**

Aircraft: **Army/Curtiss R3C-2**
Manufacturer: **Curtiss Aeroplane and Motor Co.**
Type: **Competition**
Year: **1925**
Engine: **Curtiss V-1400, 12-cylinder V, liquid-cooled, 610 hp**
Wingspan: **20 ft (6.10 m)**
Length: **20 ft 8 in (6.29 m)**
Height: **10 ft 4 in (3.15 m)**
Weight (empty): **2,135 lb (968 kg)**
Weight (loaded): **2,738 lb (1,242 kg)**
Maximum speed: **246 mph (396 km/h)**
Ceiling: **21,200 ft (6,400 m)**
Range: **250 mile (400 km)**
Crew: **1**

Ford 4AT Trimotor

The first great US contribution to the world of civil aviation was known as the 'Tin Goose'. Second in fame only to the Douglas DC-3, which was to make its appearance ten years later, the Ford Trimotor holds a place of honor in the history of the airplane. Two hundred 'Tin Geese' came out of the Ford factory between June 11, 1926, and June 7, 1933. But that was enough to establish an American airline system, and they saw service in some hundred companies on five continents. The 'Tin Goose' became

legendary, and this legend is still alive, thanks to the creation in 1966 of a prototype of a modern version of that plane, the Bushmaster 2000.

The immediate ancestor of the Ford Trimotor was the 1924 Stout Air Pullman, a monoplane designed and built by William B. Stout and George H. Prudden, the former the owner and the latter the engineer of a small firm, the Stout Metal Airplane Company. Henry Ford became interested in the company and bought it in 1925. He initiated research for the construction

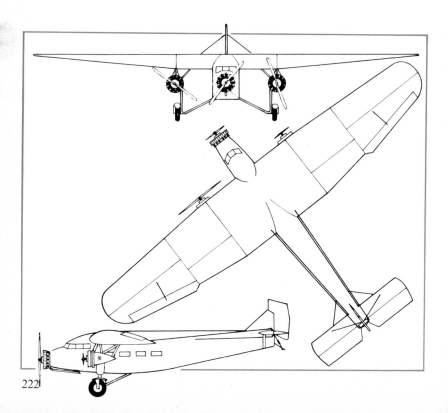

of a three-engine transport plane. The result was the prototype of the 4AT, which made its maiden flight on June 11, 1926. It was a high-wing monoplane, powered by three 200 hp Wright Whirlwind engines. It was an all-metal plane covered in corrugated sheet aluminium, similar to the fashion of the German Junkers. The 4AT was an extremely tough plane for all weather conditions.

Production began at once, with two models in particular: the 4AT powered by Wright J-6 engines, and the 5AT powered by 420 hp Pratt and Whitney Wasps. Almost all the American airlines used the Ford Trimotor, and civilian lines in Canada, Mexico, Central and South America, Europe, Australia, and even China followed suit. The army took thirteen planes and the navy took nine to be used as transport craft. The 'official' career of the Trimotors lasted until 1934, when they were replaced by the more modern Douglas DC-2, but they continued to be used by private

Aircraft: **Ford 4 AT Trimotor**
Manufacturer: **Ford Motor Co.**
Type: **Civil transport**
Year: **1926**
Engine: **Three Wright J.6 Whirlwind, 9-cylinder radial, air-cooled, 200 hp each**
Wingspan: **74 ft (22.56 m)**
Length: **49 ft 10 in (15.19 m)**
Height: **11 ft 9 in (3.58 m)**
Weight: **10,100 lb (4,600 kg)**
Cruising speed: **107 mph (172 km/h)**
Ceiling: **16,400 ft (5,000 m)**
Range: **570 mile (920 km)**
Crew: **2**
Passengers: **11–14**

owners and small airlines until after World War II. Perhaps the most important enterprise of the Trimotor was Richard Byrd's flight over the South Pole on November 29, 1929. The fifteenth production model of the 4AT, the 'Floyd Bennett' carried Byrd and three companions around the pole and back to base at Little America.

Vought 02U-1 Corsair

The first Corsair was also the first plane designed for the navy with an engine that was to become world-famous, the Pratt and Whitney Wasp. (There were two later Corsairs, one during World War II and the other a jet aircraft.) The Corsair prototype made its first flight in 1926, and delivery of the aircraft to naval units began the following year. What made the Vought-built plane remarkable was its great versatility. It had been ordered as a reconnaissance plane, but it also saw service as a light bomber and as an observation plane in support of battleships and cruisers. It was a two-seat biplane, all metal in structure, and could accommodate both an undercarriage and pontoons. It soon became standard equipment in naval reconnaissance units. A total of 291 aircraft, in various models, were produced until 1930. In 1927, Vought 02U-1 Corsairs set four world records for speed and altitude.

Aircraft: **Vought 02U-1 Corsair**
Manufacturer: **Chance Vought Co.**
Type: **Reconnaissance**
Year: **1927**
Engine: **Pratt and Whitney Wasp, 9-cylinder radial, air-cooled, 450 hp**
Wingspan: **34 ft 6 in (10.51 m)**
Length: **24 ft 5 in (7.45 m)**
Height: **10 ft 1 in (3.08 m)**
Weight: **3,635 lb (1,649 kg)**
Maximum speed: **150 mph (241 km/h)**
Ceiling: **18,700 ft (5,700 m)**
Range: **610 mile (980 km)**
Armament: **2–3 machine guns**
Crew: **2**

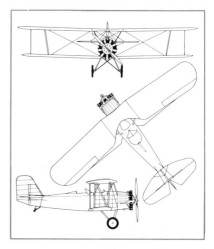

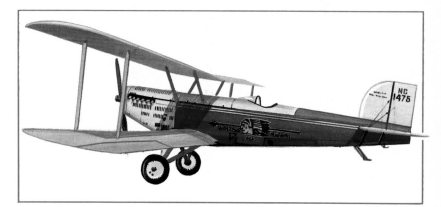

Douglas M-4

Aircraft: **Douglas M-4**
Manufacturer: **Douglas Aircraft Co.**
Type: **Civil transport**
Year: **1927**
Engine: **Liberty 12 A, 12-cylinder V, liquid-cooled, 420 hp**
Wingspan: **39 ft 8 in (12.09 m)**
Length: **28 ft 11 in (8.81 m)**
Height: **10 ft 1 in (3.08 m)**
Weight: **4,968 lb (2,253 kg)**
Maximum speed: **145 mph (233 km/h)**
Ceiling: **17,000 ft (5,200 m)**
Range: **700 mile (1,130 km)**
Crew: **1**
Cargo: **2,058 lb (933 kg)**

The M-4 was the last of the M series of aircraft that the Douglas company began producing in 1925 for the US air mail service. The M-4 saw duty with several small private companies that carried mail. One of these was the Western Air Express, founded in the spring of 1926 by Harris M. 'Pop' Hanshue, which grew into one of the most famous air transport companies in the United States. The Douglas M-4 was a development of the earlier M-1 and M-2 models. They were all conventionally-built biplanes, driven by old Liberty engines and were capable of carrying over 800 pounds payload, chiefly mail. What makes these aircraft important is that they were pioneers. They opened routes in near-primitive conditions, they flew millions of miles across America; performing an important service. They flew mostly at night, over long distances, and without landing facilities. Man and machine were all but abandoned to their own devices. Yet a host of the great names in aviation began their careers in the postal service. Suffice it to mention the name of Charles Lindbergh, who flew the mail run from St. Louis to Chicago.

225

Ryan NYP Spirit of St. Louis

The trans-Atlantic crossing of the Spirit of St. Louis has entered the realm of legend. At 7.52 a.m. on May 20, 1927, Charles A. Lindbergh took off from Roosevelt Field, in Mineola, New York, with his Spirit of St. Louis loaded with fuel. His goal was Paris, 3,520 miles (5,670 km) away on the other side of the ocean. Thirty-three hours and 39 minutes later he landed at Le Bourget just outside Paris. The Atlantic had been crossed before; it had been crossed non-stop as well. But Lindbergh's was the first solo flight, a landmark in the history of aviation.

Lindbergh left college at the University of Wisconsin to enrol in a flying school in Lincoln, Nebraska.

He barnstormed for a while in a surplus World War I plane, and spent a year at the army flying school. In 1926 he became an airmail pilot. A $25,000-prize had been offered for the first non-stop flight from New York to Paris, and Lindbergh wanted to compete for it. He was convinced that a non-stop solo Atlantic crossing was possible if he could find the right plane and the money to build it. His enthusiasm was met with general skepticism. A solo flight in a single-engine plane seemed impossible. After many difficulties Lindbergh finally found a small company in San Diego as well as financial backers. Ryan Airlines Inc. were already building two high-wing

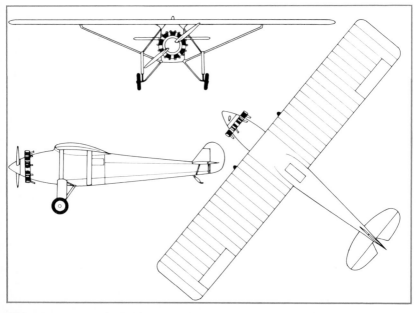

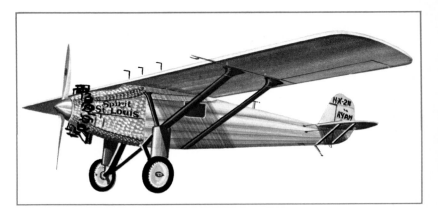

monoplanes, the M-1 and the M-2. These planes were combination mail and passenger carriers. On February 26, 1927, three days after signing a contract, the head designer, Donald H. Hall set to work on building a special version of the monoplane for Lindbergh's flight. Two months later the plane was ready. The aircraft was constructed of wood and metal and covered with wood, fabric, and aluminium. The aircraft was powered by a 220 hp Wright Whirlwind radial engine, which drove a two-blade metal propeller. The fuel tanks were loaded in the fuselage in front of the cockpit.

Lindbergh began flight tests on April 26, 1927, and on May 10, the Spirit of St. Louis flew from San Diego to St. Louis in 14 hours and 25 minutes, a new record for the run. Two days later, Lindbergh took off from St. Louis and landed at Curtiss Field 7 hours and 20 minutes later. The last days before the flight were devoted to flight checks and tests. And

Aircraft: **Ryan NYP Spirit of St. Louis**
Manufacturer: **Ryan Airlines Inc.**
Type: **Trans-Atlantic monoplane**
Year: **1927**
Engine: **Wright Whirlwind J-5-C, 9-cylinder radial, air-cooled, 200 hp**
Wingspan: **46 ft (14.02 m)**
Length: **27 ft 5 in (8.36 m)**
Height: **8 ft (2.44 m)**
Weight (empty): **2,150 lb (975 kg)**
Weight (loaded): **5,245 lb (2,379 kg)**
Cruising speed: **112 mph (180 km/h)**
Ceiling: **16,400 ft (5,000 m)**
Range: **4,100 mile (6,600 km)**
Crew: **1**

then the great day itself came. The events of that day are forever recorded in the history books.

The Ryan NYP Spirit of St. Louis is now housed in the Smithsonian Institution in Washington, D.C., alongside another famous aircraft, the Wright Brothers' 1903 plane, Flyer 1, the first powered, heavier-than-air machine to make a successful sustained and controlled flight.

Lockheed Vega 1
Lockheed Vega 5B

Perhaps the most famous of the 131 Vegas that the Lockheed company began building in 1927 was Wiley Post's monoplane, the Winnie Mae. Setting out from New York on June 23, 1931, with Harold Gatty as navigator, Post flew around the world in 8 days, 15 hours, and 51 minutes. Two years later Post set out to break this record, this time flying solo. He took off on July 15, 1933, and 7 days, 18 hours, and 49 minutes later he completed this round-the-world flight. Total time in the air was 115 hours, 36.5 minutes. The record he set on the first solo round-the-world flight remained unmatched for fourteen years.

The first Vega made its maiden flight on July 4, 1927. It was Lockheed's first high-wing monoplane. It was designed by John K. Northrop and built expressly for the 'Dole Derby', a trans-Pacific race from Calfornia to Hawaii. It was an impressive aircraft with fine aerodynamic form, smooth lines, and excellent overall performance. The all-wood cigar-shaped fuselage could accommodate five people. The one-piece wing-system was also built of wood and had no struts or cables. Power was provided by a 220 hp Wright Whirlwind radial engine. The prototype, painted bright orange and christened Golden Eagle, met a tragic

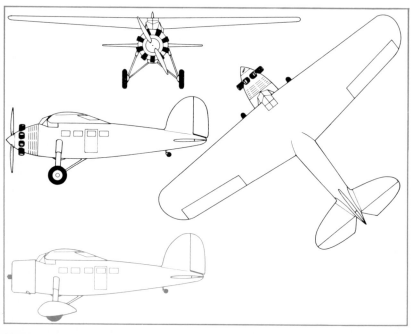

end. During the race to Hawaii, the plane disappeared over the Pacific Ocean with its two crew-members, Jack Frost and Gordon Scott.

A second Vega was prepared as a demonstration plane, and soon orders began coming in. The third Vega took part in George Hubert Wilkins' Arctic exploration flight of 1928, and another was used in Antarctica. The Vega also won races and set records. These included a new endurance record which was set in May 1929 when the plane successfully maintained its flight for thirty-seven hours without having to refuel.

Although the Vega's structure remained the same, improvements were continually made. An important improvement was the installation of the NACA cowl over the engine. It changed the appearance of the aircraft and notably increased its aerodynamic qualities. All the Vegas, from model 1 to model 5, maintained the same size, although weight, performance, and appearance changed.

Aircraft: **Lockheed Vega 1**
Manufacturer: **Lockheed Aircraft Co.**
Type: **Civil transport**
Year: **1927**
Engine: **Wright Whirlwind J-5, 9-cylinder radial, air-cooled, 220 hp**
Wingspan: **41 ft (12.50 m)**
Length: **27 ft 6 in (8.38 m)**
Height: **8 ft 6 in (2.59 m)**
Weight: **3,470 lb (1,570 kg)**
Cruising speed: **118 mph (190 km/h)**
Ceiling: **15,000 ft (4,600 m)**
Range: **900 mile (1,450 km)**
Crew: **1**
Passengers: **4**

Aircraft: **Lockheed Vega 5B**
Manufacturer: **Lockheed Aircraft Co.**
Type: **Civil transport**
Year: **1930**
Engine: **Pratt and Whitney Wasp, 9-cylinder radial, air-cooled, 450 hp**
Wingspan: **41 ft (12.50 m)**
Length: **27 ft 6 in (8.38 m)**
Height: **8 ft 6 in (2.59 m)**
Weight: **4,750 lb (2,150 kg)**
Cruising speed: **170 mph (273 km/h)**
Ceiling: **20,000 ft (6,100 m)**
Range: **680 mile (1,100 km)**
Crew: **1**
Passengers: **7**

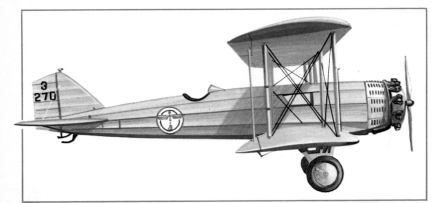

Boeing 40A

Aircraft: **Boeing 40 A**
Manufacturer: **Boeing Aircraft Co.**
Type: **Civil transport**
Year: **1927**
Engine: **Pratt and Whitney Wasp, 9-cylinder radial, air-cooled, 420 hp**
Wingspan: **44 ft 2 in (13.46 m)**
Length: **33 ft 2 in (10.10 m)**
Height: **12 ft 3 in (3.73 m)**
Weight: **6,000 lb (2,720 kg)**
Cruising speed: **105 mph (169 km/h)**
Ceiling: **14,500 ft (4,420 m)**
Range: **650 mile (1,050 km)**
Cargo: **1,200 lb (540 kg) of mail (2 passengers)**

One of the few non-military designs created by Boeing, the 1925 model 40, was to result in one of the most important aircraft in the history of air mail flying. The 1927 model 40A was built expressly for the Boeing Air Transport Corporation, an airline founded by the manufacturer to carry mail on the San Francisco–Chicago route. This biplane could carry more than half a ton of mail, as well as two passengers housed in the front part of the fuselage. What made the 40A different from its predecessor was the passenger cabin, structural improvements, and the adoption of a 420 hp Whitney and Pratt Wasp engine in place of the outmoded Liberty. The first 40A took to the air in May 1927, and twenty-three more aircraft were delivered to the transport company on June 29, just in time for the July 1 inauguration of the postal route.

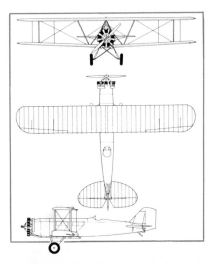

Fairchild FC-2W

Aircraft: **Fairchild FC-2W**
Manufacturer: **The Fairchild Engine &
   Airplane Co.**
Type: **Civil transport**
Year: **1927**
Engine: **Pratt and Whitney Wasp, 9-
   cylinder radial, air-cooled, 450 hp**
Wingspan: **50 ft (15.24 m)**
Length: **31 ft (9.45 m)**
Height: **9 ft (2.74 m)**
Weight: **4,600 lb (2.080 kg)**
Cruising speed: **120 mph (193 km/h)**
Ceiling: **18,000 ft (5,500 m)**
Range: **1,000 mile (1,600 km)**
Crew: **1**
Passengers: **4**

The Fairchild FC-2W was one of the
first work-horses of American civil
aviation. This tough, safe, reliable round plane would transport
anything that could fit into its fuselage. It was a mail and cargo plane,
but it was also the plane that John
Henry Mears and Captain Charles
B. D. Collyer chose for their 1928
round-the-world flight. The two men
set off in a FC-2W from New York on
June 29, 1928, and were back again on
July 22. The plane, christened City of
New York, made the trip in 23 days,
15 hours, 21 minutes, and 3 seconds.

The Fairchild FC-2W was a deri-
vation of an earlier plane, the FC-2,
but although it had the same general
form of its predecessor it was designed
expressly for transport. It was a high-
wing monoplane with mixed structure
covered in fabric. The fuselage was of
metal tube construction, while the

skeleton of the wing was wood. The
wings could be folded which made it
an easy matter to house the plane in
cold regions. The plane was powered
by a 450 hp Pratt and Whitney Wasp,
which assured high performance even
when the plane was heavily loaded.
The FC-2W was also used by the Bell
Telephone Laboratories in a series of
important scientific experiments in
radio communication.

Sikorsky S-38A

The robust and functional S-38A was the second successful amphibious plane that Igor Sikorsky, the great Russian aircraft designer, built in America. Together with other exiles he had moved to America after the Russian Revolution. In a few years his talent put him in the forefront of the American aviation industry. The first plane he built outside Russia was the 1923 S.29, a popular transport plane because of its safety and reliability.

The S-38A appeared five years later. An offshoot of his earlier amphibian plane (the S.36), it was built for Pan American Airways, which wanted a plane for its Central American flights. The plane had an unusual structure. The slender seaworthy fuselage, which could accommodate 8–10 passengers, supported the wing system with a strong simple structure. The tail was connected to the wings and to the fuselage by two connecting rods. Two Pratt and Whitney Wasp engines, of 420 hp each, were mounted above the fuselage between the upper and lower wings. A retractable undercarriage made it possible for the aircraft to come down on land as well as water. The S-38 had greater cargo capacity,

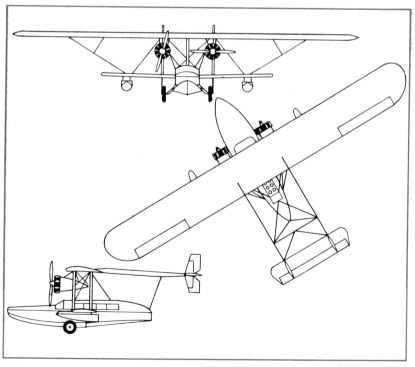

higher cruising speed, and greater range than its predecessor, which had also been ordered by Pan American for its Caribbean flights.

Sikorsky built eleven S-38s, the first of which went into service with Pan American in June 1928. Pan American put three planes in service, and the Curtiss Flying Service also bought three. One flew with the N.Y.R.B.A. line, another saw service with Western Air Express, and two saw service in the US Navy. A variety of models were produced, including the S-38B, with continuing success.

Before the S-38A, the Russian designer had created several aircraft, none of which had enjoyed particular commercial success. After the 1923 S.29, he produced the S.30, a twin-engine biplane for ten passengers. He received his first orders, however, with the S.31, a single-engine biplane for 3–4 passengers. Models S.32, S.33, and S.34 never got beyond the prototype stage. The S.35 was involved in a tragedy. The plane had been ordered

Aircraft: **Sikorsky S-38 A**
Manufacturer: **Sikorsky Aircraft**
Type: **Civil transport**
Year: **1928**
Engine: **Two Pratt and Whitney Wasp, 9-cylinder radial, air-cooled, 420 hp each**
Wingspan: **71 ft 8 in (21.84 m)**
Length: **40 ft 3 in (12.27 m)**
Height: **13 ft 10 in (4.21 m)**
Weight: **10,480 lb (4,750 kg)**
Cruising speed: **103 mph (165 km/h)**
Ceiling: **16,000 ft (4,900 m)**
Range: **600 mile (960 km)**
Crew: **2**
Passengers: **8**

by René Fonck, who hoped to win the $25,000 prize offered by Raymond Orteig for the first nonstop New York–Paris flight (the prize later won by Charles Lindbergh with his Spirit of St. Louis). The plane crashed on take-off, and the S.35 design was abandoned.

Boeing 80A

The three-engine plane proved to be the most sensible commercial formula of the second post-World War I generation, and the Boeing company began producing its 80 series in 1928. It was a series of transport planes, fifteen in all, manufactured exclusively for the airline founded by the manufacturer, the Boeing Air Transport Company. The planes marked a transition phase. The Boeing 80 and the 80A remained in service until 1933, the year they were replaced by the first new and technologically modern aircraft, the 247 model, a radically new plane that revolutionized the world of civil aviation.

The model 80 project got under way in early 1928. It was designed specifically for passenger transport on Boeing Air Transport's San Francisco–Chicago run. The prototype took to the air for the first time in August of the same year. It was a large, three engine biplane, all metal in structure and powered by three 410 hp Pratt and Whitney Wasps. The plane could accommodate twelve passengers in four rows, double seats on the left-hand side of the aircraft and single seats on the right. At the back of the cabin was a fold-up seat for the flight

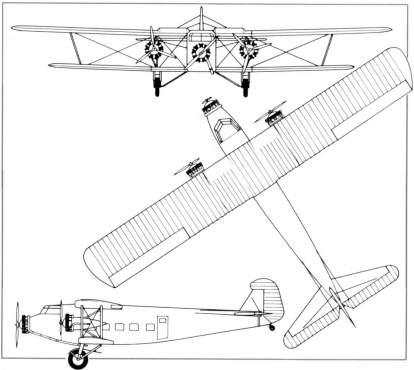

stewardess, a new idea in airline service at the time.

Only four Model 80As and 80Bs were built and put in service with the airline. Meanwhile an improved model had been designed, and most of the production was then centred on this aircraft, the 80A. While it maintained the general structure of its predecessor, it represented a decided improvement. Aside from minor structural alterations, the most important change was in the engines. With 525 hp Pratt and Whitney Hornets, the plane gave better general performance and could carry eighteen passengers.

Twelve 80As were begun, but only ten were completed to these specifications. The eleventh 80A was extensively modified and turned into an 'executive' aircraft, the Model 226. The twelfth plane had the forward part of the fuselage altered to accommodate an open cockpit. This aircraft was known as the Model 80B.

Aircraft: **Boeing 80 A**
Manufacturer: **Boeing Airplane Co.**
Type: **Civil transport**
Year: **1928**
Engine: **Three Pratt and Whitney Hornet, 9-cylinder radial, air-cooled, 525 hp each**
Wingspan: **80 ft (24.38 m)**
Length: **56 ft 6 in (17.22 m)**
Height: **15 ft 3 in (4.65 m)**
Weight: **17,500 lb (7,900 kg)**
Cruising speed: **125 mph (201 km/h)**
Ceiling: **14,000 ft (4,300 m)**
Range: **460 mile (740 km)**
Crew: **2–3**
Passengers: **18**

The ten original 80As were also modified in the course of their working career: they were equipped with two auxiliary fins and rudders. This structural modification reduced the aircraft's fuel capacity, and the planes were rechristened 80A-1. All were pulled out of service with the arrival of the Boeing 247, but one survived until World War II. It was transformed into a cargo plane, with the addition of a large loading door, and saw service in Alaska.

Fokker F.32

The largest Fokker designed and built in America was the F.32. It was 69 feet 10 inches (21.28 m) long, with a wingspan of 99 feet (30.18 m) the F.32 was a four-engine plane that could carry thirty-two passengers. The F.32 was also the last civil transport plane that Anthony Fokker built in the United States. He went to America in 1920, and nine years later the Fokker Aircraft Corporation of America was absorbed by the General Motors Corporation. The F.32 was a worthy swan song for the 'Flying Dutchman'. The five F.32s sold to Western Air Express saw several years of service on the San Francisco–Los Angeles route, where they made a name for themselves for reliability and performance.

The large four-engine plane was designed in 1929 and made its first flight in September of that year. Two airlines, Universal Air Lines and Western Air Express, were interested in the plane. Indeed, Western Air Express asked Fokker to give the plane a special designation irrespective of the factory series number and the number of passengers the aircraft could carry. Thus, what should have been the F.12 was called the F.32 strictly for publicity reasons. But the aircraft was unlucky at the beginning. Two months after its first flight,

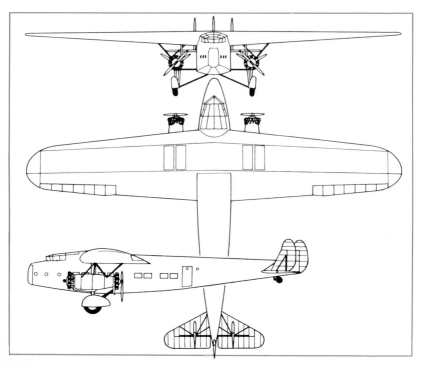

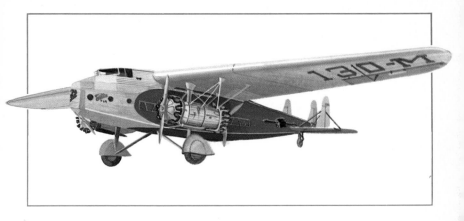

the prototype (earmarked for Universal Air Lines) crashed on take-off near Roosevelt Field, Long Island. The accident was blamed on a sudden failure of two engines. Universal cancelled its order on the grounds that the plane was unsafe. But Western Air Express still had faith in the aircraft and placed a first order for two planes. Satisfied with the aircraft, the company ordered three more.

The aircraft had the usual Fokker structure, wood and steel-tube, and was designed as a day and night transport. The first model carried thirty-two passengers, but the second one carried only sixteen. However, these sixteen passengers were accommodated in berth seats. The fuselage of the earlier version was divided into four cabins, each of which contained eight seats. Balsa wood sound-proofing of the cabins was an innovation of that time. The four engines were installed in two pairs, another innovation. The four 525 hp Pratt and Whitney Hornets were

Aircraft: **Fokker F.32**
Manufacturer: **Fokker Aircraft Co. (USA)**
Type: **Civil transport**
Year: **1929**
Engine: **Four Pratt and Whitney Hornet, 9-cylinder radial, air-cooled, 525 hp each**
Wingspan: **99 ft (30.18 m)**
Length: **69 ft 10 in (21.28 m)**
Height: **16 ft 6 in (5.03 m)**
Weight: **22,500 lb (10,200 kg)**
Cruising speed: **123 mph (198 km/h)**
Ceiling: **18,000 ft (5,500 m)**
Range: **740 mile (1,190 km)**
Crew: **2**
Passengers: **32**

housed in pairs in pods suspended from the wings, with two tractor and two pusher propellers. Although this resolved several structural and aerodynamic problems, the engines remained the plane's weak point. And a thoroughly satisfactory solution to the problem of cooling the two rear engines was never found.

The F.32 also had a brief encounter with the military. A special military transport model, the YC-20, was tested by the US Army, but it never went into production.

Travel Air 'Mystery Ship'

Aircraft: **Travel Air 'Mystery Ship'**
Manufacturer: **Travel Air**
Type: **Competition**
Year: **1929**
Engine: **Wright R-975, 9-cylinder radial, air-cooled, 400 hp**
Wingspan: **29 ft 2 in (8.89 m)**
Length: **20 ft 2 in (6.15 m)**
Height: **7 ft 9 in (2.36 m)**
Weight (empty): **1,480 lb (670 kg)**
Weight (loaded): **1,940 lb (880 kg)**
Maximum speed: **209 mph (336 km/h)**
Ceiling: **30,000 ft (9,100 m)**
Range: **525 mile (845 km)**
Crew: **1**

It was in 1929 that an aircraft propelled by a radial engine broke the 200 mph (322 km/h) barrier. The 1929 National Air Races speed contest was won by a small agile monoplane that was brought to the racing grounds shrouded in mystery and only unveiled at the moment of take-off. The Travel Air 'Mystery Ship', as it came to be known, took over the open race with an average speed of 194.86 mph (313.59 km/h) and at its fastest clocked 208.66 mph (335.79 km/h). The 'Mystery Ship' had been designed by Herbert Rawdon and Walter Burnham in the early summer of 1928, and construction was completed in August of the following year, just in time for the National Air Races. Aside from its excellent aerodynamic qualities, the secret of the plane's victory was the engine. It was a 300 hp Wright R-975 Whirlwind radial, modified to increase its power output by one third.

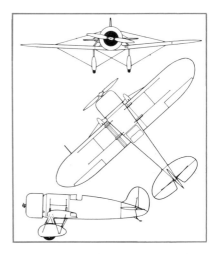

Stinson SM-1F Detroiter

The large family of Detroiters that the Stinson Aircraft Company began manufacturing in 1926 turned out to be one of the most famous series of light aircraft produced in America between the mid-1920s and the mid-1930s. Aside from giving a boost to the development of private flying, the Stinsons contributed to the formation of several small air transport companies, which relied on these tough and versatile planes for all sorts of commercial activities. Some of these small companies developed into large airlines, including Braniff Airways, which started out on June 20, 1928, with a single Stinson SM-1 and one line out of Tulsa, Oklahoma. The 1929 SM-1F was probably the most important variation of the SM-1. It was a high-wing monoplane, with the typical Stinson configuration, all-metal construction and covered in mixed materials.

Aircraft: **Stinson SM-1 F Detroiter**
Manufacturer: **Stinson Aircraft Co.**
Type: **Civil transport**
Year: **1929**
Engine: **Wright J-6, 9-cylinder radial, air-cooled, 300 hp**
Wingspan: **46 ft 8 in (14.22 m)**
Length: **32 ft 8 in (9.95 m)**
Height: **9 ft (2.74 m)**
Weight: **4,300 lb (1.950 kg)**
Cruising speed: **113 mph (182 km/h)**
Ceiling: **17,000 ft (5,200 m)**
Range: **680 mile (1,095 km)**
Crew: **1**
Passengers: **5**

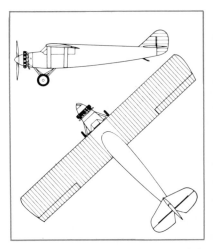

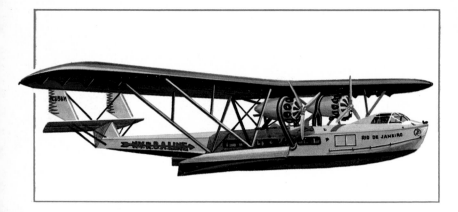

Consolidated Commodore

The New York, Rio and Buenos Aires Air Line Inc., the NYRBA, was founded in 1929 to provide air service to major South American cities. The company ran into financial difficulties and was absorbed by Pan American Airways in 1930. The ten Consolidated Commodores that had inaugurated the NYRBA routes remained in service under the Pan American banner until 1935. And Pan American ordered four new Commodores as well.

The Consolidated Commodore was a large monoplane flying boat. It had a central-hull structure and was powered by two 575 hp Pratt and Whitney engines. The skeleton was all-metal, and the skin was metal and fabric. The aircraft could carry twenty passengers about 1,000 miles (1,600 km) at a cruising speed of about 105 mph (170 km/h). The passengers were accommodated in three spacious cabins.

Aircraft: **Consolidated Commodore**
Manufacturer: **Consolidated Aircraft Co.**
Type: **Civil transport**
Year: **1929**
Engine: **Two Pratt and Whitney Hornet B, 9-cylinder radial, air-cooled, 575 hp each**
Wingspan: **100 ft (30.48 m)**
Length: **61 ft 6 in (18.74 m)**
Height: **15 ft 8 in (4.77 m)**
Weight: **17,600 lb (8,000 kg)**
Cruising speed: **108 mph (175 km/h)**
Ceiling: **10,000 ft (3,200 m)**
Range: **1,000 mile (1,600 km)**
Crew: **3**
Passengers: **18–22**

The two forward cabins normally seated eight passengers each, and the rear cabin seated four. The Commodore's inaugural flight with the NYRBA took place in July 1929. Under the Pan American banner, the planes were used on the longest nonstop over-sea route of the time, the Jamaica–Panama run, which was inaugurated in 1930. When Pan Am absorbed the NYRBA, its flights linked fifteen countries with a network of over 8,900 miles (14,400 km).

Lockheed 9D Orion

The Lockheed Orion was the first commercial aircraft to fly over 200 mph (322 km/h). It was the finest plane of the family that had begun with the 1927 Vega. The Orion made an immense contribution to the development of civil aviation. Small, developing companies took advantage of this plane's excellent performance to extend and strengthen their lines. The first company to order the Orion was Bowen Airlines in 1931, but the plane soon found a vast market. The plane truly revolutionized the world of smaller air transport companies. Thirty-five Lockheed Orions were built. It was a low-wing monoplane with a retractable undercarriage. The first Orions were powered by 400 hp Pratt and Whitney Wasp engines, while later ones were driven by 650 hp Wright Cyclone engines. In later models of the plane the passenger capacity was increased to six.

Aircraft: **Lockheed 9D Orion**
Manufacturer: **Lockheed Aircraft Co.**
Type: **Civil transport**
Year: **1931**
Engine: **Pratt and Whitney Wasp, 9-cylinder radial, air-cooled, 500 hp**
Wingspan: **42 ft 10 in (13.05 m)**
Length: **27 ft 6 in (8.38 m)**
Height: **9 ft (2.74 m)**
Weight: **5,200 lb (2,360 kg)**
Cruising speed: **191 mph (307 km/h)**
Ceiling: **23,700 ft (7,200 m)**
Range: **560 mile (900 km)**
Crew: **1**
Passengers: **4**

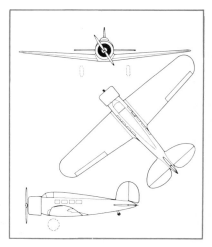

Boeing 221A Monomail

Aircraft: **Boeing 221 A Monomail**
Manufacturer: **Boeing Airplane Co.**
Type: **Civil transport**
Year: **1931**
Engine: **Pratt and Whitney Hornet B, 9-cylinder radial, air-cooled, 575 hp**
Wingspan: **59 ft 2 in (18.03 m)**
Length: **41 ft 2 in (12.55 m)**
Height: **12 ft 6 in (3.81 m)**
Weight: **8,000 lb (3,630 kg)**
Cruising speed: **137 mph (220 km/h)**
Ceiling: **14,000 ft (4,200 m)**
Range: **540 mile (870 km)**
Crew: **1**
Passengers: **8**

The Boeing Monomail represented an important advance on the road to modern civil aviation. The original version of this aircraft, which incorporated some revolutionary technical improvements, appeared in 1930 and was known as the Model 200. It was an all-metal aircraft, both skeleton and skin, with a fine aerodynamic design. The undercarriage was retractable. Its mail and cargo carrying capacity was excellent for its size, and it was a high-performance plane. It was an extremely successful plane commercially. The original Model 200 was designed exclusively for mail and cargo, but a passenger version was developed afterwards. This was the 221 which could carry six passengers along with the mail. In 1931 the 221 was further modified so that it could accommodate eight passengers. This was the final model, the 221A.

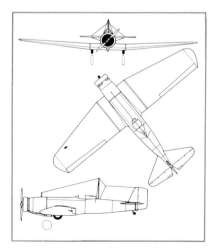

242

Stinson Trimotor SM-6000

Aircraft: **Stinson Trimotor SM-6000**
Manufacturer: **Stinson Aircraft Co.**
Type: **Civil transport**
Year: **1931**
Engine: **Three Lycoming R-680, 9-cylinder
    radial, air-cooled, 215 hp each**
Wingspan: **60 ft (18.29 m)**
Length: **32 ft 10 in (10.00 m)**
Height: **12 ft (3.81 m)**
Weight: **8,600 lb (3,900 kg)**
Cruising speed: **115 mph (185 km/h)**
Ceiling: **15,000 ft (4,570 m)**
Range: **345 mile (555 km)**
Crew: **1**
Passengers: **10**

After the great commercial success Stinson Aircraft had with its light planes, the company decided about 1930 to develop larger civil transport planes to offer the airlines. Keeping costs low was a fundamental principle of Stinson's policy, and the Trimotor SM-6000 (the first in a popular series of three-engine aircraft) was put on the market at an extremely competitive price. Stinson hoped to attract the major airlines, but instead the company attracted the smaller airlines as customers. Among these was the Ludington Line (New York–Philadelphia–Washington Airways), which bought ten SM-6000s for its New York–Washington run. The company had eleven daily flights at one-hour intervals.

The Stinson Trimotor SM-6000 was a short-range transport plane. A high-wing monoplane, with all-metal skele-

ton and fabric skin, it was powered by three 215 hp Lycoming engines. The aircraft could carry ten passengers at a cruising speed of 115 mph (185 km/h). The planes were tough and safe. Since the New York–Washington flight was relatively short and because of the frequency of flights, the pilot had to double as ticket-taker and steward on the ground.

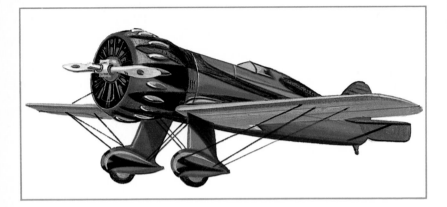

Wedell Williams

The Wedell Williams won the Thompson Trophy in 1933 and 1934 with average speeds of 237.95 mph (382.93 km/h) and 248.13 mph (399.31 km/h) respectively. The plane won the Bendix Transcontinental Air Race three times. (This prestigious trophy was offered for the first time in 1931 by Vincent Bendix, the famous inventor and industrialist.) In 1932 it won the race with an average speed of 245 mph (394.27 km/h); in 1933 it won with 214.78 mph (345.64 km/h) and in 1934 with 216.24 mph (347.99 km/h). On September 4, 1933, the plane set a world speed record for land-based planes with a speed of 305.24 mph (491.22 km/h). The Wedell Williams was one of the outstanding racing planes of the 1930s. It was designed by James Robert Wedell, a man who was passionately interested in flying. (He had lost an eye in a motorcycle accident.)

Aircraft: **Wedell Williams**
Manufacturer: **Wedell Williams**
Type: **Competition**
Year: **1931**
Engine: **Pratt and Whitney Wasp Jr., 9-cylinder radial, air-cooled, 550 hp**
Wingspan: **26 ft 2 in (7.98 m)**
Length: **21 ft 3 in (6.48 m)**
Height: **8 ft (2.44 m)**
Weight (empty): **1,500 lb (680 kg)**
Weight (loaded): **2,200 lb (1,000 kg)**
Cruising speed: —
Maximum speed: **305 mph (491 km/h)**
Ceiling: —
Range: —
Crew: **1**

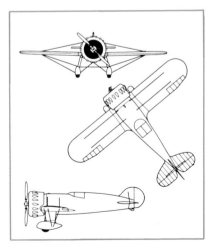

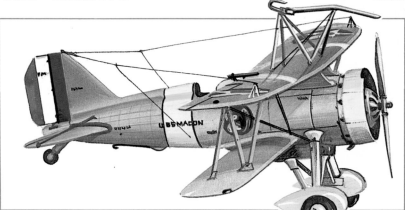

Curtiss F9C

At the beginning of the 1930s the US Navy developed the idea of 'parasite' planes in an attempt to put dirigibles to military use. The idea was to create a small plane that could be transported, launched, and recovered in flight by one of the large dirigible airships already in existence or under construction. The plane's mission was not only defence of the airship but also reconnaissance and observation. The Curtiss F9C, the Sparrowhawk, was the first aircraft expressly designed for this purpose. The dirigible had a complicated mechanism for launching and landing, as well as a five-plane hangar at the rear of the airship car. The eight T9Cs made several test flights aboard the dirigibles Akron and Macon and demonstrated the validity of the concept of parasite planes. Tests were finally abandoned after the two dirigibles were destroyed.

Aircraft: **Curtiss F9C**
Manufacturer: **Curtiss Aeroplane and Motor Co.**
Type: **Fighter**
Year: **1931**
Engine: **Wright Whirlwind, 9-cylinder radial, air-cooled, 420 hp**
Wingspan: **25 ft 6 in (7.77 m)**
Length: **20 ft 1 in (6.12 m)**
Height: **7 ft 1 in (2.16 m)**
Weight: **2,752 lb (1,248 kg)**
Maximum speed: **177 mph at 4,000 ft (284 km/h at 1,220 m)**
Ceiling: **19,200 ft (5,800 m)**
Range: **360 mile (590 km)**
Armament: **2 machine guns**

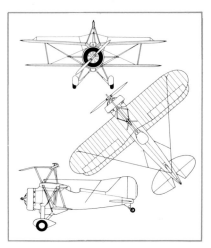

Boeing F4B-4

Boeing's most famous fighter biplane was the outcome of the company's independent attempt to design a fighter plane that could be used by both the army and the navy. This aircraft, the F4B, turned out to be one of the major combat planes of the period between the two world wars. The prototype took to the air on June 25, 1928, and the US Navy ordered twenty-seven aircraft, named F4B-1, for service on the aircraft carriers Lexington and Langley. This first model was followed by other improved versions, the F4B-2 (of which forty-one were built), the F4B-3 (twenty-one built), and the final version, the F4B-4 (of which initially, ninety-two were ordered). Delivery of the F4B-4 began in January 1932, and F4B-4s saw service until the end of 1937, when they were replaced by more modern Grumman biplanes. A total of 586 planes were built.

Aircraft: **Boeing F4B-4**
Manufacturer: **Boeing Airplane Co.**
Type: **Fighter**
Year: **1932**
Engine: **Pratt and Whitney Wasp, 9-cylinder radial, air-cooled, 550 hp**
Wingspan: **30 ft (9.14 m)**
Length: **20 ft 1 in (6.12 m)**
Height: **9 ft 4 in (2.84 m)**
Weight: **3,611 lb (1,637 kg)**
Maximum speed: **188 mph at 6,000 ft (302 km/h at 1,800 m)**
Ceiling: **26,900 ft (8,200 m)**
Range: **585 mile (940 km)**
Armament: **2 machine guns**
Crew: **1**

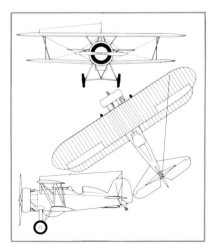

Keystone B-4A

Aircraft: **Keystone B-4A**
Manufacturer: **Keystone Aircraft Co.**
Type: **Bomber**
Year: **1932**
Engine: **Two Pratt and Whitney Hornet, 9-cylinder radial, air-cooled, 575 hp each**
Wingspan: **74 ft 9 in (22.78 m)**
Length: **48 ft 10 in (14.88 m)**
Height: **15 ft 9 in (4.80 m)**
Weight: **13,200 lb (6,000 kg)**
Maximum speed: **121 mph (195 km/h)**
Ceiling: **14,000 ft (4,300 m)**
Range: **855 mile (1,376 km)**
Armament: **3 machine guns; 2,500 lb (1,130 kg) of bombs**
Crew: **5**

In the middle of the 1920s, the Keystone Aircraft Corporation built LB type twin-engine bombers for the United States Army. The first production plane, called the LB-5, served as the basis for the entire series, which consisted of a number of variant models. New models appeared with slight structural modifications, newer engines than the 420 hp Liberty, which became outmoded, and with double rudders in some cases to improve the range of the rear gunner. Almost 250 Keystone bombers were built in all versions, including 25 B-4As. The B-4A had a single tail and was powered by 575 hp Pratt and Whitney Hornets. The B-4A had the same biplane configuration as the other models in the series, but together with the final model, the B-6A it was the best performer in the Keystone bomber family.

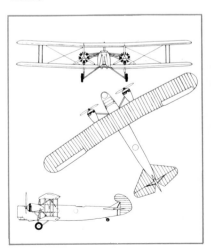

Gee Bee R-1
Gee Bee Z

The Gee Bee won the Thompson Trophy in 1931 and 1932 with average speeds of 236.24 mph (380.17 km/h) and 252.75 mph (406.74 km/h) respectively. In scarcely a year between these two victories the small squat monoplane became the most famous racing plane in America. It was not only because of its original appearance and the excitement of its victories that the Gee Bee was so famous. It was the racing plane par excellence for American racing fans in the 1930s, because it was a tough, 'mean' plane to handle. A pilot could get top performance out of the plane only if he had great ability and courage. The plane's reputation was well founded. Lowell Bayles who had won the Thompson Trophy in 1931 crashed in his Gee Bee Z on December 5 of the same year while trying to set a speed record. The Gee Bee R-1, the Thompson winner in 1932, crashed in 1933, killing Russell Boardman, the pilot. In 1933 a Gee Bee T flown by Florence Klingensmith blew up in flight. And in 1935 model R-1/R-2 crashed on take-off during the Bendix Trophy race, killing its owner-pilot, Cecil Allen.

The Gee Bee Z was designed by Robert Hall in July 1931, little more than a month before the Thompson Trophy race. The aircraft was a development of a line of racing planes built by Granville Brothers Aircraft of Springfield, Massachusetts. (Their most successful aircraft had been the Gee Bee X and Y models of 1930–31.) The Springfield Air Racing Association was set up to provide the financial backing for the Gee Bee Z.

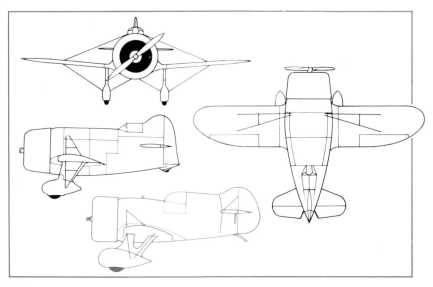

The aircraft was deliberately built to accommodate the 535 hp Pratt and Whitney Wasp Jr. engine. The fuselage was squat precisely because it had to align with a very large engine cowling (more than a yard in diameter) in the most aerodynamic way possible. And to offset the weight of the engine, the cockpit was moved back as far as possible. The plane's unusual appearance did not fail to impress both the technical experts and the general public.

After the 1931 Thompson Trophy win and the plane's fatal accident, two improved Gee Bees were built. The R-1 and the R-2 were similar in design but different in engine power. Structurally, the two planes were identical to the Gee Bee Z. They were larger aircraft with different covering and different engines. The Gee Bee R-1, piloted by Jimmy Doolittle, won the 1932 Thompson Trophy race and became perhaps the most famous of all the Gee Bees. From the wreckage of the R-1 (which crashed in 1933) and

Aircraft: **Gee Bee R-1**
Manufactuer: **Granville Brothers Aircraft**
Type: **Competition**
Year: **1932**
Engine: **Pratt and Whitney Wasp Jr., 9-cylinder radial, air-cooled, 800 hp**
Wingspan: **25 ft (7.62 m)**
Length: **17 ft 9 in (5.41 m)**
Height: **8 ft 1 in (2.47 m)**
Weight (empty): **1,840 lb (835 kg)**
Weight (loaded): **3,075 lb (1,395 kg)**
Maximum speed: **296.246 mph (476.741 km/h)**
Ceiling: —
Range: —
Crew: **1**

Aircraft: **Gee Bee Z**
Manufacturer: **Granville Brothers Aircraft**
Type: **Competition**
Year: **1931**
Engine: **Pratt and Whitney Wasp Jr., 9-cylinder radial, air-cooled, 535 hp**
Wingspan: **23 ft 6 in (7.16 m)**
Length: **15 ft 1 in (4.60 m)**
Weight (empty): **1,400 lb (835 kg)**
Weight (loaded): **2,280 lb (1,030 kg)**
Maximum speed: **286 mph (460 km/h)**
Ceiling: —
Range: **1,000 mile (1,600 km)**
Crew: **1**

the R-2 (which was damaged on take-off) a new plane was built, the R-1/R-2, and this new aircraft was destroyed in its first race.

Curtiss T-32 Condor

The Curtiss T-32 Condor was the first aeroplane in the world with sleeping births, and the last civil transport biplane produced by the American aircraft industry. A total of forty-five T-32s were built and saw service with Eastern Air Transport and with American Airways. When a new generation of airliners began to make their appearance, including the Boeing 247, the aircraft found employment outside the United States.

The Condor T-32 had been preceded by the Model 18, a plane developed in 1929 alongside the Fokker F.32. The first Condor, however, was developed from a military aircraft, the Curtiss B-2 bomber, twelve of which were constructed for the US Army Air Corps. The Model 18 kept the bomber's general structure of steel tubes with fabric covering as well as the earlier plane's engines, a pair of 600 hp, liquid-cooled Curtiss Conquerors. The civil aircraft also maintained the bomber's biplane configuration with double rudders. The Curtiss Model 18 could carry eighteen passengers. Six 18s were built and saw service with Transcontinental Air Transport (TAT) and Eastern Air Transport. Eastern put its Condors in service on December 10, 1930, and in a few months' time had extended its service to the major east coast cities.

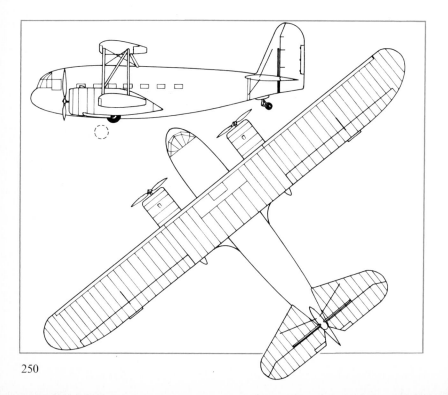

In order to expand and improve its services, Eastern Air Transport urged the Curtiss company to develop an improved Condor. This aircraft was the T-32. It was not a variation on the 18, however, but an all-new plane. It was a twin-engine biplane, like its predecessor, but its design was much more modern and advanced. The wings had a different structure and configuration, the tail was more orthodox (with a single rudder), and the fuselage was enlarged within a more aerodynamic design. The two liquid-cooled Conqueror engines were replaced by a pair of 760 hp Wright Cyclone radials, and the plane was equipped with a retractable undercarriage. Thanks to these structural improvements and the considerable increase in power, the T-32 was able to perform at a better overall level than its predecessor.

Several versions of the T-32 were produced. As a day transport, it could carry fifteen passengers; as a night flyer it could carry twelve. Passengers

Aircraft: **Curtiss T-32 Condor**
Manufacturer: **Curtiss Aeroplane and Motor Co.**
Type: **Civil transport**
Year: **1933**
Engine: **Two Wright Cyclone, 9-cylinder radial, air-cooled, 760 hp each**
Wingspan: **82 ft (24.99 m)**
Length: **48 ft 7 in (14.81 m)**
Height: **16 ft 4 in (4.98 m)**
Weight: **17,500 lb (7,900 kg)**
Cruising speed: **145 mph (233 km/h)**
Ceiling: **23,000 ft (7,000 m)**
Range: **650 mile (1,050 km)**
Crew: **2**
Passengers: **15**

on night flights had berths, and this innovation added prestige to Eastern Air Transport. But the plane's commercial success was short-lived. For both Eastern and American Airways, which employed Condors, soon found stiff competition from the new Boeing 247. The airlines had to keep pace with their rivals, and the Condors were sold abroad. In 1939 two of these Condors took part in Admiral Byrd's Antarctic expedition. Some continued in foreign service until well after World War II, and the last known operational Condor, owned by the Peruvian air force, was not scrapped until 1956.

Boeing 247

The appearance of the Boeing 247 marked the end of an era. For more than ten years the typical transport plane had been a three-engine aircraft, usually high-wing, with fixed under-carriage and generally modest performance. And this type of plane had made an incalculable contribution to the development of civil aviation – suffice it to mention such names as Fokker, Ford, Junkers, and Savoia Marchetti. Nevertheless all these planes became automatically obsolete when faced with the advanced design, technology, and high performance of the Boeing 247. The twin-engine concept and the modern structure of the new aircraft provided hitherto un-matched aerodynamic qualities and also reduced operating costs. And economy was a major consideration in the survival of airlines in the years of the great depression.

The introduction of the 247 gave an enormous impetus to American air transport. United Air Lines, which had a monopoly of the new aircraft, soon outdistanced all its competitors. To be able to compete, TWA turned to Douglas Aircraft to commission an aeroplane that could match the 247, and this led to the development of the DC-2 and DC-3, perhaps the most

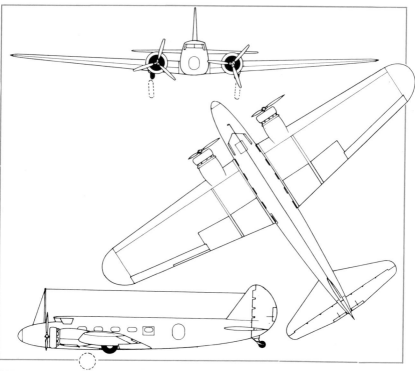

famous family of planes in the history of aviation.

The first of seventy Boeing 247s to be built made its maiden flight on February 8, 1933, and on March 30 went into service with United Air Lines. By the end of June, the company had thirty planes in service on the more important US routes. The Boeing 247 was a development of a 1931 military design, that of the B-9 bomber. The B-9 had been developed for the US Army Air Corps but never got beyond the prototype stage. The structure of the 247 was based on that of the B-9. A low-wing, all metal monoplane, the 247 had a retractable undercarriage and was powered by a pair of 550 hp Pratt and Whitney Wasp radial engines. The plane could carry ten passengers at a cruising speed of about 155 mph (250 km/h). The final variant of the type, which incorporated structural modifications and variable-pitch propellers, was called the 247D, of which thirteen were built.

Aircraft: **Boeing 247**
Manufacturer: **Boeing Airplane Co.**
Type: **Civil transport**
Year: **1933**
Engine: **Two Pratt and Whitney Wasp, 9-cylinder radial, air-cooled, 550 hp each**
Wingspan: **74 ft (22.56 m)**
Length: **51 ft 4 in (15.64 m)**
Height: **15 ft 5 in (4.69 m)**
Weight: **12,650 lb (5,740 kg)**
Cruising speed: **155 mph (250 km/h)**
Ceiling: **18,400 ft (5,600 m)**
Range: **485 mile (780 km)**
Crew: **2–3**
Passengers: **10**

On June 1, 3 the United 247 set a record for flying from one coast of America to the other: 19 hours and 45 minutes. TWA's Ford Trimotor took 26 hours and 45 minutes. The Boeing 247 also took part in the famous London–Melbourne race in October 1934. A Boeing 247D was specially prepared for the famous racing pilot Roscoe Turner. The plane arrived second in the transport category and third over-all in the race. The plane was outraced by a KLM Douglas DC-2, the plane that was first to be its toughest rival and finally its successor.

Grumman FF-1

The FF-1 was the first fighter that Grumman built for the US Navy. It was the first aircraft-carrier plane with a retractable undercarriage. The little FF-1s career was not outstanding, for the sixty planes built (27 as fighters, and 33 as reconnaissance planes) were only in service for about three years. Nevertheless, this plane marked the beginning of a long and profitable collaboration between the Grumman Aircraft Engineering Corporation and the US Navy. Over the next thirty years this collaborative effort was to result in some of the finest naval aircraft ever designed. The prototype of the FF-1 took to the air in late 1931 and was soon followed by a reconnaissance version (SF-1). The undercarriage was manually retractable; the wheels were raised almost vertically into a housing just in front of the lower wing. The FF-1 and the SF-1 saw first-line service until 1936.

Aircraft: **Grumman FF-1**
Manufacturer: **Grumman Aircraft Engineering Co.**
Type: **Fighter**
Year: **1933**
Engine: **Wright Cyclone, 9-cylinder radial, air-cooled, 700 hp**
Wingspan: **34 ft 6 in (10.51 m)**
Length: **24 ft 6 in (7.46 m)**
Height: **11 ft 1 in (3.63 m)**
Weight: **4,830 lb (2,190 kg)**
Maximum speed: **207 mph at 4,000 ft (333 km/h at 1,220 m)**
Ceiling: **21,000 ft (6,400 m)**
Range: **920 mile (1,480 km)**
Armament: **3 machine guns**
Crew: **2**

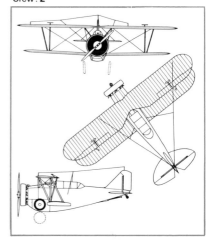

Northrop Delta

The Northrop Delta was one of the last single-engine transport planes built in the 1930s. The plane was designed specifically for TWA mail pilots, who were looking for a plane that would eliminate problems of visibility when landing at night or in bad weather. What Northrop did was to adapt an excellent design it had already developed, the Gamma model. The Gamma was an all-metal low-wing monoplane with fixed undercarriage and a 775 hp Wright Cyclone radial engine. The Delta had a more spacious fuselage for mail and passengers than the Gamma, and the cockpit was much farther forward. The Delta performed very well, and the plane had a certain commercial success. TWA bought three in 1934, and nine other aircraft were sold to private operators. The final Northrop-built plane went to the US Coast Guard, which transformed it into a VIP plane.

Aircraft: **Northrop Delta**
Manufacturer: **Northrop Co.**
Type: **Civil transport**
Year: **1934**
Engine: **Wright Cyclone, 9-cylinder radial, air-cooled, 775 hp**
Wingspan: **47 ft 9 in (14.55 m)**
Length: **33 ft 1 in (10.08 m)**
Height: **9 ft (2.74 m)**
Weight: **7,350 lb (3,330 kg)**
Cruising speed: **200 mph (320 km/h)**
Ceiling: **23,400 ft (7,130 m)**
Range: **1,650 mile (2,650 km)**
Crew: **2**
Passengers: **8**

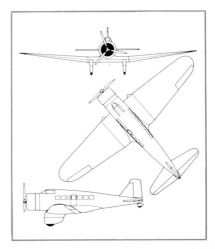

Lockheed 10A Electra

The Lockheed Electra was an elegant twin-engine monoplane. It was the last in a line of celebrated planes that had started with the 1927 Vega and achieved its greatest success with the 1931 Orion. The Electra was also the first in a new series of light commercial aircraft that was to give the world such famous planes as the Lockheed 14 and the Lockheed Lodestar.

The Electra design was developed in 1933, in direct competition with the imminent new and revolutionary Boeing 247. Design went ahead for about a year while Lockheed engineers and technicians tried to work out all the problems connected with building an all-metal aircraft (skeleton and skin). Until then Lockheed's experience had been with wood-structure or at least wood-covered planes. The Electra was Lockheed's first all-metal plane. A number of aerodynamic tests were run at the University of Michigan's wind tunnel, and it was here in March 1933 that the original tail and rudder design was shown to be unsatisfactory. New plans were prepared, and a twin-tail

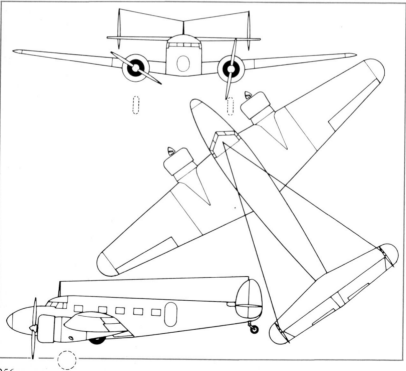

solution was adopted. This twin-tail was to remain characteristic of all the planes that were subsequently developed from the Electra.

The prototype was ready on February 23, 1934. During one of its first test flights the plane almost crashed. The landing was bad because one of the wheels of the undercarriage had not functioned properly. Nevertheless the aircraft was extremely impressive and could compete with Boeing's 247. With the same number of passengers as the Boeing, the Electra could fly faster. The Electra had greater range and a higher ceiling. And it was the lowest-priced plane on the market, $36,000. No other multi-engine commercial aircraft in America cost so little. The first company to order the new plane was Northwest Airlines; the first plane was delivered in July 1934. It was put in service on the St. Paul–Chicago run, and Northwest ordered nine more planes. Other airlines soon followed suit. In one month twenty-two aircraft were ordered. Al-

Aircraft: **Lockheed 10A Electra**
Manufacturer: **Lockheed Aircraft Co.**
Type: **Civil transport**
Year: **1934**
Engine: **Two Pratt and Whitney Wasp Jr., 9-cylinder radial, air-cooled, 420 hp each**
Wingspan: **55 ft (16.76 m)**
Length: **38 ft 7 in (11.76 m)**
Height: **10 ft (3.05 m)**
Weight: **9,000 lb (4,080 kg)**
Cruising speed: **203 mph (327 km/h)**
Ceiling: **20,000 ft (6,100 m)**
Range: **850 mile (1,370 km)**
Crew: **2**
Passengers: **12**

together 148 aircraft were manufactured. They saw service with Braniff, Pan American, and the Chicago and Southern, and were ordered by airlines in Great Britain, Australia, and New Zealand. Amelia Earhart was flying a Lockheed Electra with Lt. Commander Fred Noonan, in an around-the-world attempt, when she disappeared in the South Pacific.

Vultee V-1A

The Vultee V-1A, which was considered one of the most advanced and fastest airline planes of the early 1930s, marked the end of the era of single-engine transport. The era of the Lockheed Vega and Orion, the Northrop Delta and Gamma, and the Boeing Monomail, to name only the most famous of the planes that had contributed so much to the growth of US airlines, had come to an end. Air transport companies were concerned with economy of operation.

The Vultee V-1 was very tough, fast, and technically advanced for its time. It was an all-metal, low-wing monoplane with a retractable undercarriage. Powered by a 735 hp Wright Cyclone radial engine, the plane could carry eight passengers and two crewmembers at a cruising speed of 215 mph (346 km/h). American Airlines ordered the plane in 1934 and on September 9 put it in service on the route between the Great Lakes and

Aircraft: **Vultee V-1A**
Manufacturer: **Vultee Aircraft Inc.**
Type: **Civil transport**
Year: **1934**
Engine: **Wright Cyclone F.2, 9-cylinder radial, air-cooled, 735 hp**
Wingspan: **50 ft (15.24 m)**
Length: **37 ft (11.28 m)**
Height: **9 ft 3 in (2.81 m)**
Weight: **8,500 lb (3,850 kg)**
Cruising speed: **215 mph (346 km/h)**
Ceiling: **20,000 ft (6,100 m)**
Range: **1,000 mile (1,600 km)**
Crew: **2**
Passengers: **8**

Texas. The plane's commercial success, however, was overshadowed by the appearance of the first 'modern' liner, the Boeing 247, which revolutionized the whole concept of commercial air transport because of its low operating costs. The small, fast, luxurious airliner was a thing of the past.

The Vultee also made a name for itself in sport flying, as well as in speed and endurance trials. It achieved a certain notoriety in September 1936 by flying from New York to London and back with a load of 50,000 ping-pong balls. The Atlantic crossing took 18 hours and 38 minutes at an average speed of 210 mph (338 km/h).

Boeing P-26A

The Boeing P-26 is remembered in the history of military aviation for two reasons. It was the first monoplane fighter adopted by the US Army Air Corps and the first that was all-metal. A total of 136 Peashooters, as the P-26s were called, were built, and for almost five years they were front-line equipment in the United States, the Panama Canal Zone, and in Hawaii. The P-26 design was the joint effort of Boeing and the US Army. The prototype took to the air on March 20, 1932. After a series of tests and trial flights, the army placed an initial order for 111 aircraft; another 26 were ordered subsequently. The production model, an improved version of the prototype, was known as the P-26A. This aircraft went into service early in 1934. The last twenty-five planes were designated P-26B and P-26C. The controls of the P-26B were improved, and the P-26C had a fuel injection system.

Aircraft: **Boeing P-26 A**
Manufacturer: **Boeing Airplane Co.**
Type: **Fighter**
Year: **1934**
Engine: **Pratt and Whitney Wasp, 9-cylinder radial, air-cooled, 600 hp**
Wingspan: **27 ft 11 in (8.52 m)**
Length: **23 ft 7 in (7.18 m)**
Height: **10 ft (3.05 m)**
Weight: **2,955 lb (1,340 kg)**
Maximum speed: **234 mph at 7,500 ft (377 km/h at 2,300 m)**
Ceiling: **27,400 ft (8,300 m)**
Range: **620 mile (1,000 km)**
Armament: **2 machine guns; 110 lb (50 kg) of bombs**

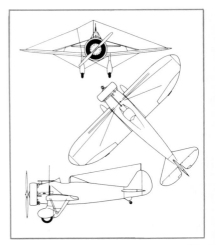

1934 – Curtiss A-12 Shrike USA

Curtiss A-12 Shrike

The Curtiss A-12 Shrike was a typical product of the aeronautical thinking of the 1930s, and, like the Boeing P-26, represented an important contribution to the development of the modern combat plane. An all-metal, low-wing monoplane was asked for by the US Army Air Corps to replace the antiquated Curtiss Falcon-type attack biplane. The new aircraft was a long time coming. After long testing and comparison with a rival project designed by General Aviation/Fokker, the Curtiss company received an order for thirteen aircraft propelled by a liquid-cooled Conqueror V-12 engine. The following year another model was developed, this one powered by a radial engine. But it was only in 1934 that the first finished planes, powered by Wright Cyclones, were delivered to their units. A total of forty-six planes were built, and they were kept in service for just a little over two years.

Aircraft: **Curtiss A-12 Shrike**
Manufacturer: **Curtiss Aeroplane and Motor Co.**
Type: **Ground attack**
Year: **1934**
Engine: **Wright Cyclone, 9-cylinder radial, air-cooled, 690 hp**
Wingspan: **44 ft (13.41 m)**
Length: **32 ft 3 in (9.83 m)**
Height: **9 ft 4 in (2.84 m)**
Weight: **5,900 lb (2,670 kg)**
Maximum speed: **175 mph (282 km/h)**
Ceiling: **15,150 ft (4,620 m)**
Endurance: **3½ hr**
Armament: **4 machine guns; 400 lb (180 kg) of bombs**
Crew: **2**

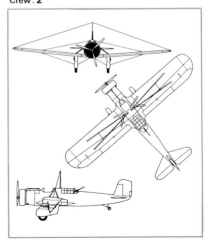

260

Douglas DC-2
Douglas DC-3

The Douglas DCs have been in service for more than forty years. A total of about eleven thousand aircraft have been built in military and civil versions. The DCs are the most important family of transport planes in the history of aviation. The DC was born as a direct competitor of the Boeing 247. With the Boeing aircraft, United Air Lines dominated American commercial aviation. TWA set out to find a competitive aircraft, and so was born the DC family. The DC-1 was immediately followed by an improved version, the DC-2. Then it was American Airways' turn. Neither the Boeing 247 nor the Douglas DC-2 was available to that company, and a third Douglas, the final version, the DC-3 was produced. This was the best known and most popular of the DCs. Not only were the planes a commercial success but they earned Douglas Aircraft great prestige in transport aircraft construction. And ever since the 1930s the initials DC (Douglas Commercial) have been applied to a long line of distinguished aircraft.

What TWA originally asked for was a three-engine, all-metal plane with cruising speed of about 150 mph (240 km/h), a range of about 1,000 miles (1,600 km), and a ceiling of 20,000 feet (6,000 m); a plane that could carry at least twelve passengers with maximum comfort. TWA ap-

proached all the leading American aircraft manufacturers, but the Douglas Aircraft Company was the first to respond. Five days after receiving TWA's letter, Douglas was in touch with the airline. And after three weeks of meetings, when a twin-engine plane was decided on, the contract was signed. The date was September 20, 1932. TWA ordered a prototype DC-1 with an option for sixty aircraft.

Ten months later, on July 1, 1933, the plane was in the air. It was an elegant, low-wing monoplane with the main features of its direct rival and several new features as well. The new plane delivered more than TWA had asked for. The DC-1 could accommodate twelve passengers in a much more spacious and comfortable cabin than the 247s. The aircraft was delivered to TWA in September, and the company immediately ordered forty of the improved model, the DC-2. (The DC-2 was already in an advanced stage of construction.)

The DC-2 first took to the air on May 11, 1934, and one week later it was flying the TWA Columbus–Pittsburgh–Newark run and outdoing the 247 for speed. On August 1, the DC-2 was put on the longest (18 hours) and most important run, New York to Los Angeles. There was nothing United could do to match the overwhelming superiority of TWA's DC-2s. United and all the other airlines had to wait for Douglas to complete TWA's order. Now TWA led the market.

The Douglas DC-2 was successful in Europe as well. The first European company to buy the DC-2 was the Dutch airline KLM. After winning the

1934 – Douglas DC-2

London–Melbourne race in October 1934, the Dutch company ordered a total of fourteen DC-2s. Other airlines in Europe followed KLM's lead. Douglas built a total of about 200 DC-2s before closing down the production line in 1936, when the DC-3 made its appearance.

The DC-3 was developed for American Airways, which was looking for a plane to replace its Curtiss Condors on night flights. The DC-3, a larger and more powerful variation of the DC-2, made its first flight on

Aircraft: **Douglas DC-2**
Manufacturer: **Douglas Aircraft Co.**
Type: **Civil transport**
Year: **1934**
Engine: **Two Wright Cyclone F.3, 9-cylinder radial, air-cooled, 710 hp each**
Wingspan: **85 ft (25.91 m)**
Length: **61 ft 11 in (18.90 m)**
Height: **16 ft 3 in (4.96 m)**
Weight: **18,000 lb (8,200 kg)**
Cruising speed: **170 mph (273 km/h)**
Ceiling: **23,700 ft (7,200 m)**
Range: **1,200 mile (1,900 km)**
Crew: **2–3**
Passengers: **14**

December 17, 1935. American Airways was the first to receive delivery of the new plane and put it in service on

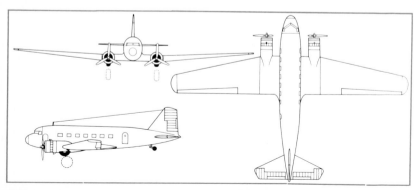

the New York–Chicago non-stop run in June 1936. The DC-3 was an enormous success. In the end there were DC-3s with every airline in America and in most of the leading European airlines as well. Before the United States entered World War II, a total of over 800 aircraft had been built and sold. More than ten times that number were built during the war. The inimitable qualities of the DC-3 made it the most versatile and practical aircraft in the history of military transport. Lord, V.C., won his award for bravery

Aircraft: **Douglas DC-3**
Manufacturer: **Douglas Aircraft Co.**
Type: **Civil transport**
Year: **1936**
Engine: **Two Pratt and Whitney, 9-cylinder radial, air-cooled, 1,200 hp each**
Wingspan: **95 ft (28.96 m)**
Length: **64 ft 6 in (19.65 m)**
Height: **16 ft 11 in (5.15 m)**
Weight: **25,200 lb (11,400 kg)**
Cruising speed: **180 mph (290 km/h)**
Ceiling: **23,200 ft (7,070 m)**
Range: **1,300 mile (2,100 km)**
Crew: **2**
Passengers: **14–32**

while flying a combat mission in a Royal Air Force transport version of the famous 'Gooney Bird'.

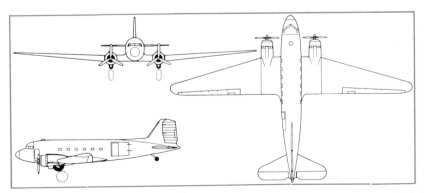

Sikorsky S-42

The Sikorsky S-42 marked the beginning of the golden age of the clippers, the large multi-engine flying boats that flew important trans-oceanic routes until the outbreak of World War II. The plane was built at the request of Pan American Airways, which needed a capacious, long-range, fast plane for its sea routes.

The direct predecessor of the S-42 was the S-40, of which Sikorsky had built three in the early 1930s for Pan American. At the time, the S-40 was the largest aircraft that had been built in the United States. It could carry forty passengers in a luxurious cabin and had a range of over 900 miles (1,500 km). Some time after the S-40 was put in service on Caribbean flights, Pan American announced that it was looking for something even more ambitious: a four-engine seaplane that could carry twelve passengers over 2,500 miles (4,000 km). Two manufacturers offered designs, Martin and Sikorsky. The Martin company offered its model M-130 (which was built after the S-42), and Pan American accepted Sikorsky's design as well, even though the S-42 had a shorter range than Pan American had asked for. The Sikorsky was ready before the Martin, and the prototype

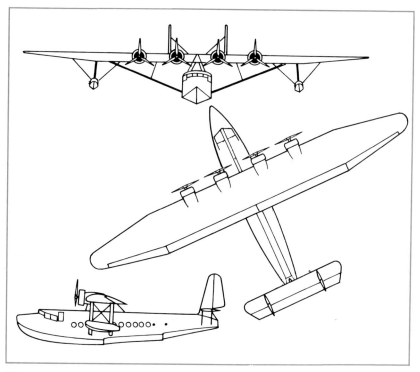

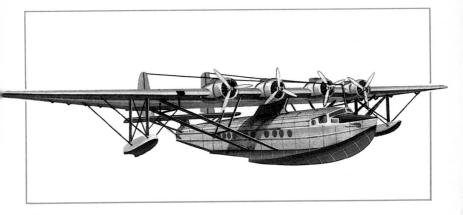

took to the air on March 29, 1934. It was a large, all-metal central-hull flying boat. A high-wing monoplane, it had auxiliary pontoons towards the end of each wingtip. Power was provided by four 700 hp Pratt and Whitney Hornet engines driving three-blade, variable-pitch, metal propellers.

During the test flights, the Sikorsky S-42 set ten altitude records with varying loads. Pan American ordered ten planes, three in the S-42B version with extra fuel tanks. The new clippers were put in service in April 1935 on the San Francisco–Hawaii line. Subsequently Pan American used the planes on flights to South America and the Far East.

The S-42s could not meet the range requirements of the company, even with fewer passengers. The standard load was thirty-two passengers plus a five-man crew. On night flights, fourteen passengers were to be accommodated in sleeping berths. A maximum of forty passengers could oe

Aircraft: **Sikorsky S-42**
Manufacturer: **Sikorsky Aircraft**
Type: **Civil transport**
Year: **1935**
Engine: **Four Pratt and Whitney Hornet, 9-cylinder radial, air-cooled, 750 hp each**
Wingspan: **114 ft 2 in (34.79 m)**
Length: **67 ft 8 in (20.62 m)**
Height: **17 ft 4 in (5.28 m)**
Weight: **38,000 lb (17,200 kg)**
Cruising speed: **170 mph (274 km/h)**
Ceiling: **16,000 ft (4,900 m)**
Range: **1,200 mile (1,900 km)**
Crew: **5**
Passengers: **32**

carried on shorter flights, but this required turning the forward baggage and cargo area into a supplementary cabin. Thus the Sikorsky S-42 was used on medium-distance flights, while the longer runs were assigned to the three M-130s that Pan American bought from Martin. The two aircraft were used together and on several occasions, the S-42s were used for surveillance over the long ocean distances that were flown by the larger M-130s.

Martin M-130
China Clipper

The three M-130s that Pan American used on its overseas luxury flights were named China Clipper, Philippine Clipper, and Hawaii Clipper. But all three planes soon came to be known collectively as the China Clippers. These aircraft made it possible for Pan American to inaugurate the first air route from America to China. The flight went from San Francisco to Manila and from there to Hong Kong.

The last leg of the flight, however, was made on planes of the China National Aviation Corporation, of which Pan American was part-owner.

The Martin M-130 China Clipper was built to the same Pan American specifications as the Sikorsky S-42. The Sikorsky could not meet Pan American's specifications for a range of 2,500 miles (4,000 km), but the M-130 did. Pan American had planned a direct route across the Pacific, from San Francisco to Manila. The flight was in five legs, San Francisco–Honolulu (2,380 miles; 3,880 km), Honolulu–Midway Island (1,360 miles; 2,200 km), Midway Island–Wake Is-

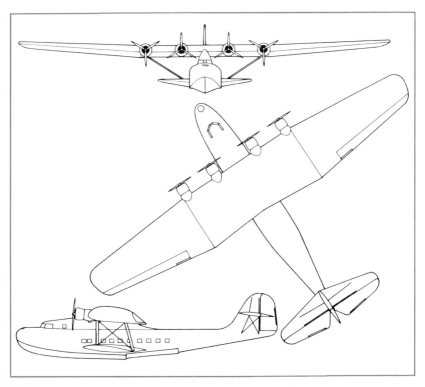

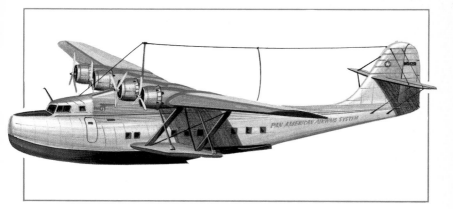

land (1,260 miles; 2,030 km), Wake
Island–Guam (1,450 miles; 2,335 km),
and Guam–Manila (2,000 miles; 3,220
km).

The China Clipper was a large, all-
metal flying boat. A high-wing plane
with a central hull, the Clipper was
powered by four 830 hp Pratt and
Whitney Twin Wasp engines. Fully
loaded, the plane weighed about
twenty-four tons, and its cruising
speed was 165 mph (270 km/h). Its
range was increased to 3,200 miles
(5,150 km) because of the special installation of fuel tanks in the two
auxiliary pontoons. Thus they did not
intrude on passenger or cargo space.
The pontoon tanks held about 1,700
gallons (7,700 l) of fuel, a little less
than half the total fuel load. The plane
could carry from twelve passengers on
the longest distances to a maximum of
forty-eight on short runs. On night
flights, eighteen persons could be accommodated in sleeping berths in the
three main cabins.

Tests of the China Clipper began

Aircraft: **Martin M-130 China Clipper**
Manufacturer: **Glenn L. Martin Co.**
Type: **Civil transport**
Year: **1935**
Engine: **Four Pratt and Whitney Twin
　Wasp, 14-cylinder radial, air-cooled,
　830 hp each**
Wingspan: **130 ft 3 in (39.70 m)**
Length: **90 ft 7 in (27.60 m)**
Height: **24 ft 7 in (7.49 m)**
Weight: **52,000 lb (23,600 kg)**
Cruising speed: **165 mph (266 km/h)**
Ceiling: **17,000 ft (5,200 m)**
Range: **3,200 mile (5,150 km)**
Crew: **5**
Passengers: **48**

toward the end of 1935, and between
November 22 and December 6 of the
same year, the plane made its first
commercial round-trip Pacific crossing. Scheduled flights began on October 21, 1936. The flight took five
days with sixty hours in the air. By
1940 the two surviving aircraft had
flown a total of 10,000 hours. (The
Hawaii Clipper crashed at sea.) In
1942 the two clippers were turned over
to the United States Navy and saw
service as military transport planes.

Martin B-10B

The Martin B-10, one of the last bombers of the period between the two World Wars, incorporated the best technical developments achieved in the 1930s in military aviation. But its operational life was fairly short. The development of more modern bombers, including the Boeing B-17, made it immediately out-of-date. Though it was not successful in its career with the US Army Air Corps, the Martin B-10 was successful abroad. A total of about one hundred and ninety aircraft, in various models, were sold in South America (Argentina), the Far East (China, Dutch East Indies, and Siam), and Europe (Turkey). One B-10 was sold to Russia.

The B-10 was a development of its immediate predecessor, the Boeing B-9, which was the first all-metal monoplane bomber in the United States. The B-10 was also an all-metal midwing monoplane with retractable undercarriage and two radial engines, but it was the first bomber to carry bombs inside the fuselage and the first to have a machine-gun turret. The prototype, factory Model 123, was developed privately by the Glenn L.

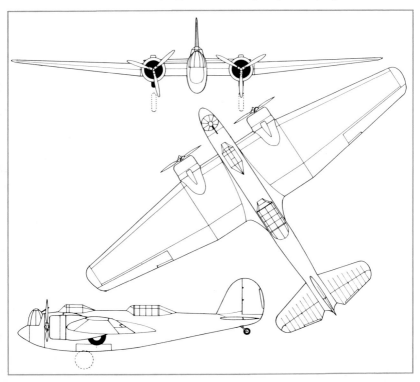

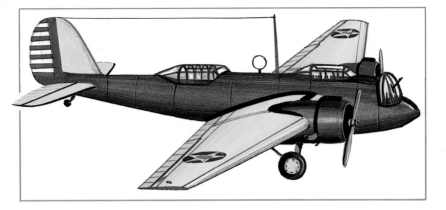

Martin Co. in hopes of offering it to
the US Army Air Force as a bomber
that could compete with those already
in service. The manufacturer's strong
point was the bomber's maximum
speed, 197 mph (317 km/h), faster
than the fighters of the time.

In March 1932 the prototype was
delivered to the military authorities
for testing. The manufacturer was not
surprised that the new bomber's speed
impressed the authorities. The Martin
company received a first order for
forty-eight planes in 1933. Variant
models were requested, with different
engines and different fuel capacities.
The first deliveries to the US Army Air
Corps were made in the summer of
1934, and at the beginning of the
following years units in the United
States, the Panama Canal Zone, and
Hawaii began to be equipped with the
new bomber.

Delivery of the largest single variant
(103 aircraft), the B-10B, began in
1935. The B-10B incorporated several
minor modifications, and all the air-

Aircraft: **Martin B-10B**
Manufacturer: **Glenn L. Martin Co.**
Type: **Bomber**
Year: **1935**
Engine: **Two Wright Cyclone, 9-cylinder
   radial, air-cooled, 775 hp each**
Wingspan: **70 ft 6 in (21.49 m)**
Length: **44 ft 9 in (13.63 m)**
Height: **11 ft 5 in (3.48 m)**
Weight: **16,400 lb (7,430 kg)**
Maximum speed: **213 mph (343 km/h)**
Ceiling: **24,200 ft (7,300 m)**
Range: **600 mile (960 km)**
Armament: **3 machine guns; 2,260 lb
   (1,025 kg) of bombs**
Crew: **4**

craft of this series were equipped with
Wright Cyclone engines. The planes
were kept in service until the Douglas
B-18 and the Boeing B-17 appeared on
the scene. Then Martin B-10s were
sold on the export market with such
success that the production line was
kept open until 1939. Martin bombers
also saw combat duty. Chinese Mar-
tins flew war missions against the
Japanese.

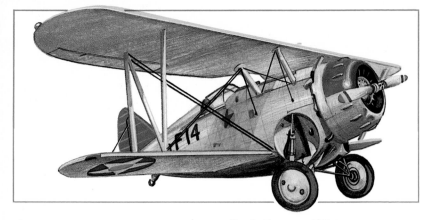

Grumman F3F-1

After its success with the FF-1, the Grumman company received another contract from the US Navy for a more modern carrier-borne fighter. This was the F2F-1, fifty-four of which were built. An improved model was developed in March 1935, the F3F-1. Two prototypes of this new aircraft crashed, but the third performed brilliantly in test flights, and the navy ordered fifty-four planes. The next version was equipped with a more powerful engine. This plane was considered the finest single-seat fighter in the navy, and eighty-one planes were constructed. Of the final version, the F3F-3, twenty-seven aircraft were built. F3Fs were in service until the outbreak of World War II and were the last fighter biplanes built for the navy. Grumman subsequently built its first carrier-borne monoplane fighter for the navy, the F4F Wildcat, which found its place in history during the first two years of the war.

Aircraft: **Grumman F3F-1**
Manufacturer: **Grumman Aircraft Engineering Co.**
Type: **Fighter**
Year: **1935**
Engine: **Pratt and Whitney Twin Wasp Jr., 14-cylinder radial, air-cooled, 700 hp**
Wingspan: **32 ft (9.75 m)**
Length: **23 ft 3 in (7.08 m)**
Height: **9 ft 4 in (2.84 m)**
Weight: **4,121 lb (1,869 kg)**
Maximum speed: **231 mph (372 km/h)**
Ceiling: **28,500 ft (8,600 m)**
Range: **530 mile (850 km)**
Armament: **2 machine guns; 110 lb (50 kg) of bombs**

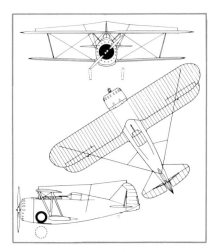

1922 Army Curtiss R-6. Wingspan: 18 ft 11 in (5.76 m). Length: 18 ft 8 in (5.68 m). Maximum speed: 231 mph (371 km/h). Engine: 460 hp Curtiss CD. This elegant biplane was considered one of the most handsome planes ever built. It was designed by Curtiss for the US Army Air Service and made its first appearance at the Pulitzer Trophy races in 1922. The R-6 won the race with an average speed of 205.9 mph (331.4 km/h).

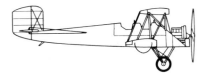

1924 Consolidated PT-1. Wingspan: 34 ft 9 in (10.59 m). Length: 27 ft 8 in (8.43 m). Maximum speed: 103 mph (166 km/h). Engine 180 hp Wright E. This was the US Army Air Service's first basic trainer. Hundreds of these small tough planes were manufactured in a variety of models that differed from each other chiefly in engine type. The US Navy also ordered a variant model with floats as well as wheels.

1924 Verville-Sperry R-3. Wingspan: 30 ft 2 in (9.19 m). Length: 23 ft 2 in (7.06 m). Maximum speed: 220 mph (354 km/h). Engine: 50 hp Curtiss CD-12. This extremely aerodynamic monoplane took part in two Pulitzer Trophy races before winning the 1924 competition at an average speed of 216 mph (347.6 km/h), with H. H. Mills at the controls. The engine was modified for the race, along with the cooling system, which was installed on the wings.

1928 Curtiss P-6 Hawk. Wingspan: 31 ft 6 in (9.60 m). Length: 23 ft 2 in (7.06 m). Maximum speed: 198 mph (319 km/h). Engine: 600 hp Curtiss Conqueror. This plane was derived from the 1924 Curtiss P-1, the US Army Air Services first pursuit plane. The plane performed exceptionally well in several races in 1928, reaching a speed of 201 mph (323 km/h). A total of seventy planes were constructed over the next few years.

1931 Laird Super Solution. Wingspan: 21 ft (6.40 m). Length: 17 ft 9 in (5.41 m). Maximum speed: 241 mph (387 km/h). Engine: 525 hp Pratt and Whitney Jr. This small biplane racer, designed by Matty Laird, beat two Lockheed Orions in their first race. It was the 1931 competition in the Bendix Trophy Series, and James Doolittle flew the Super Solution from Burbank, California, to Cleveland, Ohio, in 9 hours, 10 minutes, and 21 seconds at an average speed of 223.04 mph (358.93 km/h).

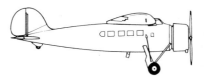

1932 Consolidated Fleetster. Wingspan: 45 ft (13.72 m). Length: 31 ft 9 in (9.68 m). Maximum speed: 169 mph (271 km/h). Engine: 575 hp Pratt and Whitney Hornet B. This was one of the most popular light civil aircraft before the appearance of the more modern Boeing 247 and the DC-2. The Fleetster saw service in various airlines on short-range flights.

National Civil Aviation Registration Letters

Argentina	LV,LQ		Hungary	HA
Australia	VH		Iceland	TF
Austria	OE		Iran	EP
Belgium	OO		Iraq	YI
Bolivia	CP		Ireland	EI. EJ
Brasil	PP,PT		Italy	I
Bulgaria	LZ		Japan	JA
Canada	CF		Liberia	EL
Chile	CC		Liechtenstein	HB
China	B		Luxembourg	LX
Colombia	HK		Mexico	XA, XB,
Costa Rica	TI		New Zealand	ZK, ZL, ZM
Cuba	CU		Nicaragua	AN
Czechoslovakia	OK		Norway	LN
Denmark	OY		Panama	HP
Dominican Rep.	HI		Paraguay	ZP
Ecuador	HC		Peru	OB
El Salvador	YS		Poland	SP
Finland	OH		Portugal	CS,CR
France	F		Romania	YR
Germany	D		Soviet Union	URSS
Great Britain	G		Spain	EC
Colonies and			Sweden	SE
protectorates	VP, VH, VR		Switzerland	HB
Greece	SX		Turkey	TC
Guatemala	TG		United States	
Haiti	HH		of America	N
Holland	PH		Uruguay	CX
Honduras	HR		Venezuela	YV

Union of Soviet Socialist Republics

In the years following World War I the Russian aircraft industry was behind the rest of Europe. The revolution and crucial domestic problems all but halted the development of Russian aviation. Even during World War I Russia had built foreign aircraft under licence, French planes in particular. The few original designs were not competitive. Furthermore Russia was totally dependent on imported engines.

Towards the end of 1918 a new organization was established, the Central Aerohydrodynamic Institute (TsAGI) to develop Russian aircraft and end the country's dependence on foreign industries. The Central Institute was set up for the design and development of aircraft and engines, to carry out aerodynamic and hydrodynamic research, and to coordinate in one body the work of engineers and technicians. A decade later the Central Institute had reached the level of, and in some cases outstripped, comparable organizations in other countries. The Russian government gave strong backing to the development of aviation, and the whole sector was dramatically overhauled in 1920. The five existing aircraft plants were reorganized and expanded, all available personnel was mobilized, and expansion policies were initiated.

In this general atmosphere some highly talented designers came to the fore. These were the years in which some world-famous names began to appear, Tupolev, Polikarpov, Grigorovich, Yakovlev, and others. Although military aviation was emphasized, there was also distinct progress in civil aviation. It would have been impossible to ignore the great tradition established by Igor Sikorsky, which had put Russia in the vanguard of world aviation in 1913. Tupolev, in particular, felt Sikorsky's influence, and several of Tupolev's designs for transport planes had a decisive influence on Russian civil aviation. Russian civil aviation developed slowly. The first civil air line was the Deruluft, a collaborative effort with Germany that started in 1921. The Dobrolet company appeared in 1924, the first all-Russian air line. Both companies concentrated on domestic routes. Finally the Aeroflot company was founded, and it is still the official Russian air line.

Tupolev ANT-14

Fifteen years after the first 'giant' in aviation history (the Sikorsky Ilya Mourometz), the Soviet Union considered the formula again with its 'monster' Tupolev ANT-14. This plane was a worthy successor to the grandfather of all the jumbos. The ANT-14 wingspan was over 132 feet (40 m), and, powered by five engines, it could carry forty-two people at a cruising speed of 121 mph (195 km/h).

The plane was designed by Andrei Nikolaevich Tupolev, who became head designer of the Russian Central Aerohydrodynamic Institute (TsAGI) in 1922. He had helped organize the Institute in 1918, together with N. Zhukovski, with the aim of developing aeronautical research in Russia after the revolution. Tupolev's first project, and the first plane built by the Institute, was a small, low-wing monoplane, a single-seat plane powered by a 45 hp Anzani engine. In 1923 Tupolev designed the ANT-2, a small all-metal transport plane. In 1925 he designed a two-seater biplane for civil and military use, the ANT-3, and in the same year he designed his first multi-engine aircraft, the ANT-4. In 1928 he designed the ANT-5, his first fighter plane.

The immediate predecessor of the ANT-14 was the ANT-9, a multi-

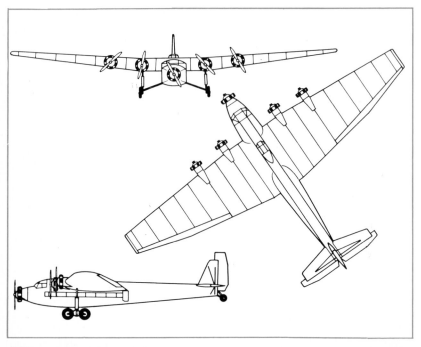

engine plane that Tupolev developed between 1928 and 1929. By now an old hand at all-metal aircraft construction, Tupolev built a large, high-wing, three-engine monoplane, propelled by three 230 hp Gnome–Rhône Titan radials, that could carry eight passengers. The ANT-9 followed the pattern of the best similar planes then being produced abroad. It was a high-performance plane, and its ability to land and take off on primitive airstrips made it ideal for flights to wilder areas of the Soviet Union. The plane was used extensively in propaganda flights, and a special squadron for these activities was named after the Russian writer Maxim Gorki.

In 1929 Tupolev designed a larger version of the ANT-9, the 14. This five-engine, all-metal, high-wing monoplane was powered by five M-22 radial engines (copies of the Gnome–Rhône Jupiter). It could carry thirty-six passengers and six crew-members over long distances. With its range of 740 miles (1,200 km)

Aircraft: **Tupolev ANT-14**
Manufacturer: **State Industries**
Type: **Civil transport**
Year: **1931**
Engine: **Five M-22 (Gnome-Rhône Jupiter), 9-cylinder radial, air-cooled, 480 hp each**
Wingspan: **132 ft 7 in (40.40 m)**
Length: **86 ft 11 in (26.48 m)**
Height: **17 ft 9 in (5.40 m)**
Weight: **37,800 lb (17,100 kg)**
Cruising speed: **121 mph (195 km/h)**
Ceiling: **13,800 ft (4,220 m)**
Range: **740 mile (1,200 km)**
Crew: **6**
Passengers: **36**

it could fly from Moscow to Vladivostock. The prototype made its maiden flight on August 14, 1931, and limited production was begun. One ANT-14 flew the Moscow–Berlin route for a while, and another, the Pravda, joined the Maxim Gorki Squadron. Equipped with skis, the plane was also used in scientific explorations in Siberia and the Arctic.

Polikarpov R-5

One of the more notable all-round planes of the period between the two World Wars was the Polikarpov R-5. It could outdo all its contemporaries, including the famous Fokker C V. A total of six thousand aircraft were built in many military and civil variations. The R-5 prototype was built in 1928 by a team led by Nikolai N. Polikarpov. It was a two-seat biplane, built in wood and metal and powered by a 680 hp M-17 engine, 12-cylinder V. The plane carried two machine guns in the military version, a forward gun, which was fixed and synchronized, and the other on an adjustable mount. The plane could carry a maximum of 530 pounds (240 kg) of bombs. Beginning in 1931 many Soviet air units were equipped with Polikarpov R-5s. In civil aviation, the plane saw light transport service with Aeroflot, and was also employed as an ambulance plane.

Aircraft: **Polikarpov R-5**
Manufacturer: **State Industries**
Type: **Reconnaissance**
Year: **1931**
Engine: **M-17, 12-cylinder V, liquid-cooled, 680 hp**
Wingspan: **50 ft 10 in (15.50 m)**
Length: **34 ft 8 in (10.55 m)**
Height: **10 ft 8 in (3.25 m)**
Weight: **6,515 lb (2,955 kg)**
Maximum speed: **142 mph at 9,800 ft (228 km/h at 3,000 m)**
Ceiling: **21,000 ft (6,400 m)**
Range: **500 mile (800 km)**
Armament: **2 machine guns; 530 lb (240 kg) of bombs**
Crew: **2**

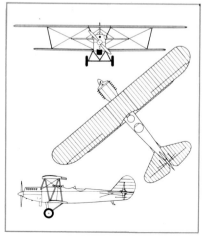

276

Tupolev ANT-9/M-17

The ANT-9/M-17 was the last variation on the successful 1929 model, and it played an important part in the history of Soviet air transport. For several years it was the basic plane of the Dobrolet and Deruluft airlines. (Dobrolet was the first all-Soviet airline, founded in 1924; while Deruluft was a joint Russo–German company, founded on November 11, 1921.) The plane was subsequently used by Aeroflot. The plane's structure was identical with that of its predecessor. An all-metal, high-wing monoplane, covered in corrugated duralumin, the plane could carry nine passengers and two crew-members. The fundamental difference from its predecessor was the engines. The three 230 hp Gnome–Rhône radials of the ANT-9 were replaced by a pair of 680 hp M-17 engines, 12-cylinder V, liquid-cooled. The two engines generated considerably more power, and the elim-

Aircraft: **Tupolev ANT-9/M-17**
Manufacturer: **State Industries**
Type: **Civil transport**
Year: **1932**
Engine: **Two M-17, 12-cylinder V, liquid-cooled, 680 hp each**
Wingspan: **77 ft 10 in (23.73 m)**
Length: **55 ft 9 in (17.00 m)**
Height: **16 ft 5 in (5.00 m)**
Weight: **13,600 lb (6,200 kg)**
Cruising speed: **108 mph (175 km/h)**
Ceiling: **14,700 ft (4,500 m)**
Range: **620 mile (1,000 km)**
Crew: **2**
Passengers: **9**

ination of the third, central engine made the plane more aerodynamic and thus improved its performance. Like the ANT-9, the M-17 variation was used extensively on the Moscow–Berlin route. Some seventy planes were built in all. One of the ANT-9/M-17s was used for propaganda flights by the Maxim Gorki squadron.

Kalinin K-7

The tendency of Russian designers to project ever more gigantic aeroplanes is well illustrated by the 1933 Kalinin K-7, an enormous bomber with a most unusual structure that was built experimentally by a team headed by K. Alexeivich Kalinin. The plane was powered by six engines that generated a total of 4,500 hp. The wingspan was 173 ft 10 inches (53 m), and its loaded weight was some 40 tons, including about 9 tons of bombs. The plane carried an eleven-man crew, and its armament consisted of three 20-mm cannons and six machine-guns. Despite the originality of some of its features, the plane never got beyond the prototype stage. The prototype crashed because of structural weaknesses, and the whole project was abandoned.

The Kalinin K-7 was a monoplane with a twin tail. The enormous wing-system was eliptical in plan and housed the six 750 hp M-34F engines. The undercarriage was distinctive. The wheels were set in two large fairings that also housed the bomb load. The guns were installed at the nose, at the tail, and in the under-carriage fairings.

The plane made its first flight on

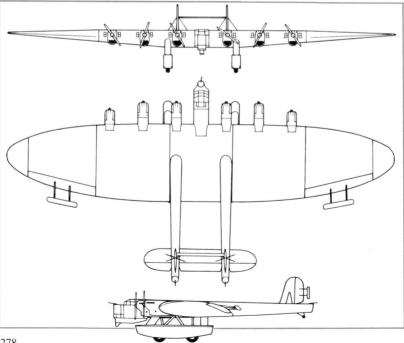

August 11, 1933, and went through a long series of tests. On paper the plane should have had a maximum speed of 140 mph (225 km/h), a range of 600 miles (1,000 km) fully loaded, and a ceiling of 13,000 feet (4,000 m). These calculations were never confirmed in flight, because the plane crashed on November 21 and was totally destroyed. Investigations revealed that flutter in one of the two rudders had caused vibration of the whole tail assembly, and the structural failure of the whole tail boom.

Before abandoning the project altogether, the designers of the K-7 had two offers. One was to build two more bomber prototypes with the weak structural elements redesigned and strengthened. The other was to develop a passenger version of the plane. This plane was to have had a passenger capacity of one hundred and twenty-eight on daylight flights and sixty-four berthed passengers on night flights. But in 1935 the Kalinin team was broken up and the K-7 programme

Aircraft: **Kalinin K-7**
Manufacturer: **State Industries**
Type: **Heavy bomber**
Year: **1933**
Engine: **Six M-34F, 12-cylinder V, liquid-cooled, 750 hp each**
Wingspan: **173 ft 10 in (53.00 m)**
Length: **91 ft 10 in (28.00 m)**
Height: **—**
Weight: **83,700 lb (38,000 kg)**
Maximum speed: **140 mph (225 km/h)**
Ceiling: **13,000 ft (4,000 m)**
Range: **620 mile (1,000 km)**
Armament: **3 cannons (20 mm); 6 machine guns; 19,800 lb (9,000 kg) of bombs**
Crew: **11**

declared obsolete. The failure of the K-7 programme, however, did not discourage other designers from attempting larger and larger planes. A contemporary of the Kalinin K-7 was that other giant, the Tupolev ANT-20, which was considered the largest land plane in the world when it was built.

Polikarpov I-15

The Polikarpov I-15 fighters, which first appeared in 1933, saw combat in two wars and remained in service for about ten years. These fast and manoeuvrable biplanes first saw action in the Spanish Civil War, and later variations, with more powerful engines, battled the Japanese on the Manchurian and Mongolian borders. Many I-15s remained in service after the outbreak of World War II, albeit not on front-line duty.

Nikolai Polikarpov, one of the most brilliant Russian designers, specialized at an early age in combat aircraft. In 1923 he had already designed the first Soviet fighter, the I-1, which went into production. Sub-sequently, he designed the I-2 in 1924 and the I-3 in 1928. Then he built the I-5, the immediate predecessor of the I-15. The I-5 made its first flight in April 1930, and its performance was so fine that a large number were immediately ordered. The I-5 was a fast and manoeuvrable biplane powered by a 450 hp M-22 engine. What was most striking, however, was the plane's armament: four forward machine guns. It was the heaviest armed fighter of its time. A total of eight hundred Polikarpov I-5s were built.

Early in 1933 Nikolai Polikarpov began work on a more advanced model of this plane, the I-15. The new plane had a modified upper wing-

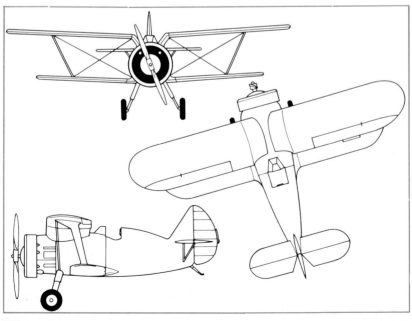

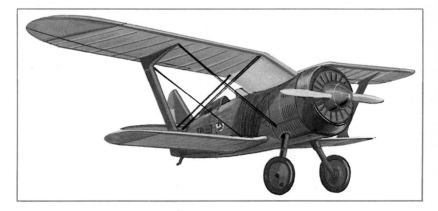

system, the struts and undercarriage were highly simplified, and the plane was powered by a larger engine: the 700 hp M-25 was a Russian version of the American Wright Cyclone. The I-15 had the same armament as its predecessor: four fixed synchronized machine guns that fired through the propeller disc. The prototype first took to the air in October 1933, and production began early in 1934. Deliveries began late in 1934. The plane was the equal of, if not superior to, the best contemporary planes of its class. For example, it outclassed the American Boeing P-26A and the Italian Fiat CR.32 in its speed of climb to high altitude and in its manoeuvrability, although its maximum speed was somewhat slower than either of these two aircraft.

The plane saw combat during the Spanish Civil War. The first twenty-five I-15s reached Spain in November 1936. A total of five hundred saw service on the Republican side. A variant model of the I-15 (the I-15bis)

Aircraft: **Polikarpov I-15**
Manufacturer: **State Industries**
Type: **Fighter**
Year: **1934**
Engine: **M-25 (Wright Cyclone), 9-cylinder radial, air-cooled, 700 hp**
Wingspan: **32 ft (9.75 m)**
Length: **20 ft (6.10 m)**
Height: **9 ft 7 in (2.92 m)**
Weight: **3,000 lb (1,370 kg)**
Maximum speed: **229 mph (368 km/h)**
Ceiling: **32,100 ft (9,800 m)**
Range: **310 mile (500 km)**
Armament: **4 machine guns**
Crew: **1**

was produced with different armament, different fuel capacity, and a modified upper-wing. Another model, the I-15ter, was built in 1938. It had the original wing-system, a 1,000 hp engine, and fully retractable undercarriage. Production of this model continued until 1940, and the later I-15ters were given a still more powerful engine, the 1,100 hp M-63.

Tupolev ANT-20
Maxim Gorki

When the Tupolev ANT-20 first appeared, in the spring of 1934, it was the largest land-based plane in the world. Its story is quite unusual in the annals of aviation history. In 1932 the Union of Soviet Writers and Publishers (YURGAZ) ordered a plane to celebrate the anniversary of Maxim Gorki's literary debut. A squadron bearing the writer's name was also planned for propaganda purposes. Six million roubles were collected by public subscription. The Tupolev ANT-20 met all the requirements. Illuminated writings and symbols were displayed under the wings, and the fuselage and wings accommodated a small printing plant, a photographic studio, a cinema, and a radio transmitting station. The plane survived for only a year. On May 18, 1935, the Maxim Gorki collided in the air with a I-4 fighter and crashed.

Tupolev began building the giant aircraft in March 1933, with an entire factory at his disposal. Eight hundred people were involved, including technicians, engineers, and workers. It was a long and painstaking job. The plane's unusual dimensions made preliminary tests of single structural elements mandatory. But considering all the problems, the Maxim Gorki was built in good time. By the end of 1933 the aircraft was all but finished. All that was left was the final assembly, which was carried out at Moscow's Central Airport in April 1934. The plane's first flight was on May 19.

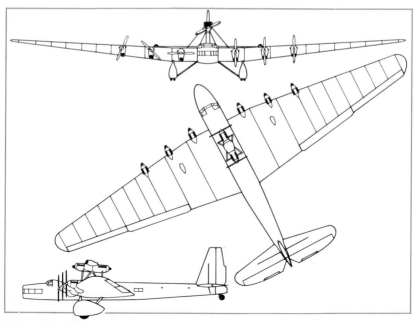

The Maxim Gorki was an all-metal monoplane covered in corrugated duralumin. Tupolev had long followed the German Junkers' example in this. The plane was powered by eight 12-cylinder V, liquid-cooled, 900 hp AM-34 RN engines. Six engines were mounted on the front of the wings and two were mounted over the centre of the fuselage. The plane carried a standard crew of twenty and between forty-three and seventy-six passengers. On occasion, eighty passengers were carried, but the crew was then reduced to eight. The wings housed the small printing plant, the photographic laboratory, crew quarters, and rest rooms. The fuselage carried the radio station and telephone office as well as all the auxiliary apparatus needed for the electrical generators.

After the Maxim Gorki crashed, with 49 victims, a subscription was begun to build three other planes. Tupolev modified his design and produced the ANT-20bis, which was

Aircraft: **Tupolev ANT-20 Maxim Gorki**
Manufacturer: **State Industries**
Type: **Civil transport**
Year: **1934**
Engine: **Eight AM-34 RN, 12-cylinder V, liquid-cooled, 900 hp each**
Wingspan: **206 ft 8 in (63.00 m)**
Length: **106 ft 6 in (32.47 m)**
Height: **36 ft 11 in (11.25 m)**
Weight: **92,600 lb (42,000 kg)**
Cruising speed: **137 mph (220 km/h)**
Ceiling: **19,600 ft (6,000 m)**
Range: **1,200 mile (2,000 km)**
Crew: **8**
Passengers: **43**

powered by six 1,100 hp M-100 engines. This aircraft could carry sixty-four passengers, and one was employed by Aeroflot from May 1940 on its Moscow–Mineralnie Vodi route. According to Russian sources, sixteen ANT-20bis were built, eight of which were still flying in 1945.

Tupolev ANT-25

Russia made an important contribution to sporting aviation in the 1930s. The ocean crossings, the long-distance flights, and the air expeditions that had stimulated Western countries aroused Russian interest as well. And so was born the Tupolev ANT-25, an aircraft designed expressly for record flying. The technical characteristics of this new plane were to influence future Soviet aircraft construction.

As soon as the aircraft was built, it began breaking records. On September 12, 1934, it broke the world closed-circuit distance record, flying 7,712 miles (12,411 km) in 75 hours and 2 minutes. In 1936 it made a trans-polar flight of 5,799 miles (9,332 km) in 56 hours and 20 minutes, crossing areas never explored by man. The first non-stop flight from Moscow to Portland, Oregon, was completed on June 20, 1937, a distance of 5,299 miles (8,529 km) flown in 63 hours and 25 minutes. And on July 12 of the same year, a new world record was established for straight distance flying: the ANT-25 flew from Moscow to San Jacinto, California, in 62 hours and 17 minutes, a distance of 6,260 miles (10,075 km).

The ANT-25 project was developed at Stalin's direct order in 1933. Tupolev was to design a long-range aircraft that would be able to set records for its class. Tupolev set to work with Sukhoi, Kondorsky, Beliaev, and Pogoski. They developed a thoroughly original aircraft, even though the configuration had already been used in the

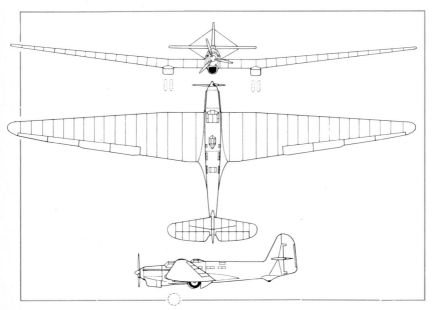

construction of French and British planes. The most striking feature of the ANT-25 was its wing-system. The wingspan was almost three times the length of the aircraft. The increased wingspan made it possible for the aircraft to carry larger quantities of fuel and to obtain a maximum of support with a minimum of power. In fact, the plane was powered by a single 675 hp M-34R engine, 12-cylinder V, liquid-cooled. The performance of the plane was outstanding. Theoretically the plane could remain in the air for 100 hours.

The plane's tests fully confirmed the designers' expectations. The plane could take off in about 3,200 feet (990 m) after 46.5 seconds of warm-up, with a load of 16,000 pounds (7,200 kg). When it took off on its record-breaking flight in July 1937 (pilot: Mikhail Gromov; co-pilot: Andrei Yumashev; navigator: Sergei Danelin), its loaded weight was over 12 tons, considerably more than normal. The three-man crew had rel-

Aircraft: **Tupolev ANT-25**
Manufacturer: **State Industries**
Type: **Long range monoplane**
Year: **1934**
Engine: **M-34R, 12-cylinder V, liquid-cooled, 675 hp**
Wingspan: **111 ft 6 in (33.98 m)**
Length: **43 ft 11 in (13.38 m)**
Height: **18 ft (5.49 m)**
Weight: **22,802 lb (10,343 kg)**
Cruising speed: **103 mph (165 km/h)**
Maximum speed: **149 mph (240 km/h)**
Ceiling: **23,000 ft (7,000 m)**
Range: **8,000 mile (13,000 km) (maximum theoretical)**
Crew: **3**

atively comfortable quarters. The fuselage housed the cockpit, complete with blind-flying instruments, a small cabin for sleeping, the navigator's cabin, and another cockpit, simpler than the other with basic controls. The plane was equipped with several safety devices. There were rubberized fabric coverings that could be inflated to float the aircraft in case of forced landing on water. And the plane was equipped with inflatable boats, electrically heated suits, food supplies sufficient for thirty days, and arms, and ammunition.

285

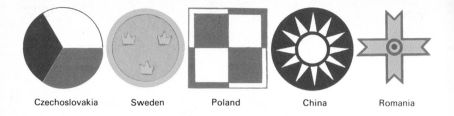

Czechoslovakia   Sweden   Poland   China   Romania

Other Countries

The first years of peace and the birth of civil aviation increased the gap that already existed between the countries which had developed an aircraft industry and those which had remained behind. In terms of aviation, post-War Europe was divided into two geographical groupings. One included Great Britain, France, Italy, Holland, and, notwithstanding the restrictions imposed by the peace treaty, Germany. The other represented the rest of Europe. At the outset there were great differences, both in quantity and in quality, between the two groups. One group had taken part in the pioneering efforts in the field and had made gigantic developments during the First World War. The less advanced countries had to take a back seat until they could make up for lost time.

Despite these initial disadvantages, the gap was slowly closed to a large extent, thanks to worldwide enthusiasm for flying. Thus in Czechoslovakia, some of the planes built by the Vojenska Tovarna Na Letadla (Letov) and by the Aero Tovarna Letadel (Aero) companies were on a level with those of the most advanced productions elsewhere. Poland's nat-

ional company, the Panstwowe Zaklady Litnicze (P.Z.L.) produced several high-performance aircraft, including one of the finest fighters of the period between the two World Wars. And Romania developed a flourishing industry that produced light aircraft and racing planes that were well-known throughout Europe.

Air transport kept pace with these developments. The groundwork for future airline development was already laid down in the first half of the 1920s. Several companies were established, even though they had to rely on imported aircraft. The SNETA airline was founded in Belgium in 1919, and SABENA was started in 1923. Norway's Det Norske Luftfarts Rederi (DET) was founded in 1920, as were Denmark's Det Danske Luftfatselskab (DDL) and Latvia's Latvijas Gaisa Satikmes. Spain's CEA (Compania Española de Tràfico Aéro) appeared in 1921, and Hungary's Magyar Legiforgalmi Malert was founded in 1922. By 1923 the CSA (Ceskoslovenske Statni Aerolinie) was operating in Czechoslovakia, while Aeronaut flew in Estonia, and Aero O/Y served Finland.

Aero A-11

Aircraft: **Aero A-11**
Manufacturer: **Aero Tovarna Letadel**
Type: **Reconnaissance**
Year: **1923**
Engine: **Walter W.IV, 8-cylinder V, liquid-cooled, 240 hp**
Wingspan: **41 ft 11 in (12.77 m)**
Length: **26 ft 11 in (8.20 m)**
Height: **10 ft 2 in (3.10 m)**
Weight: **3,260 lb (1,480 kg)**
Maximum speed: **133 mph at 8,200 ft (214 km/h at 2,500 m)**
Ceiling: **23,600 ft (7,200 m)**
Range: **460 mile (750 km)**
Armament: **1 machine gun**
Crew: **2**

One of the most versatile Czechoslovakian planes was the model A-11, built by Aero Tovarna Letadel in 1932. One of the first companies to enter the aircraft business (1918), it first built Austrian Phönix fighters under licence. The A-11 was one of the first of Aero's own designs and was developed to replace the old Letov reconnaissance planes. The Aero A-11 was a two-seat biplane, conventional in size and structure. It was powered by a 240 hp Walter W-IV engine, a licence version of the German BMW IV. The plane was so satisfactory that 440 aircraft were built in more than 20 variant models. What made this such a versatile plane was that a host of different engines, even radials, could be mounted on it. There were day and night reconnaissance versions of the plane, as well as trainers, light bombers, seaplanes, and target carriers.

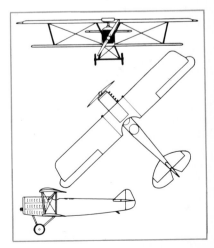

Svenska J 6A Jaktfalk

Although only eighteen Jaktfalks were built, this small fast Swedish fighter plane was an excellent design. The plane was finer than the British Bristol Bulldog, which was considered a 'classic' in the 1930s. The Jaktfalk was built by Svenska Aero A.B. for the Swedish air force. The prototype, powered by a 465 hp Armstrong Siddeley Jaguar radial engine satisfied the military authorities, but they asked for two more pre-production models equipped with Jupiter engines. Tests comparing the Jaktfalk's performance with that of the Bristol Bulldog were carried out, and the Swedish authorities ordered fifteen production models of the Jaktfalk. The Svenska Aero A.B. company went bankrupt after delivering eight aircraft. The remaining seven planes were built by the ASJA company, which took over the Svenska company. These planes were known as J 6Bs. The Jaktfalk remained in service until 1941.

Aircraft: **Svenska J 6A Jaktfalk**
Manufacturer: **Svenska Aero A.B.**
Type: **Fighter**
Year: **1931**
Engine: **Bristol Jupiter VIIF, 9-cylinder radial, air-cooled, 500 hp**
Wingspan: **28 ft 10 in (8.80 m)**
Length: **24 ft 7 in (7.50 m)**
Height: **11 ft 4 in (3.46 m)**
Weight: **3,240 lb (1,470 kg)**
Maximum speed: **193 mph at 14,700 ft (310 km/h at 4,500 m)**
Ceiling: **26,200 ft (8,000 m)**
Range: **340 mile (550 km)**
Armament: **2 machine guns**
Crew: **1**

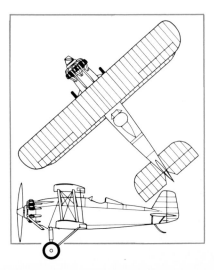

P.Z.L. P.7

The P.Z.L. P.7, designed by Zygmunt Pulawski in 1930, was one of the most famous fighter planes of the period between the two World Wars. For many years all the front-line squadrons of the Polish Air Force were equipped with this fast, highly manoeuvrable, well-armed, all-metal monoplane. The aircraft saw service until the outbreak of World War II. The P.7 fighter was derived from the 1929 P.1 and had the same general structure and covering of its predecessor. The chief difference was the engine: the P.1's Hispano–Suiza 12-cylinder V engine was replaced by a 485 hp Jupiter VIIF radial built under licence by Skoda. A typical single-seat high-wing monoplane, the P.7 began to be delivered to Polish squadrons in the late summer of 1932. The first squadron to receive delivery was the famous Eskadra Kosciuszkowska (the 'Kosciuszko Squadron'). A total of one hundred and fifty P.7s were built.

Aircraft: **P.Z.L. P.7**
Manufacturer: **Panstwowe Zaklady Lotnicze**
Type: **Fighter**
Year: **1932**
Engine: **Bristol Jupiter VIIF (Skoda), 9-cylinder radial, air-cooled, 485 hp**
Wingspan: **33 ft 10 in (10.31 m)**
Length: **23 ft 6 in (7.46 m)**
Height: **9 ft (2.74 m)**
Weight: **3,050 lb (1,380 kg)**
Maximum speed: **203 mph at 16,400 ft (327 km/h at 5,000 m)**
Ceiling: **32,800 ft (10,000 m)**
Range: **430 mile (700 km)**
Armament: **2 machine guns**
Crew: **1**

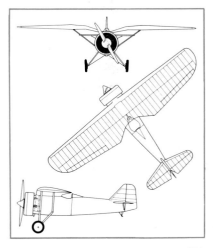

Nin Hia

One of the few planes designed in China, the Nin Hia was a small two-wing seaplane designed for reconnaissance. It was specially created for service on the cruiser *Nin Hai* and was named after the ship. The project was developed in 1933 by T. T. Mar of the Naval Air Establishment. It was a single-engine, single-seat aircraft with a conventional wood structure covered in a fabric. The plane was powered by a 130 hp, 7-cylinder Jimpu radial engine. It was not a catapult-launched plane, but it could be easily housed aboard ship, as it had wings that folded along the fuselage. The

Aircraft: **Nin Hia**
Manufacturer: **Naval Air Establishment**
Type: **Reconnaissance**
Year: **1933**
Engine: **Jimpu, 7-cylinder radial, air-cooled, 130 hp**
Wingspan: **30 ft 2 in (9.20 m)**
Length: **22 ft 11 in (7.00 m)**
Height: **9 ft 8 in (2.96 m)**
Weight: **1,803 lb (817 kg)**
Maximum speed: **177 mph (110 km/h)**
Ceiling: **12,200 ft (3,700 m)**
Range: **418 mile (673 km)**
Crew: **1**

two floats were built of wood, with four watertight compartments, and lacquered to prevent corrosion. The Nin Hia carried no armament. Its maximum speed was 110 mph (177 km/h), its climbing speed was 8 feet (2.50 m) per second, and its range was 418 miles (673 km).

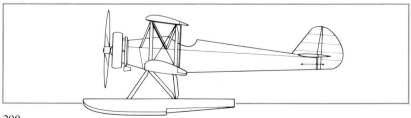

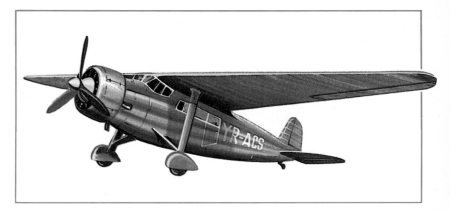

ICAR IAR-36 Commercial

The first commercial aeroplane built in Romania was the ICAR 'Commercial', a high-wing monoplane, with metal skeleton and mixed skin, that could carry six passengers as well as two crew members. The aircraft was designed and built by the ICAR company (Intreprindere de Constructii Aeronautice Romane), which was founded in 1932. The company specialized in light aircraft for private flying, training, and aerobatics. The Commercial was built in 1934 and proved itself an excellent plane. Powered by a 360 hp Armstrong Siddeley Serval Mk. 1 radial engine, the plane could reach a maximum speed of about 155 mph (250 km/h). The plane could reach an altitude of almost 10,000 feet (3,000 m) in 17 minutes. The plane was used between 1936 and 1938 on domestic flights of the L.A.R.E.S. air line (Liniile Aeriene Romane Exploatate de Stat).

Aircraft: **ICAR IAR-36 Commercial**
Manufacturer: **ICAR**
Type: **Civil transport**
Year: **1934**
Engine: **Armstrong Siddeley Serval Mk.1, 9-cylinder radial, air-cooled, 340 hp**
Wingspan: **50 ft 6 in (15.40 m)**
Length: **32 ft 2 in (9.80 m)**
Height: **9 ft 2 in (2.80 m)**
Weight: **4,960 lb (2,250 kg)**
Cruising speed: **130 mph (210 km/h)**
Ceiling: **16,500 ft (5,000 m)**
Range: **430 mile (700 km)**
Crew: **2**
Passengers: **6**

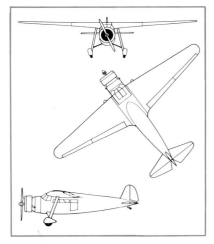

Major Civil Aircraft

1919

1920

The birth of civil aviation coincided with the end of World War I. The development of civil aircraft was slow but constant until just before World War II. At first, surplus military aircraft were overhauled. Then the design of and manufacture of civil aircraft began. The early airmail lines gave birth to the major air lines that spread civil aviation throughout the world. Some of the more important commercial aeroplanes are shown in this chart. They all made decisive contributions to the development of air transport.

**Farman F.60 Goliath
(France)**

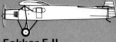

**Fokker F.II
(Holland)**

**Junkers F 13
(Germany)**

**Vickers Vimy Comm.
(Great Britain)**

**Breguet 14 T
(France)**

**de Havilland D.H. 4A
(Great Britain)**

1921

Fokker F.III
(Holland)

1922

H.P. W8b
(Great Britain)

1923

Dornier Do J Wal
(Italy)

1924

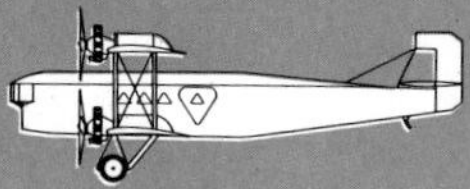

Blériot 135
(France)

1925

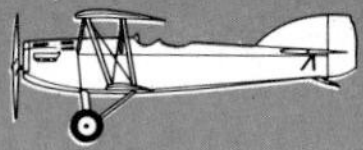

Potez 25 A.2
(France)

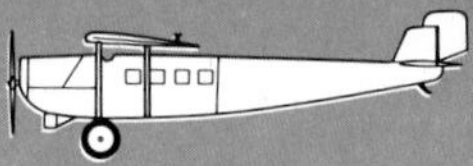

Dornier Komet III
(Germany)

Junkers G24
(Germany)

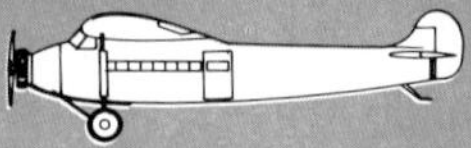

Fokker F VIIa
(Holland)

1926

A.W. 155 Argosy I
(Great Britain)

D.H.66 Hercules
(Great Britain)

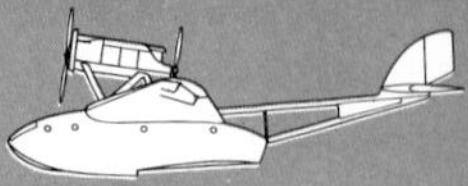

SM. 55C
(Italy)

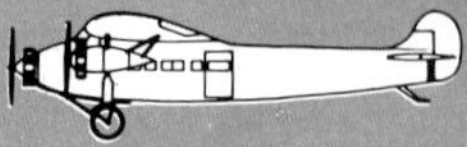

Fokker F.VIIa-3m
(Holland)

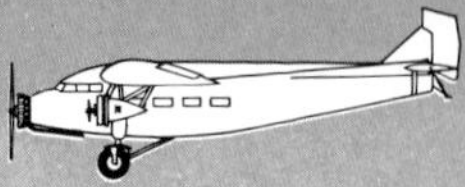

Ford 4AT Trimotor
(United States)

Major Civil
Aircraft

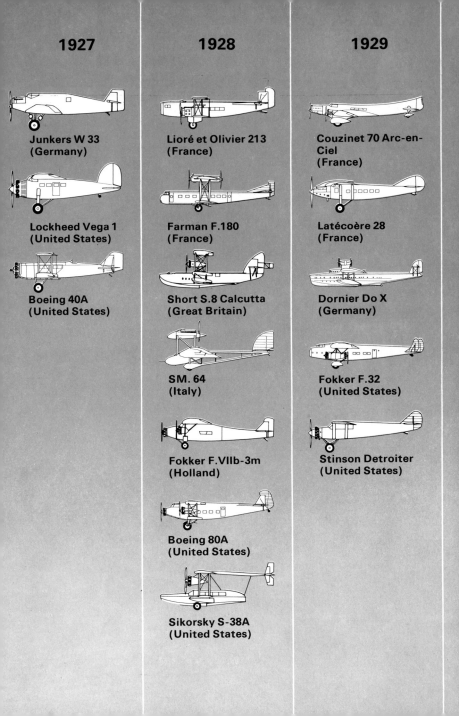

1927

Junkers W 33
(Germany)

Lockheed Vega 1
(United States)

Boeing 40A
(United States)

1928

Lioré et Olivier 213
(France)

Farman F.180
(France)

Short S.8 Calcutta
(Great Britain)

SM. 64
(Italy)

Fokker F.VIIb-3m
(Holland)

Boeing 80A
(United States)

Sikorsky S-38A
(United States)

1929

Couzinet 70 Arc-en-
Ciel
(France)

Latécoère 28
(France)

Dornier Do X
(Germany)

Fokker F.32
(United States)

Stinson Detroiter
(United States)

1930

Junkers G 38
(Germany)

1931

H.P. 42 E
(Great Britain)

Lockheed Orion
(United States)

Tupolev ANT-14
(USSR)

1932

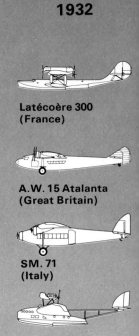

Latécoère 300
(France)

A.W. 15 Atalanta
(Great Britain)

SM. 71
(Italy)

SM. 66
(Italy)

Major Civil
Aircraft

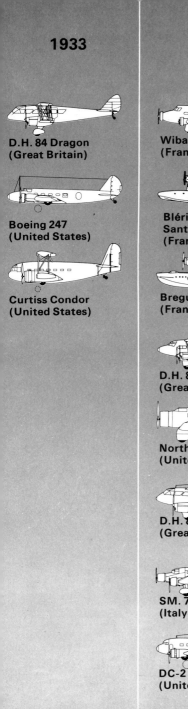

1933

D.H. 84 Dragon
(Great Britain)

Boeing 247
(United States)

Curtiss Condor
(United States)

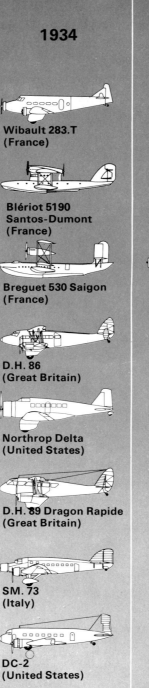

1934

Wibault 283.T
(France)

Blériot 5190
Santos-Dumont
(France)

Breguet 530 Saigon
(France)

D.H. 86
(Great Britain)

Northrop Delta
(United States)

D.H. 89 Dragon Rapide
(Great Britain)

SM. 73
(Italy)

DC-2
(United States)

1935

Latécoère 521
(France)

Dewoitine D.338
(France)

Ca.133
(Italy)

Martin China Clipper
(United States)

Sikorsky S-42
(United States)

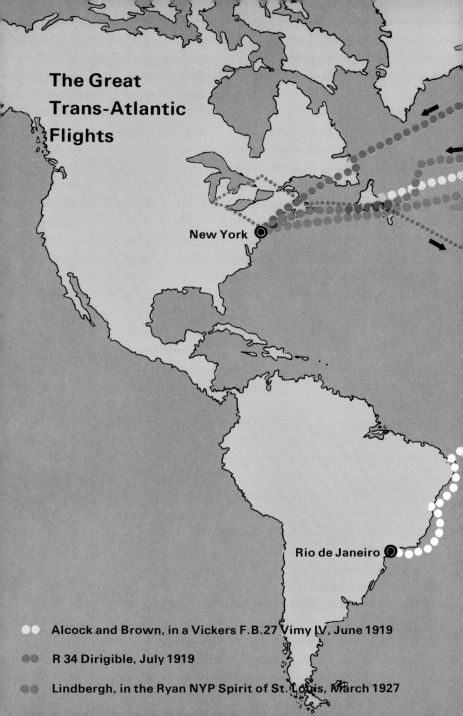

The Great Trans-Atlantic Flights

New York

Rio de Janeiro

Alcock and Brown, in a Vickers F.B.27 Vimy IV, June 1919

R 34 Dirigible, July 1919

Lindbergh, in the Ryan NYP Spirit of St. Louis, March 1927

Paris

Rome

Balbo, commanding fourteen SIAI-Marchetti SM.55As,
December 1930–January 1931

Balbo, commanding twenty-five SIAI-Marchetti SM.55Xs,
July–August 1933

Dirigibles

The first practical demonstration that the dirigible airship could compete with the aeroplane as a means of transport took place in the summer of 1919 when the British airship R 34 made a round-trip crossing of the Atlantic between England and the United States. This flight marked the beginning of the second 'lighter-than-air' period, an era that lasted twenty-one years and intensified competition with that heavier transport, the aeroplane.

During World War I (especially in Germany) the dirigible had been a successful combat vehicle, and it subsequently had a certain success in the civilian world. Great Britain, Germany, and the United States were the countries that most contributed to the development of lighter-than-air machines. The Americans concentrated on military airships, while the British and Germans devoted their efforts to the field of civil transport. Germany's success with the Zeppelin was turned to the development of bigger and better airships. And as early as 1921 Great Britain considered establishing a special company for airship connections between the British Isles and India, Australia, New Zealand, and South Africa. Plans were even considered for a joint venture involving Great Britain, Germany, and the United States in developing long-distance passenger dirigibles. Because of technical difficulties and bureaucratic complications, British progress was slow. The British dirigible programme came to a brusque end on October 5, 1931, when the R 101 airship crashed near Paris during a test flight.

Germany was way ahead of Great Britain. The Graf Zeppelin was christened on July 8, 1928, while the two intercontinental dirigibles the British had projected were still being built. Two months later the Graf Zeppelin made its first Atlantic crossing to America. The large German airship made many crossings in the following years, to both North and South America. In 1936, an even more ambitious airship made its appearance; this was the LZ 129 Hindenburg, which had been under construction for two years. This enormous dirigible together with the Graf Zeppelin, should have ensured regular and continuous flights to North America. But the Hindenburg disaster on May 6, 1937, at Lakehurst put an end to further German plans for bigger and more luxurious dirigibles. The Americans had withdrawn from dirigible construction four years earlier, when the Akron crashed with 76 persons on board. The age of the dirigible was over.

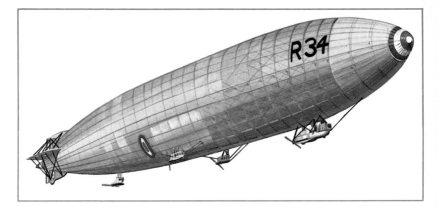

R 34

Airship: **R 34**
Country: **Great Britain**
Year: **1919**
Engine: **Five Sunbeam Maori, 250 hp each**
Volume: **1,958,550 ft³ (55,460 m³)**
Length: **643 ft 5 in (196 m)**
Diameter: **78 ft 8 in (24 m)**
Weight (empty): **81,400 lb (36,900 kg)**
Maximum speed: **62 mph (100 km/h)**
Range: **4,800 mile (7,750 km)**
Crew: **23**

The first Atlantic dirigible crossing took place in 1919. The R 34 flew from East Fortune, Scotland, to Mineola, Long Island, in one hundred and ten hours. The R 34 was the second Class 33 dirigible built between 1918 and 1919. The R 34's history-making flight got under way at 1.42 on the morning of July 2, 1919, a little more than two weeks after Alcock and Brown flew their Vickers Vimy across the Atlantic. The R 34 flight, with a thirty-man crew, was smooth as far as Nova Scotia, where the airship ran into a storm. For a time it seemed as if the dirigible would have to make a forced landing. But the weather improved, and at 1.54 in the afternoon on July 6 the airship landed at Mineola. It had enough fuel left for another forty minutes in the air. The return trip began at 3.54 in the morning on July

10. Aided by favourable winds, the R 34 flew back in eighty hours. The R 34 flight was the first victory of a lighter-than-air ship over an aeroplane and paved the way for future dirigible crossings. The R 34 was severely damaged in an accident in bad weather early in 1921 and never flew again.

N 1 Norge

In the middle of the 1920s dirigibles and aeroplanes competed for the conquest of the North Pole. Again the lighter-than-air craft came in a close second, as it had in the Atlantic crossing. The Norge flew over the North Pole on May 12, 1926, only three days after Richard Byrd and Floyd Bennett had made the flight in their Fokker F.VIIa-3m, the Josephine Ford.

The Norge, originally known as N 1, was designed by the Italian Umberto Nobile in 1925 and had aroused a good deal of interest through its Mediterranean flights. The Norwegian explorer Roald Amundsen wanted to buy the dirigible and invited Nobile to take part in a flight over the North Pole. Nobile accepted the invitation on condition that he fly the airship. The Norge took off from Italy on April 10, 1926. The third member of the crew was the American Lincoln Ellsworth, who had financed the pur-

Airship: **N 1 Norge**
Country: **Italy**
Year: **1926**
Engine: **Three Maybach, 245 hp each**
Volume: **670,980 ft³ (19,000 m³)**
Length: **347 ft 9 in (106 m)**
Diameter: **64 ft (19.50 m)**
Weight: **—**
Maximum speed: **71 mph (115 km/h)**
Range: **3,300 mile (5,300 km)**

chase of the airship. On May 7, the airship touched down at Spitsbergen, Norway, where final preparations were made. It was there that the crew of the Norge met Byrd and Bennett, after their return flight from the Pole. The Norge took off at 10.00 a.m. on May 11. The first part of the voyage was uneventful, but the Norge later ran into bad weather and fog. It was May 14 when the ship landed in Alaska.

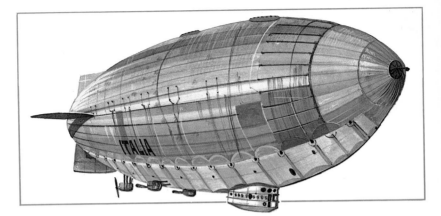

N 4 Italia

Airship: **N 4 Italia**
Country: **Italy**
Year: **1928**
Engine: **Three Maybach, 250 hp each**
Volume: **653,300 ft³ (18,500 m³)**
Length: **341 ft 4 in (104 m)**
Diameter: **60 ft 8 in (18.50 m)**
Weight: —
Maximum speed: **71 mph (115 km/h)**
Range: **3,100 mile (5,000 km)**

Umberto Nobile's second polar expedition was made in the N 4, the Italia, sister-ship of the Norge. The crash of the Italia led the Italian authorities to remove all dirigibles from service.

The N 4 was built in 1927 by the Stabilimento Costruzioni Aeronautiche along the lines of the N 1, the Norge. The Italia had slightly different dimensions and was a little lighter. Otherwise it was identical to the Norge. After his polar flight with Amundsen and Ellsworth, Nobile wanted to make his own expedition to the North Pole, and a public subscription was started in Milan to finance construction of a new dirigible. The Italia reached Spitsbergen on May 6, 1928, after a three-stage flight across Central Europe and the Barents Sea. A first attempt at the Pole was obstructed by bad weather. The airship took off again at 4.28 a.m. on May 23. The flight over the Pole was successful, but bad weather and ice made the dirigible crash at 10.33 a.m. on May 25. Seven people died, and the survivors were trapped for forty-eight days before rescue came.

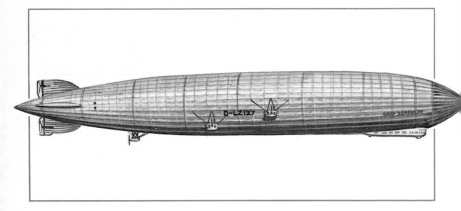

LZ 127 Graf Zeppelin

Airship: **LZ 127 Graf Zeppelin**
Country: **Germany**
Year: **1928**
Engine: **Five Maybach, 550 hp each**
Volume: **3,308,600 ft³ (93,600 m³)**
Length: **776 ft 3 in (236.60 m)**
   100 ft (30.48 m³)
Diameter: **100 ft (30.48 m³)**
Weight: **148,100 lb (67,200 kg)**
Cruising speed: **68 mph (109 km/h)**
Range: **6,200 mile (10,000 km)**
Crew: **45**
Passengers: **20**

Probably the most famous passenger dirigible was the Graf Zeppelin. It was christened on July 8, 1928, the ninetieth birthday of the father of lighter-than-air craft, Count Ferdinand von Zeppelin. The LZ 127 was expressly designed for intercontinental passenger service. The airship could carry only twenty passengers, but their accommodation was luxurious. The Graf Zeppelin was 776 feet 3 inches (236.60 m) long; its diameter was 110 feet 7 inches (33.70 m); and it weighed 147,900 pounds (67,100 kg). Its range was over 7,000 miles (11,200 km). The five 580 hp Maybach engines were fed with a gaseous fuel known as 'blaugas' ('blue gas'). One-third of the airship's volume was filled with 'blaugas', the rest with hydrogen. The airship, manned by a crew of forty-five, had a cruising speed of 68 mph (109 km/h).

The Graf Zeppelin's maiden voyage began on October 11, 1928. The airship took off from Friedrichshafen for its first trans-Atlantic flight to America with sixty-three persons aboard and a cargo of goods and mail, including 60,000 letters specially franked and cancelled for the occasion. Over the years the Graf Zeppelin made hundreds of flights, including about one hundred across the South Atlantic, between Friedrichshafen and Pernambuco. In 1935 alone, the Graf Zeppelin made eighty-two flights and carried 1,429 passengers plus fourteen tons of mail and goods.

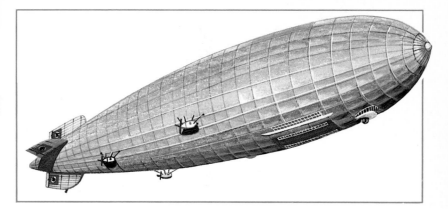

LZ 129 Hindenburg

The career of the most famous dirigible ever built lasted just a year. On May 6, 1936, the LZ 129 Hindenburg began regular passenger service with the Deutsche Zeppelin–Reederei on the Frankfurt–New York line. On May 6, 1937, the airship caught fire over Lakehurst, New Jersey, and was totally destroyed. Thirty-five of the ninety-seven people aboard were killed, and the Hindenburg disaster marked the virtual end of dirigible passenger service.

The Hindenburg was the next-to-last Zeppelin ever built. The last was the LZ 130, the Graf Zeppelin II. Both airships powered by four diesel engines, were especially designed for passenger service to the United States. The Hindenburg was 803 feet 9 inches (245 m) long, 135 feet 2 inches (41.20 m) in diameter, and weighed 287,000 pounds (130,000 kg). Its maximum speed was 84 mph (135 km/h)

Airship: **LZ 129 Hindenburg**
Country: **Germany**
Year: **1936**
Engine: **Four Daimler-Benz, 1,320 hp each**
Volume: **7,063,000 ft³ (200,000 m³)**
Length: **803 ft 9 in (245 m)**
Diameter: **135 ft 2 in (41.20 m)**
Weight: **287,000 lb (130,000 kg)**
Maximum speed: **84 mph (135 km/h)**
Range: **8,700 mile (14,000 km)**
Crew: **40**
Passengers: **50**

and it carried a crew of forty with a passenger capacity of fifty. The passenger compartment was in the forward part, just behind the crew cabin. Passenger accommodations included a dining room, a reading room, and a promenade deck with large windows. In the one year the airship was in service, it made some twenty Atlantic crossings carrying about a thousand passengers were only to reappear on the aviation scene decades later with the replacement of helium by non-flammable gas.

Engines

The years between the two World Wars saw remarkable progress in engine technology. By the end of World War I the first development of aircraft engines was fully consolidated. The dominant were either in-line or vee, thanks chiefly to the fine achievements of Great Britain and France. But the 1920s witnessed the rapid popularization of a radically different power plant, the radial engine, which had been overshadowed by the other types throughout the war. The radial engine had two distinct advantages. It was simpler in structure and lighter in weight. Once the radial engine had increased its generating capacity, it proved to be an almost ideal engine, especially for military use, where strength and reliability were top priorities. An entire industry specialized in the manufacture of radial engines, particularly in the United States. Over the years the

Napier Lion – 1918 (GB)

The Napier Lion was developed towards the end of the First World War and was one of the most important British engines of the era. It was designed by A. J. Rowledge. A 12-cylinder W engine, it had three banks of four engines, each set at 60°. Liquid-cooled, it could generate 450 horse power at 1,925 revolutions per minute. Several versions of the engine were built with ever-greater power. A racing version generated 1,320 horse power at 3,600 revolutions per minute.

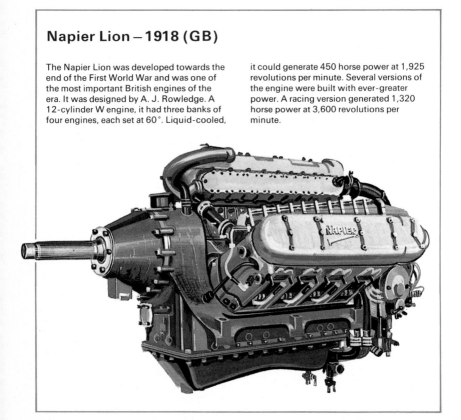

quality of the radial engine was so improved that it finally took the place of the in-line or vee engines. In the United States, thanks chiefly to the excellent engines manufactured by Pratt and Whitney and by Wright, the radial engine replaced all others both in civil and in military aviation.

In Europe, however, the other engine types continued to be developed and improved. One reason for their success was the popularity of such important races as the Schneider Trophy. Racing required slender aerodynamic aircraft, and only the in-line engine could satisfactorily slim down the aircraft's nose. Some of the finest engines of the period were developed for racing, such engines as the Rolls-Royce R and the Fiat AS.6. These jewels of engineering and technology brought the in-line engine to a level of quality that was to reach a climax during World War II with the famous Rolls-Royce Merlin and Griffon vee-engine series.

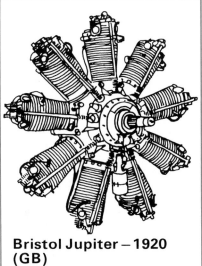

Bristol Jupiter – 1920 (GB)

This was one of the most popular engines of the 1920s and was built under licence in no less than sixteen countries. Designed by Roy Fedden, it was a nine-cylinder radial engine that could generate 375–400 horse power in its original version. Over the years the design proved its reliability, and 500 hp versions were developed. Another famous radial engine was derived from the Jupiter. This engine was the Pegasus, the final versions of which generated more than 1,000 hp.

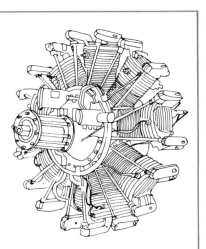

Wright Whirlwind – 1925 (USA)

This engine played a fundamental role in the development of aviation in the United States and powered planes involved in some history-making flights, including Lindbergh's trans-Atlantic flight. The 9-cylinder radial generated 220 horse power in its original version, and was the father of a long series of engines that the Wright company built during two decades.

Pratt and Whitney Wasp – 1925 (USA)

One reason for the radial engine's success was the excellent work of Pratt and Whitney. The Wasp was their first outstanding engine. It had the standard nine cylinders of the period and generated fairly high power (400 hp in its first version). It was particularly popular in military aviation.

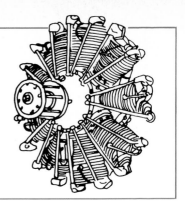

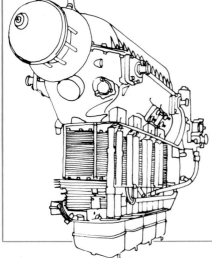

de Havilland Gipsy Major I – 1927 (GB)

The Gipsy Major was an air-cooled, four-cylinder, in-line engine that generated 130 horse power. The long career of the Gipsy engines began with this model, and included several world-famous engines. Almost all the Gipsy Majors were used in the light aircraft manufactured in England during the 1930s and made a significant contribution to the development of British civil aviation. Among the famous planes that were powered by Gipsy engines were the D.H. 82A Tiger Moth and the D.H. 84 Dragon.

Rolls-Royce R – 1931 (GB)

The engine that won Great Britain the Schneider Trophy was built in 1929 but only reached its finest form in 1931. The Rolls-Royce R was a liquid-cooled, 12-cylinder, vee engine that could generate 2,300 horse power at 3,200 revolutions per minute. The R model was built by Rolls-Royce expressly for the Supermarine seaplane racers. It was the progenitor of the famous Merlin engines.

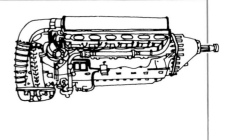

Wright Cyclone – 1931 (USA)

The success of the Whirlwind was confirmed and extended by one of its most important offspring, the Wright Cyclone. A nine-cylinder radial engine, like its predecessor, the Cyclone was bigger and more powerful than the Whirlwind. It dominated the 700 hp class and was extremely successful, particularly in military aviation.

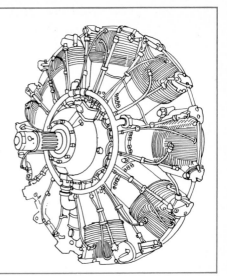

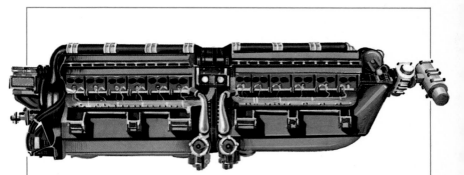

Fiat AS.6 – 1931 (I)

This engine was responsible for Italy's conquest of the world seaplane speed record, a record that still stands. It was a twenty-four-cylinder vee engine constructed with two AS.5 engines. This liquid-cooled engine generated over 3,000 hp at 3,300 revolutions per minute. It was used in only a few races during the 1930s.

Summary of Aviation History
1919–1935

1919 **February 5.** The first civil air line was opened in Europe: Deutsche Luft-Reederei began its service between Berlin and Weimar.

March 22. The first European international route, between Paris and Brussels, was inaugurated by the Lignes Aériennes Farman.

April 19. The first successful free-fall parachute jump was made by Leslie Leroy Irvin at McCook Field, Dayton, Ohio.

May 8–31. Commander A. C. Read's Curtiss NC-4 made the first Atlantic crossing.

June 14–15. John Alcock and Arthur Whitten Brown made the first non-stop Atlantic crossing in a modified Vickers Vimy bomber.

July 2–6. The British R 34 made the first dirigible crossing of the Atlantic and also the first round-trip crossing (July 9–13).

August 25. The British Aircraft Transport and Travel company inauguarated the first daily, commercial, international flights, between London and Paris.

November 12–December 10. Two Australian brothers, Ross and Keith Smith, both officers, made the first flight between Great Britain and Australia in a Vickers Vimy.

1920 **February 14–May 30.** Ferrarin and Masiero, flying two SVA biplanes, made the first Rome–Tokyo flight, 11,250 miles (18,105 km) in 109 hours.

1921 **February 21–24.** The first solo flight from coast to coast of the United States was made by William D. Coney. He flew from San Diego, California, to Jacksonville, Florida.

1922 **March–June.** S. Cabral and G. Coutinho made the first flight across the South Atlantic.

1923 **May 2–3.** A Fokker T-2 made the first non-stop flight across the United States. O. G. Kelly and J. A. Macready flew from New York to San Diego in 26 hours and 50 minutes.

1924 **April–September.** The first round-the-world flight. Four Douglas DWCs took off from Seattle and flew west.

April 1. Imperial Airways, the British national air line was founded.

1925 **April–November.** Francesco De Pinedo flew his Savoia-Marchetti S.16ter seaplane about 33,000 miles (53,000 km) across three continents.

1926 **January 6.** The German air line Deutsche Lufthansa was founded.

February 1. The first Italian air line, the Transadriatica began operations, on the Rome-Venice route.

May 9. Richard Byrd and Floyd Bennett flew over the North Pole for the first time. The plane was the Fokker F.VIIa-3m.

May 11–14. The North Pole was flown over by a dirigible for the first time. Aboard the Norge were Amundsen, Ellsworth, and Nobile.

1927 **May 20–21.** The first solo non-stop Atlantic crossing was made by Charles A. Lindbergh on board his Ryan monoplane, the NYP Spirit of St. Louis.

1928 **March 30.** The 500-km/h barrier was broken by Mario de Bernardi in a Macchi M.52 seaplane. He reached a speed of 318.58 mph (512.69 km/h) over Venice.

April 13. Hermann Koehl von Hunefeld and J. Fitzmaurice, on board a Junkers W 33, made the first east-west crossing of the North Atlantic.

July 3. Ferrarin and Del Prete, on board the SIAI-Marchetti SM.64 established a world non-stop distance record by flying from Montecelio, Italy, to Touros, Brazil, in 48 hours and 14 minutes, a distance of 4,467 miles (7,188 km).

1929 **August 8–29.** The German dirigible Graf Zeppelin completed the first round-the-world airship flight. It took off from Lakehurst, New Jersey, and touched down at Friedrichshafen, Tokyo, and Los Angeles before landing again at Lakehurst.

September 30. The first rocket-propelled aeroplane flight. The pilot was the German Fritz von Opel.

October 21. The Dornier Do X, on Lake Constance, was the first plane to take off with more than 100 persons aboard. There were 169 passengers.

November 29. The first flight over the South Pole was made by Richard Byrd in a Ford Trimotor.

1930 **May 5–24.** Amy Johnson was the first woman to fly from Great Britain to Australia. She flew a D.H.60G Gipsy Moth from Croydon to Darwin.

1931 **January.** The first formation crossing of the South Atlantic was made. Italo Balbo commanded a flight of fourteen SM.55 seaplanes.

October 3. The first non-stop flight from the United States to Japan was made by Clyde Pangborn and Hugh Herndon aboard a Bellanca.

1932 **May 20–21.** The first woman to fly solo across the Atlantic was Amelia Earhart in a Lockheed Vega.

August 25. Amelia Earhart was the first woman to fly non-stop across America coast-to-coast.

1933 **July.** Twenty-five SM.55 seaplanes made the first North Atlantic crossing in formation. They were under the command of Italo Balbo.

July 15. Wiley Post made the first solo round-the-world flight in a Lockheed Vega. He flew 15,596 miles (25,099 km) in 7 days, 18 hours, and 49 minutes.

1934 **August 8.** The first non-stop flight from Canada to Great Britain was made by a D.H. Dragon piloted by L. Reid and J. R. Ayling.

October 23. Francesco Agello established a world seaplane speed record of 440.698 mph (709.202 km/h) in a Macchi MC.72.

1935 **November 13.** The first woman to make a solo flight across the South Atlantic was Jean Batten. She flew a Percival Gull from Lympne to Natal, Brazil.

Index

(The numbers in **bold type** *refer to illustrations)*

Bibliography

C. Dollfus–H. Bouche, *Histoire de l'aéronautique*, Paris, L'Illustration, 1932.

Luigi Mancini, *Grande enciclopedia aeronautica*, Milan, Edizioni Aeronautica, 1936.

Jean Mermoz, *Mes vols*, Paris, Flammarion, 1937.

Igor I. Sikorsky, *The Story of the Winged-S*, London, Robert Hale, 1939.

J. Hébrard, *Vingt-cinq années d'aviation militaire (1920–1945)*, vol. I, II, Paris, Editions Albin Michel, 1946.

Charles Lindbergh, *The Spirit of St. Louis*, New York, Scribner, 1953.

J. Hébrard, *L'aviation des origines à nos jours*, Paris, Robert Laffont, 1954.

D. M. Desoutter, *All about Aircraft*, London, Faber & Faber Ltd., 1955.

John W. Underwood, *The World's Famous Racing Aircraft*, Los Angeles, Floyd Clymer, 1955.

A History of D. Napier & Son, Engineers, Ltd., 1808–1958, London, Weidenfeld and Nicolson, 1958.

A. J. Jackson, *British Civil Aircraft 1919–59*, vol. I, II, London, Putnam & Co. Ltd., 1959–60.

Henry R. Palmer Jr., *This was Air Travel*, Superior Publishing Company, 1960.

Piaggio & C., *75 anni di attività*, Genoa.

John W. R. Taylor, *Warplanes of the World*, London, Ian Allan Ltd., 1960.

Francis K. Mason, *Hawker Aircraft since 1920*, London, Putnam & Co. Ltd., 1961.

Fokker–The Man and the Aircraft, Letchworth, Herts, Harleyford Publications Ltd., 1961.

United States Army and Air Force Fighters 1916–1961, Letchworth, Herts, Harleyford Publications Ltd., 1961.

Joseph P. Juptner, *U.S. Civil Aircrafts*, vol. I–IV, Fallbrook, California, Aero Publishers Inc., 1962–67.

G. Bignozzi – B. Catalanotto, *Storia degli aerei d'Italia*, Rome Editrice Cielo, 1962.

Maynard Crosby, *Flight Plan for Tomorrow. The Douglas Story: A Condensed History*, Santa Monica, Douglas Aircraft Co., 1962.

A. J. Jackson, *De Havilland Aircraft*, London, Putnam & Co., Ltd., 1962.

Robert A. Kilmarx, *A History of Soviet Air Power*, London, Faber & Faber, 1962.

O. Thetford, *Aircraft of the Royal Air Force since 1918*, London, Putnam & Co. Ltd., 1971 (5th edition).

A. J. Jackson, *British Civil Aircraft since 1919* Vols. I, II and III, London, Putnam & Co. Ltd., 1973–4 (2nd edition).

T. G. Foxworth, *The Speed Seekers*, London, Macdonald & Janes, 1975.

D. Mondey, *The Schneider Trophy*, London, Robert Hale, 1975.